T0313909

KRUPP

KRUPP

A HISTORY OF THE LEGENDARY GERMAN FIRM

HAROLD JAMES

Princeton University Press   Princeton & Oxford

PUBLISHED BY PRINCETON UNIVERSITY PRESS,
41 WILLIAM STREET, PRINCETON, NEW JERSEY 08540

IN THE UNITED KINGDOM: PRINCETON UNIVERSITY PRESS,
6 OXFORD STREET, WOODSTOCK, OXFORDSHIRE OX20 1TW

PRESS.PRINCETON.EDU

Library of Congress Cataloging-in-Publication Data

James, Harold, 1956–
Krupp: a history of the legendary German firm / Harold James.
p. cm.
Includes bibliographical references and index.
ISBN 978-0-691-15340-7 (hardcover : alk. paper) 1. Fried. Krupp GmbH—History.
2. Krupp family—History. 3. Steel industry and trade—Germany—History.
I. Title.
HD9523.9.F697J36 2012
338.7′6691420943—dc23
2011024639

BRITISH LIBRARY CATALOGING-IN-PUBLICATION DATA IS AVAILABLE

THIS BOOK HAS BEEN COMPOSED IN BERLING AND DIN

PRINTED ON ACID-FREE PAPER. ∞

PRINTED IN THE UNITED STATES OF AMERICA

1 3 5 7 9 10 8 6 4 2

CONTENTS

Acknowledgments [vii]

—

Introduction: A Nation and a Name
[1]

ONE
Risk: Friedrich Krupp
[9]

TWO
Steel: Alfred Krupp
[24]

THREE
Science: Friedrich Alfred Krupp
[89]

FOUR
Diplomacy: Gustav Krupp von Bohlen und Halbach I
[123]

CONTENTS

FIVE

Tradition: Gustav Krupp von Bohlen and Halbach II

[145]

SIX

Power and Deglobalization: Gustav and Alfried Krupp von
Bohlen und Halbach

[172]

SEVEN

Reglobalization: Alfried Krupp von Bohlen und Halbach
and Berthold Beitz

[226]

—

Appendix 1: Family Tree   [295]

Appendix 2: Business Results, 1811–2010   [297]

Notes   [305]

List of Illustrations   [337]

Index   [341]

ACKNOWLEDGMENTS

I should like to thank the Alfried Krupp von Bohlen und Halbach-Stiftung (Foundation) for financial support for the research involved in producing this book. Professor Berthold Beitz, the chairman and executive member of its board of trustees, kindly received me for some agreeable conversations. I had full access to the important historical archive of the company and the family, beautifully housed in a wing of the Villa Hügel in Essen, the historic home of the Krupp business dynasty. Especially I should like to thank Dr. Ralf Stremmel of the Krupp archive for his invaluable assistance in locating archival and pictorial material. Dr. Detlef Felken and Dr. Stefanie Hölscher of the Beck Verlag Munich and Brigitta van Rheinberg of Princeton University Press have assisted with their customary care and acumen. In addition, this book reflects insights that I have been developing in the course of working on a European Union research project on corporate governance and family firms (MEXC-CT-2005-024362). The resulting book reflects solely the views and interpretations of the author.

Princeton, New Jersey, September 2011

A Nation and a Name

Alfred Krupp made the name Krupp into a German icon. For him, it was not a coincidence that the dramatic period of expansion of the small enterprise that his father had established in 1811 coincided with the creation of the German Empire. He proudly announced to Wilhelm I, the new emperor, that they were now living in the "steel age." Kaiser Wilhelm I and Bismarck were both quick to see and confirm the parallels between the new politics and the new business. But the identification between the house of Krupp and the German political order did not stop with the death of Krupp in 1887 or of Wilhelm I in 1888. Krupp's son, Friedrich Alfred, cultivated an even closer relationship with Wilhelm I's grandson, Kaiser Wilhelm II. The new business culture reflected the kaiser's own search for modernity and greatness. For Adolf Hitler, Krupp was also an icon. In *Mein Kampf* and again in 1935 at the Nuremberg party rally, Hitler exhorted German youth to be as "quick as a greyhound, as tough as leather, and as hard as Krupp steel."[1] Some people quibbled that Krupp steel was notably resilient (because slightly malleable) rather than hard, but the company liked the analogy at the time. In 1945 at the International Military Tribunal in Nuremberg, where Gustav Krupp von Bohlen und Halbach was indicted as one of twenty-four major war criminals, prosecutor Robert Jackson also used Krupp as a symbol: "Four generations of the Krupp family have owned and operated the great armament and munitions plants which have been the chief source of Germany's war supplies. For over 130 years this family has been the focus, the symbol, and the beneficiary of the most sinister forces engaged in menacing the peace of Europe." After the Second World War, Krupp remade itself as a symbol of the new success—and new openness—of the Federal Republic. Welcoming the G-7 finance ministers and central bankers to a high-level meeting in Alfred Krupp's grandiose 269-room Villa Hügel in February 2007, the German Social Democratic Party (SPD) finance minister Peer Steinbrück stated: "Since then [1870–73, when the villa was built] the name 'Krupp' and thus the Villa Hügel have not only come to symbolize German industrialization, but German history per se. They have become both a synonym for pioneering industrial work and social responsibility in times of seemingly infinite economic prosperity as well as an example of more than questionable conduct during the darkest hours of German history."[2]

On the eve of the First World War, Krupp had been by far the largest German company, with assets of 599.5 million marks in 1912, although it was only one-fifth the size of the largest American corporation, the giant U.S. Steel, and half the size of the largest British firm, the thread and textile maker J. & P. Coats. Its owner, Bertha Krupp von Bohlen und Halbach, was listed as being, with assets of 283 million marks, the wealthiest person in Germany (the kaiser was only the fifth richest). By 1937 it was still the fourth-largest German firm in terms of market capitalization (behind the steel giant Vereinigte Stahlwerke, IG Farben, and Siemens) and the forty-eighth largest corporation in the world.[3] In 2005 ThyssenKrupp was in 85th place on the Fortune Global 500 list (ordered by revenue) and in 2010, 123rd place.

Krupp seemed to stand for a particular German way of doing business. Later analysts called this "Rhineland capitalism."[4] It involved several distinctive elements that were blended together into an astonishingly durable and successful synthesis of business culture: a commitment from the beginning to export orientation (an embrace of what we would today call globalization); a close relationship with the state, as a regulator, as a purchaser of industrial products, and as a source and guarantor of credit; a long-term commitment to a skilled workforce that was tied to the enterprise by material inducements but also by a sense of loyalty to a factory community rather than just to an owner; suspicion of "capitalists," financiers, and stock markets (even though banks played a prominent part in the financing of much of German heavy industry); and also suspicion of the principle of competition. Instead, the business model relied on obtaining absolute preeminence in a well-defined market for a number of specialized and skilled products. We would speak today of niche markets. But these niche markets were scaled up in the course of the nineteenth century and of German industrialization, so that the niches expanded to fill the world.

What drives a company? To assume that the motive force is simply a rational search for profit is endlessly naive. There are alternative visions of the ultimate purpose of business and of the motivation of owners, managers, and workers. Is the driving impulse service to the nation? Is it the link to political power? Is it a question of the psychic satisfaction of the owner or the leading managers? Is it an idea about innovation? Is it a functioning within a network of trust and relationships? All these answers have been given to explain the alleged peculiarity of continental European capitalism.

Some of the major themes of the subsequent development of the Krupp company (and which are at the heart of the analysis of this book) emerged in the nineteenth century and were then hardwired into a corporate culture that became a sustaining vision: first, the absence of an exclusive focus on profitability. The idea that business was not just about the accounting result was eventually institutionalized in the concept of a foundation (Alfried Krupp von Bohlen und Halbach-Stiftung) as owner of the company, rather than anonymous shareholders or even a large and dispersed family. Thus, at the same time as the student revolution of the late 1960s swept Germany, the Krupp enterprise ceased to be a family business. But the notion of a mission that went beyond profitability had its origins in an extraordinary nineteenth-century story in which for its first twenty-five years the company lost money. Such sustained unprofitability is unfamiliar in the age of modern capital markets, though some technologically dynamic companies do survive in stock market valuations for some time without showing profits, and only on the basis of potential. The early nineteenth century had a deeper answer that still holds true in many major emerging market economies, namely, that a network of family and friends, usually tied in with kinship links, can sustain an idea that they believe in for a very long time. But in reading the early story of Krupp, one must bear in mind that almost any modern company following that trajectory would not survive for the time Krupp needed to become a profitable enterprise: it would simply fizzle and die.

There may be analogies in the nineteenth century to the very modern world of high-tech entrepreneurship, start-up ventures, and venture capital. In recent years in California's Silicon Valley, it was often said to have been a rite of passage or even a badge of honor for entrepreneurs to have one or even more bankruptcies behind them. It could be interpreted as a sign that they knew the world. But the nineteenth-century German example is different in that it was not just the individual entrepreneur who went from one business failure to a completely new field that promised more success, but that a whole business with a complicated web of human involvements and connections underwent that transition.

The second theme is that a technically advanced enterprise exists in an international and even global system. From the beginning of the Krupp story there was a focus on competition with the most advanced economy of the time, that of Great Britain, and simultaneously an acknowledgment of the importance of countries that were catching up from what used to be called "economic backwardness": nineteenth-century Russia, Brazil, Egypt, or China. Even Friedrich Krupp, the founding entrepreneur, in the beginning of the nineteenth century dreamt of a factory in Russia. In the 1950s and 1960s, Krupp and especially the highly influential plenipotentiary Berthold Beitz recognized much earlier than most other firms the potential represented by what we now call "emerging markets": especially the very big emerging markets of Brazil, India, Russia, and (a little later) also China.

Third and finally, the enterprise lived in a perpetual tension between the story (occasionally very dramatic) of family ownership and the establishment of a complex business organization. Germans like to portray German business life and even intellectual life as a series of family affairs: the story of the Krupps, Thyssens, Siemens, Haniels, and more recently Burdas, Quandts, and Porsches, or of the Wagner and Mann clans. Especially in the second half of the twentieth century, the Federal Republic's media both glamorized and demonized (but fundamentally trivialized) business leaders, and the major business families became running stories for publications such as *Stern, Bunte,* and (especially in the case of Krupp) *Der Spiegel.*

In the nineteenth century there was also a parallel story of heroic entrepreneurship, in which an exceptional individual broke through the conventions, tastes, and limitations of his (rarely her) own time and created a new reality and a new world. For these figures, the imagination triumphed. The nineteenth century was the age of Great Men: of Goethe, Chopin, Liszt, Bismarck, Gladstone, Garibaldi. The heroic entrepreneur—an Alfred Krupp, for instance—easily fitted alongside such figures.

In 1967, in a dramatic and wrenching gesture, the Krupp enterprise was taken out of the world of family business and put into a new setting, as a company owned by a foundation. The Alfried Krupp von Bohlen und Halbach-Stiftung had not one purpose but a double mission: on the one hand, it was explicitly designed to preserve a very particular enterprise and a historical business culture; and, on the other, it was dedicated to projects that were to be in the general good.

The obsession with a heroic businessman, who might be an angel or a demon, is not uniquely German. It is also found, for instance, in the work of the Irish-British writer George Bernard Shaw, whose fictional Andrew Undershaft in his play *Major Barbara* is drawn heavily from the charismatic figure of the arms dealer Basil Zaharoff

(1850–1936) as the "wicked rich one." But the Faustian character of the business leader, and the expectations that surround succeeding generations, appear with particular harshness in the case of Germany, and especially in the story of the Krupp family.

Alfred Krupp in the nineteenth century knew about the potential for criticism and hostility. But what was peculiar about Krupp's business was how insistent Alfred Krupp was that the company should bear the name of his father, Friedrich Krupp. In other words, the company was named after someone whose entrepreneurial activity was characterized by more or less constant and continual failure, bitter failure. The name Friedrich Krupp seemed to stand as a perpetual memento mori, the equivalent of the pictorial depictions of *vanitas* that in earlier centuries merchants kept in their rooms to remind themselves not just of the transformative power of the imagination but also of the fallibility of all human effort.

ONE

R I S K

Friedrich Krupp

It was Thomas Mann who wrote the most significant and evocative account of the German commercial classes and their perpetually problematic relationship to entrepreneurship and moneymaking. *Buddenbrooks* was published in 1901, when Mann was only twenty-five. Together with another book written not long after, Joseph Schumpeter's *Theorie der wirtschaftlichen Entwicklung* (1911), which eulogized the creative destruction of entrepreneurship, it has indelibly molded our approach to business history, and in particular the way we view the dynamics of the family firm. Commentators on the phenomenon of family firms, whether academics, journalists, or business people, invariably refer to a "Buddenbrooks syndrome." The concept corresponds to long-familiar slogans in England ("from clogs to clogs in three generations"), Japan ("the fortune made through the hard work of the first generation is all lost by the easygoing third"), and India ("poor, miser, rich, spendthrift") as well as Germany ("The father makes it, the son keeps it, the grandson breaks it.").[1] The novel stands appropriately, in terms of chronology, at the turn of the century: between a nineteenth century dominated in Europe by family firms and a twentieth century shaped by large, multi-owner, joint stock corporations. Mann's novel appears to

Figure 1.1 The founder: Friedrich Krupp (1787–1826). Courtesy of Historical Archives Krupp.

give a graphically memorable account of the decline of a family (that is its subtitle: *Verfall einer Familie*), which could serve as a broader metaphor for the erosion of the values of small-town Germany and the victory of a self-destructive modern materialism.

The Krupps seemed to anticipate this dynamic almost a century earlier. The family had originally moved from the Netherlands in the sixteenth century. They were a respected and prosperous family in the small-town world of early modern Essen, a small ecclesiastical territory ruled by the abbess of the Essen Damenstift (nunnery). Arndt (or Arnold) Krupe (or Krupp) had moved to Essen in the late sixteenth century presumably for religious reasons, as he was a Lutheran, and in 1587 he is mentioned as a member of the merchants' guild and from 1600 to 1623 sat on the town council.

His great-great-granddaughter, Helene Amalie Ascherfeld, at the age of nineteen in 1751 married Friedrich Jodocus Krupp, the son of the Essen mayor Arnold Krupp. Friedrich Jodocus had developed both a retail and a wholesale business in so-called *Kolonialwaren*, imported goods such as tobacco and spices, and had at least seven properties in Essen, including a residence that was both living quarters and business property on the Essen Flax Market. When he died in 1757, his widow was only twenty-four, but she soon built up the business, trading with cloth, porcelain, sugar and spices, and increasingly with coffee, and developing an extensive range of contacts in the Netherlands, Bremen, and Hamburg as well as London. Her substantial profits were largely invested in real estate. There was a separate linen-trading business, in which she bought cloth from local rural producers.[2] She also in 1759 established a snuff tobacco mill on Essen's Flax Market, which was still flourishing at the beginning of the next century. In addition, she seems to have acted as a financier.

It was financial engagement that eventually led Helene Amalie Krupp also to move into iron production, with the acquisition of the Gutehoffnungshütte, which combined a blast furnace with a small foundry. Gute Hoffnung's owner, Eberhard Pfandhöfer, originally an imaginative and innovative businessman, had engaged in a diverse series of speculative investments, descended into alcoholism, and had needed to borrow extensively, in particular from the "widow Krupp" in Essen. She later noted that "Eberhard Pfandhöfer had built in 1782 the Gute Hoffnung Iron Furnace in Sterkrade with my cash advances."[3] In particular, Pfandhöfer seems to have used her services for making transfers to the Netherlands. In 1796 Pfandhöfer was obliged to stop operations at Gute Hoffnung, though he continued to run the nearby St. Antony ironworks. Finally, in 1799, perhaps in order to secure her debts, which had risen to the quite substantial sum of eighteen thousand thalers, Helene Amalie bought the Gute Hoffnung ironworks at an auction for twelve thousand thalers, though she only managed to begin operations in June 1800. Her major advantage was that she had excellent business contacts in the Netherlands. Helene Amalie introduced some technical innovations but found that the Gutehoffnungshütte was a rather problematic possession. The products, mostly pots and small boilers as well as weights, needed to be taken overland to the port of Ruhrort on the river Rhine, and the delicate castings seem to have often been damaged during transport.[4] But in particular the ironworks depended for its water supply on a competitor, the St. Antony Hütte, located in a different small German principality.

Helene Amalie's eldest son, Peter Friedrich Wilhelm Krupp, died at the age of forty-one, and it was his son, Friedrich, who founded the business that would achieve world fame as Krupp. But his initial business move was a disappointment. By 1807 Helene Amalie Krupp had left the management of the Gute Hoffnung to her grandson. He initially aimed to change the emphasis of production to parts for steam engines, and Petronella Krupp (the widow of Peter Friedrich Wilhelm Krupp) concluded a contract for the supply of such parts for steam engines built by Franz Dinnendahl that would be used to drain coal mines. But Friedrich Krupp rapidly found that Gute Hoffnung iron was inferior in quality to that produced by St. Antony. He ran out of fuel during the winter of 1807/8 and, as his debts mounted, agreed with his grandmother to withdraw from the enterprise. In September 1808 she sold the ironworks to the brothers Haniel, who had already bought the St. Antony works and rapidly established an important business.

In the 1800s Helene Amalie also started to buy some mining shares. She clearly recognized at a relatively early stage the transformative potential of the fuel resources of the Ruhr Valley, even though the mining techniques available meant that the amount of coal that could be extracted was still quite limited.

Only a few years later, in May 1810, she died at the age of seventy-seven, leaving a substantial fortune to Friedrich Krupp, his brother Wilhelm, and his sister Helene. Friedrich almost immediately merged his own trading firm into that of his grandmother and liquidated them both in order to concentrate on specialty iron known as *Gussstahl* or *Tiegelstahl* (cast steel) production. A notary's contract of November 20, 1811, established the firm as "Friederich Krupp in Essen."

The venture looked like, and was, a wild speculation, giving up a solid business legacy for something that rested on an arcane and uncertain new mode of fabrication. The experience with the Gutehoffnungshütte might have served as a warning. In particular Friedrich was obsessed with the English ability to produce steel, which was treated as a closely guarded secret and the fundament of British prosperity and military strength. Indeed, until 1828 England prohibited its skilled craftsmen from emigrating, so that the commercial secrets would not be lost. In 1811 Krupp concluded a contract with the brothers Georg Carl Gottfried and Wilhelm Georg Ludwig von Kechel, two quite elderly former officers from the army of the principality of Nassau, who had made cast steel in 1803 in the Eifel with the brothers Poensgen (another name that would become identified with a great steel tradition in Germany) and who promised to transfer their knowledge to Krupp.

The new enterprise was described as making cast steel "in the English manner," in other words according to the crucible process that had been developed experimentally in the mid-eighteenth century by the Sheffield watchmaker Benjamin Huntsman, who had required a high-quality, homogeneous steel for making watch springs. That process involved the melting of blister steel in a clay crucible and adding carbon and other materials; skimming off the impurities in the slag; and then pouring the product and working it. It produced very tough steel, although it was difficult to work it because the hammering could take place only while the steel was still heated. The critical metallurgical discovery of the English industrial revolution concerned the importance of the carbon content of steel, in other words iron with a carbon content of less than 2 percent. As the carbon content grew higher, the steel became harder but less malleable and less easily worked and smelted.

The Huntsman process seemed to many Europeans to have the qualities of a great mystery, and numerous continental imitators set about the development of an analogous process. In particular, the properties of the substances in the flux that needed to be added to the molten iron were the subject of a great deal of speculation. The need for indigenous German cast steel was increased after 1806 because of the impact of Napoleon's Continental System, which excluded English products from the European mainland.

Friedrich Krupp started to build a works in a costly surge of construction activity in 1812/13 that included a furnace for making steel by a cementing process, a smelting workshop, and a hammer workshop. The new business was located on one of his grandmother's properties that he had bought from his brother Wilhelm. He also seriously investigated the possibility of establishing a file-making workshop on French territory on the left bank of the Rhine but then transferred the planned production to Essen after the defeat of Napoleon in Russia. Krupp went ahead with the plan to make "English steel" even though the results seemed ever more elusive. He made a decisive technical turn when, dissatisfied with the small size and the high cost of the clay crucibles that he brought from near Passau, he started to produce his own, larger, crucibles in 1812. By 1813 he was so pleased with progress that he turned the contract with the von Kechels into a lifetime guarantee of employment and participation in the profits of the enterprise. In reality, there was nothing but loss: by autumn 1814 Krupp had spent 30,000 thalers but had made only 1,422 thalers in revenue. In November 1814, just as the Napoleonic Empire was breaking apart, Krupp dismissed the von Kechels. They, it appears, were not surprised by the rupture and concluded that the problems were the fault of Friedrich Krupp for working with larger than conventional crucibles.[5] By the end of his life, Krupp's inheritance from his grandmother, which has been calculated as the large sum of 42,222 thalers, had completely evaporated. The real estate that was the core of his grandmother's legacy was sold in two big blocks in 1818–19 and in 1824.[6]

For a time Krupp contemplated giving up the factory altogether. But then he rapidly found a new partner, Friedrich Nicolai, a mechanic who had a Prussian patent for the production of cast steel and who promised to invest his own money in the Krupp enterprise. Nicolai had a colorful past, had been briefly imprisoned as a spy, and had volunteered in the Prussian army as a captain of hussars. The two concluded a contract in July 1815, in which Nicolai committed himself to produce cast steel immediately, "without more experiments," according to the qualities set in the Prussian patent. The main attraction was that he would contribute a special flux, which contained a mixture of "Markasit," a form of pyrites, manganese ore, and cow dung.[7] But Nicolai was in reality even more incompetent than the von Kechels. An atmosphere in which knowledge is regarded as a kind of alchemical mystery clearly leads to chicanery and charlatanism. In reality, Nicolai had no money of his own to invest. He did move into the Essen factory immediately after concluding the contract, directed the building of three new crucible furnaces, and added furnaces so as to preheat the iron. Nicolai also traveled to Berlin, where he managed to obtain contracts to supply cast steel. But he found the actual producing of steel much harder. When things did not work out, he blamed Friedrich Krupp's idiosyncratic crucibles, much as the Kechels had done. What success there was depended on Krupp's own increasing skill with judging the right temperatures for the smelting process and the right additives in the crucibles. This practical skill represented the major technical breakthrough on which the future of the Krupp business would depend. By 1816 the partners were no longer on speaking terms, and Nicolai was even accusing his enemies of trying to kill him. Krupp ordered an investigation of the quality of the steel produced by Nicolai, which showed that steel to be unusable.

It was only in 1815 that Krupp managed to produce small quantities of steel on the basis of the crucible process, and only in 1818 that he began to use the Osemund pig iron from the Sauerland area (also known as Grafschaft Mark), which produced a much more consistent quality of cast steel. But even that source proved quite variable, and Krupp continually changed suppliers. It was a fortuitous occurrence that the crucibles Krupp made from local clay had a high silicate content, and that this silicate was absorbed by the molten metal and affected its metallurgical qualities. It gave a hardness not just at the surface but deeper down in the metal, making the result particularly useful for steels where different levels were exposed (notably in stamps and casts): for surface hardness, English Sheffield steel was notably superior.[8]

Another problem was that the initial location of the factory was unsuitable. Transporting the coal that was needed both as fuel and as a source of carbon was difficult, and there was no room for expansion. Part of the business was thus moved to a site near the Limbeck Gate of Essen, while the hammer works had to stay where they were because they required the flow of the creek to drive them.

Figure 1.2 The Krupp works, c. 1820. Courtesy of Historical Archives Krupp.

By 1817 Krupp was producing cast steel blocks and bars as well as drills, files, and artisans' tools, especially for tanners. Most importantly he began to produce stamps for coining. The discovery of a reliable process for producing cheap, low-nominal-value token coinage was an important innovation, which laid the basis for a vast expansion of simple commercial activity in the early nineteenth century and ended centuries of economic uncertainty caused by the absence of a reliable low-value circulating medium.[9] Matthew Boulton in England had in 1786 adapted the steam engine for use in the milling of coins. In 1817 Diedrich Uhlhorn of Grevenbroich developed a lever or knuckle action that could be driven by steam and turn out thirty to sixty coins a minute. The demand for coin-making equipment thus became a key part of a new economic era.

By 1817 the Düsseldorf mint had delivered a positive verdict on the coining stamps produced from cast steel in the Krupp works, and in 1818 Krupp was producing for the Prussian mint in Berlin as well. It was this move, rather than production of tools for local craftsmen, that made Krupp's reputation. In 1817 the works sold 2,607 thalers worth of goods, in 1818 4,202, almost half of the revenue coming from the coin-stamping casts. It was a very high-value but small-scale production: in 1820, a very good business year, the amount of steel involved in the production of the casts weighed no more than some two hundred kilograms.[10] Business went so well that Krupp set off on a new round of construction, which included a small house for a supervisor that would later be celebrated as the original Krupp house, the *Stammhaus*. He planned twenty-four furnaces in the foundry, although in the end only eight were built. Krupp had very ambitious expansion plans, and in November 1817 he asked the Prussian government for an interest-free loan of the vast sum of 20,000 or 25,000 thalers to extend the factory. Such a request seemed quite hopeless. But Krupp was instructed to wait for the outcome of his court case against Nicolai, and then there could be a determination of "whether there were business grounds and the means to support the enterprise."[11]

But in 1818 the Prussian government went over to a regime in which tariffs were greatly reduced, and the factories that were producing goods to compete with English products became much more vulnerable. Krupp's factory suffered from other problems. By the spring of 1819 the Düsseldorf mint master wrote of the "sad experience" that the quality of the metal used in the coin-making equipment had deteriorated, and that only a third of the stamps supplied were usable. A substantial problem lay in access to the right quality of pig iron. But this was just the moment when the new smelting works had been completed, with more furnaces and larger crucibles. Krupp may also have been too keen to diversify his production; he started to make a variety of steel rolls and blocks, as well as steel for springs and coils, when he might better have concentrated on the market for coining equipment, which in 1819 amounted to two-thirds of Krupp's sales. There was also new competition, not only from England but also from a rival plant, which managed to win a large share of the contracts to supply Prussia's eastern provinces. In the early 1820s there was a brief flourishing of the enterprise, but affairs were always quite precarious. In fact 1820 and 1823 were the only years in which the factory produced a small operating surplus.

The enterprise was financed as a family business, with relatives lending increasingly large amounts to support it through its vulnerable infancy. There were obviously high risks: most infant industries at that time were expected to perish. In Krupp's case most of the funding came from his mother, Petronella Krupp, who in 1820 owned 18.3 percent of the 42,150-thaler debt, as well as his father-in-law, Johann Wilhelmi, who was always slightly dubious of his relative's business sense.[12]

Krupp never stopped hoping for a better outcome and for new fields of business activity. In 1820 he turned to the Russian government and asked permission to establish a cast steel works in Russia. In 1821 he was visited by the chairman of the Prussian Association for the Promotion of Commercial Skills, but the factory was idle at the time of the visit and cannot have made a good impression.

In 1824 came an utter collapse. All of Friedrich Krupp's inherited real estate was now sold off. In 1825 the *Faktor* named Tacke, the skilled and obviously very loyal foreman who had run much of the commercial side of the business, left the company, vacating a simple dwelling on the factory site; and in 1826 the man who had looked after the finances also went. In 1824 Krupp's family had to leave the imposing house on the Flax Market and move into the small supervisor's hut next to the new works. (By the 1870s Friedrich Krupp's son Alfred had turned this "original house" [Stammhaus] into the stuff of legend.) Friedrich Krupp's mother, Petronella, took over the management of the firm's finances but refused to extend further credit. It looked as if the Krupp story might simply end in the small-scale narrative of the decline of a well-established Essen *Bürger* family because of an excessive dedication to technical innovation and the absence of any business sense or responsibility. This was total entrepreneurial failure: Krupp was obsessed with technology but had no deep understanding of the importance of securing markets, establishing a reliable supply of raw materials, or of financial control.

Friedrich Krupp remains a shadowy figure: there is indeed by contrast with his predecessors and his successors no oil portrait, only a cheap scissors silhouette. A Bürger should not take undue risks or threaten the comfortable existence of his family. But Krupp's failure as a Bürger set the scene for entrepreneurial breakthrough and success. In the end, the values of *Bürgerlichkeit* and innovative entrepreneurial activity, the Schumpeterian process of creative destruction, are mutually incompatible.

In November 1812 more than a decade before his finances collapsed, Krupp had been elected to the Essen municipal council, and he continued to play a role on the council, in the militia, and as a fire officer. But in 1824 he was required to give up all these offices and was crossed off the list of "merchants with rights." Krupp was

Figure 1.3 The widow: Therese Krupp (1790–1850). Courtesy of Historical Archives Krupp.

disgraced as well as impoverished. Nervous strain exacerbated his physical illness, and his combined physical and mental collapse damaged business prospects even more. Friedrich Krupp died, probably of tuberculosis, on October 8, 1826, at the age of thirty-nine. His son Alfred, who in 1825 had begun to assist in the factory, took over the running of the business, which now belonged to yet another widow Krupp. Therese Krupp, wife of the deceased Friedrich and the mother of young Alfred, did not hesitate in continuing the operations of the factory, a decision which, as the historian Burkhard Beyer points out, indicates that she and her financially strong father-in-law believed that Friedrich had been more than a technically gifted dreamer and that there existed, despite all the setbacks, a real basis for potential prosperity.

In continental Europe, widows played a central role in the development of the steel industry. Women in fact had a much greater part in the formulation of business strategies than at a later time in the nineteenth century, when the corporation and its statutes and the bureaucratization of corporate existence left less to chance and less to the skillful operation of dynastic politics. But this widow Krupp chose a different strategy: she circulated an advertisement to the effect that "the secret of cast steel has not been lost in consequence of the death of my husband, but has passed to our oldest son, who has already supervised the factory for some time."[13] The advertisement did not comment on the fact that the son's age was fourteen. That son, who had been baptized as Alfried, was just one year younger than the ineffective (fictional) Hanno Buddenbrook at the time of his death.

T W O

S T E E L

Alfred Krupp

One year after Alfred Krupp's death in 1887, the elderly North German writer Theodor Storm published a novella, indisputably his finest, *The Rider of the White Horse* (*Der Schimmelreiter*), about a solitary and immensely hard-working man who has devoted his life to building dikes against the sea but is increasingly lonely and vulnerable, and dies in a ferocious storm and flood as his life's work (a sea dike) seems to be coming undone. Storm's Hauke Haien is a tragic and heroic figure, the benefits of whose innovations are reaped only by later generations. He is the embodiment of the Protestant work ethic. In life he is admired but also mocked by the narrow-minded, the envious, the conservative, and the superstitious. Even after his death, however, his legacy is disputed: for some, he is a heroic entrepreneur who has enriched his community; for others, he becomes a supernatural specter.

Alfred Krupp perfectly expressed Hauke Haien's philosophy of unremitting dedication to work when he wrote in 1873, in a memorandum that the company directors found so important that they had it printed and distributed among the company's twelve thousand workers: "Foremen and masters should not emerge from comfortable domesticity, self-satisfaction, bedcoats and slippers, but from practical work, from the best workers when it

Figure 2.1 Julius Grün, portrait of Alfred Krupp, 1880s. Courtesy of Historical Archives Krupp.

is necessary to come to grips with work. . . . A simple sense is necessary that is not distracted by the pursuit of studies, art, or other passions, and that does not see work as an unpleasant necessary occupation that provides food and wages, but rather pursues work with pleasure. Whoever has fought for his bread with the hardest work, and shows himself to be capable of being a master, a foreman, and even more—that is the man!"[1] The work ethic would create a community of *Kruppianer*, workers bound to the enterprise and the community by pride in the product of their labor. This was a social philosophy that provided the precise antithesis to the theories of alienation in work developed by Krupp's near contemporary Karl Marx.

Alfred Krupp defined the image of the entrepreneur in Germany. He was constantly creative, intensely individualistic, patronizingly paternalist in his relationship with his employees, skeptical and suspicious toward bankers, supplicatory and sometimes subservient to the state, and indefatigable and innovative in search of foreign markets. One of the reasons we know such a great deal about Krupp, and the ideas that drove him, is that he was an obsessive writer and correspondent who managed his business by fierce epistolary salvos. A characteristic missive explained that he had been writing letters from four in the morning and that it was already midday.[2] He was also deeply impressed, from the example of his father, by the continual possibility of failure; and he liked to explain that he had simply had more luck than his father. That failure may have made for a sense of mistrust that became ever deeper as Krupp grew older. He was, like the hero of Storm's novella, a man who found personal relations difficult.

His view of life was precisely the opposite of that entertained by the later generations of Thomas Mann's Buddenbrook dynasty. He had little time or sympathy for culture, civilization, or formal education. In particular he constantly celebrated the idea of the self-made man who did not need formal training. The school of life was better than anything the new high schools (*Gymnasien*) or the technical universities (*Technische Hochschulen*) could offer. "Together with people who lack theory I have astonished the world and made progress," he wrote in old age. But he added nostalgically: "Since theory began to dictate, we are overtaken and outstripped. The enterprises that are now most progressive do not have highly learned people at the top, not in England, not in Belgium, not in America."[3]

But this was not merely a personal story. One particular theme that was dear to Alfred Krupp was the rags-to-riches development of the enterprise, of the *Fabrik*. In the early 1870s, in the midst of a colossal expansion, when he was also building the grand Villa Hügel, Krupp wrote to the firm's management to remind them of the days when "raw material was bought on the retail market, when I was the chief executive, clerk, treasurer, smith, smelter, coke beater, night watchman at the cement oven, as well as much else, and one run-down horse served our transportation needs."[4]

He saw a parallel between his business development and the emergence of the German state. In the aftermath of German unification, he made the explicit comparison: "Achieving something depends solely on the will. If a state in the course of one year absorbs and rules many states, then we too will also be able to introduce and manage a dozen new industrial creations."[5] And: "My achievement will stand and fall with Prussia's greatness and military supremacy."[6] By 1871, when the king of Prussia became the German emperor, Krupp had become the symbol of the new Germany, built on technical achievement as well as military success.

THE TECHNICAL IMPERATIVE

The identification of Krupp with German technological supremacy would have been hard for anyone to foresee in 1826. But already at that time, it was clear that the machine age would transform the structure of demand. In 1819 the Gutehoffnungshütte started to build steam engines, and the new machinery demanded a large number of robust and durable parts. There was inevitably an increased demand for steel tools because of the spread of machinery. But Alfred Krupp had initial difficulties, for the same reasons as his father. In 1827 the quality of the raw material was poor, and this affected the cast steel produced from it. He had given costly guarantees of the quality of his products and was obliged to replace in the case of breakages. The practice was inherited from his father, who had added a quality guarantee to his price lists. Alfred Krupp then turned to the producer with the highest reputation, the brothers Brüninghaus from the Sauerland. In 1836–37 he also tried, without success, to obtain access to Swedish ores in order to try to replicate the quality of British steel. Another initial problem was that the hammers used to work the cast steel (weighing up to four hundred kilograms) were too light to make large cast objects and too heavy to make the smaller casts required for fine steel wire and smaller tools. The technology existed, but not on the right scale.

Krupp's major initial successes, like those of his father, were in the relatively small and specialist market of cast steel stamps for the production of coins. The newly widowed Therese Krupp asked in August 1828 for contracts from the Prussian mint. Like his father, Alfred Krupp engaged in ceaseless innovation, but he kept a quite firm grip on the technical processes. The memory of his father's failures and humiliations must have been a decisive inspiration for success. But it is likely that, for his first ten years of operations, the business was still losing money.[7]

In 1829–30, when winter frost made operating the hammer impossible, Krupp took advantage of the opportunity to redesign the plant and add facilities on an upper floor of the workshop for the manufacture of rollers. He could then announce that he was in the position to produce high-quality rollers, which might be used in the production of fine rolled silverware and gold and silver wire, in other words, for a wider set of applications than simply coin stamping. He also after 1831 developed ring rollers of four or five inches diameter without a seam or joint, which became quite widely used in mints for the rolling of coins. Another experiment involved the addition of copper to increase the surface hardness of the rollers. In 1831 the production of rollers increased from a value of 640 to 1,630 thalers. In the course of the 1830s, the production of rollers overtook coin-stamping products as a share of the Krupp business. They were sold to very distant markets: in 1837, two engraved rollers, for instance, were sold to Brazil.

Larger rolls and a greater volume of business required larger casts. The Huntsman crucible process had always been a small-scale operation, more protoindustrial than industrial, and from an early stage Krupp was fascinated by the possibility of extending operations by combining the steel produced by several crucibles. In 1832 he developed casts made from four separate crucibles and weighing up to 150 pounds; by 1834 eight crucibles were being used to make casts. The larger production would require heavier hammering, with more power, and in 1835 Krupp ordered a steam engine from the Gutehoffnungshütte for this purpose. The costs involved were financed largely by a cousin, Carl Friedrich von Müller, who paid in 12,473 thalers and received a stake of one third of the company.

In 1833 Krupp began to make not just rollers but complete rolling presses, and two years later he had the facility to cut cog teeth into the rollers. Another departure was that specialized rolls could produce the steel combs required to hold threads in the new power looms, or to roll precious metals. By 1836 the value of Krupp's production had increased to 23,000 thalers; the workforce had risen to eighty.

At first, Krupp had been obliged by a shortage of capital to make semifinished products that were finally worked by other producers; as he looked to increasing the size of his business, he could move more into finished products. But those demanded a different sales philosophy, and allowed a new pricing strategy. Higher prices could be justified by building a brand and investing in reputation. His brother Hermann complained at the end of the 1830s that high quality meant that there was less demand for replacement rolls, that it "was a great fault that our rolls keep for so long." Alfred saw that if there was high-quality production, it needed to be marketed properly, and that high prices could indeed be themselves a marketing technique. As he explained to a Swiss dealer, "A good roll is never too expensive."[8]

His father had been concerned above all with technical processes. Alfred Krupp, who spent much of his early years corresponding with and visiting potential customers, was acutely aware that a technical improvement would not simply sell itself; a successful entrepreneur also needed to understand how new markets could be established. The hard steel rolls that could be used to produce new instruments might also be engaged to make tableware for the expanding middle classes: to manufacture a product that would become a visible sign of the establishment of a new bourgeois culture. In 1839 Alfred and his brother developed for a Berlin silverware producer a new rolling technique for the production of cast-steel spoons and forks. By 1843 Krupp had developed an even more successful process for rolling spoons and other silverware, with equipment that could turn out 150 spoons a day.

At this moment, it seemed that there was no particular need to be in Essen or in the Ruhr Valley and that a location closer to the new sources of demand might be preferable. For a time, it even seemed as if the whole base for the Krupp operations might shift to the Habsburg Empire, and to the Habsburg capital, which was rapidly developing as a metropole of European taste. The battle of Königgrätz, the Prussian victory, and the massive shift in influence from south to north in Germany was not a preordained fact.

In 1837 Alfred Krupp had supplied coining rolls to Vienna, but there had been constant problems with their quality and a protracted legal dispute. The equipment was enormously expensive, the machine sent in 1840 alone costing 18,300 thalers. Krupp felt that the Austrian mint officials had set a deliberate trap with impossible quality demands in order simply to avoid paying the Prussian manufacturer. He needed to go to Vienna and stay there for almost two years, an absence that had bad consequences for the Gussstahlfabrik.

It was this kind of experience that drove a continual search for new products and markets, and Alfred's brother Hermann talked of the "necessity" of finding new sources of income. Those included machine toolmaking, as from the 1830s the Krupp firm had been producing its own lathe spindles; by the 1840s Krupp was selling them. In 1843 Krupp developed plans for production of silverware in Austria, mostly financed with funds provided by Alexander Schoeller, the scion of a Düren textile manufacturing family. Krupp and Schoeller opened a major plant at Berndorf, outside Vienna, which quickly, in 1845, won a silver medal for its tableware at the Vienna commercial exhibition. The plant was managed by Krupp's younger brother Hermann. In the early years, it ran up enormous losses.

In 1846 Krupp obtained a British patent for the spoon-rolling process and then began to approach other governments—in Prussia, France, Belgium, and Russia—to protect the production process. Behind the development of the spoon rolls lay a whole entrepreneurial vision: the patents Krupp applied for in England and France as well as in Prussia in the 1840s covered basically the equipment of a silverware factory. Krupp was prepared to commit himself to sell his tools to no more than one customer in each country, so that his clients would receive for their very high-priced product a national monopoly to supply middle-class tables. There was a global outreach. By 1847, for instance, Krupp was asking his Paris representative to take up contacts with Rio de Janeiro in order to investigate the possibilities of selling the spoon-making equipment there. Another area where fine-quality steel products had an obvious application was the military. In 1844 Alfred Krupp discussed with Wilhelm Jäger, an

Elberfeld manufacturer, the supply of cast steel for armor, in particular cuirasses; this new business required financing from the Elberfeld bank of von der Heydt. Relations with Jäger were complicated because of the collapse of plans to jointly develop in Elberfeld a silverware factory double the size of the one in Berndorf. Krupp was worried that the planned factory was too close to Jäger's house and that he would intervene "in his slippers and bathrobe" in entrepreneurial decisions.

Also in 1844, at the Berlin commercial exhibition, Krupp showed not just rolling equipment for goldsmiths' work but also a rifle barrel that represented a considerable technical breakthrough. The steel had been worked in a cold state: its high malleability no longer required the hot working that had originally been required in the production of cast steel. There was a synergy between military and nonmilitary production at this stage, and one new market led quite rapidly to another. Krupp immediately sent two of the new rifle barrels to the Gutehoffnungshütte to show that crucible steel could be used to produce machine parts. The malleable rifle barrel was intended to demonstrate the advantages of Krupp steel, and in 1847 Krupp started to supply crankshafts for heavy industrial equipment, including hammers. Crankshafts also became Krupp's entrée to the railroad business, when the Bonn-Cologne railway ordered shafts. Then the bigger Cologne-Minden railway followed on an experimental basis, and was so pleased that it ordered thirty-six axles in 1849, as well as some springs; and Krupp's business partner Friedrich Sölling developed increasingly close relations with the Cologne-Minden railroad company.

The diversity of Krupp's products should not lead to the impression that this was already a large enterprise. By

1844 the workforce had risen to 131, but the factory was essentially a large and successful artisan workshop, a specialized Gussstahlfabrik that made a few niche products. There was as yet no generalized large-scale application for cast-steel products. Twenty years later it had become a gigantic enterprise, with twelve thousand workers and a productive area of thirty-five hectares.

The burgeoning interest in Krupp products, however, coincided with a major economic as well as social and in the end also political crisis. In the business downturn that followed 1846, orders fell, and by 1848, when Europe was swept by revolutions, the factory was employing only seventy workers.

The real breakthrough to mass production occurred with railroad equipment, in precisely the aftermath of the revolutionary year. Krupp fought tenaciously for axle and spring orders, undertaking costly guarantees for replacement in the event of failure and breakage. The guarantees were especially important in that the high-silicate steel was weakened by a hardening process that produced an irregular structure in the metal.[9] In particular, it was the production of weldless steel tires for the wheels of locomotives and wagons that brought Krupp to a new scale of production. On an experimental basis Krupp supplied steel tires cast in a mold for the Cologne-Minden railway in 1851, but the process was too complicated and not suited for more widespread use. He then developed a scaling-up process in which, from initial diameters of only a few inches, cast steel was worked into larger and larger weldless rings—in the end, rings large enough to be used on railway wheels. Krupp first obtained an English patent for this process in 1852 and then a Prussian patent. By 1854, at the Munich

Essen. Als Marke ist eingetragen unter Nr. 1 zu der Firma **Fried. Krupp** in Essen zufolge Anmeldung vom 6. Dezember 1875, Mittags 12 Uhr, für „Stahl und Eisen, sowie Stahl- und Eisenwaaren" das Zeichen:

Essen, den 9. Dezember 1875.
Königliches Kreisgericht. I. Abtheilung.

Figure 2.2 Registration of three steel tire logo, 1875. Courtesy of Historical Archives Krupp.

commercial exhibition, Krupp was willing to guarantee these products for a distance of twenty thousand miles. These steel tires became the symbol of the Krupp enterprise, designed by Alfred Krupp himself, with three superimposed tires forming a corporate logo after 1875 (following a new law on trademarks).[10]

The manufacture of large quantities of axles and wheels required much more steel than could be supplied by the cementing process. In the early 1850s, other German manufacturers started to experiment with the application of the puddling process to steel. Slag was added to molten metal, which was then continually stirred. In 1855 Krupp built his own puddling works. By 1857 the puddling works had six furnaces, and by 1863 seventeen. In 1853 Krupp also built his first rolling mill.

But even in 1858, the large Prussian state railways were not committed to purchasing the Krupp cast-steel tires. The demand for Krupp's expanded production remained precarious. There was heavy competition with a large rival steelmaker, the Bochumer Verein, which successfully developed the process of casting steel wheels in molds (the process that Krupp had initially preferred in 1851). The competitive response required a substantial reduction in Krupp's prices for the worked tires. Providing tires gradually led to the production of entire wheel sets. In 1886 Krupp eventually acquired an enterprise, the F. Asthöwer & Cie. Steel Works in Annen in the Ruhr, that had sufficient expertise in the production of wheels and other cast steel parts.

In 1862, under conditions of great secrecy, Krupp took a quantitative leap with the Bessemer steel process, in which air was blown through the molten pig iron in a gigantic "converter" to burn out carbon and other impurities. Krupp constructed the first Bessemer work in continental Europe. He had been alerted to the new process in 1855 by his English representative, Alfred Longsdon, and immediately tried to get a Prussian patent for it. But it took a time for the problems to be eliminated. By 1862 two converters had arrived from Sheffield and entered production. Krupp contributed significantly to the process, and replaced the original open hearth with a closed cupola furnace.[11] The new process could handle quantities two hundred times greater than the old puddling process. In the same year, 1862, a rolling mill devoted to steel plate production commenced operations. In 1864 Krupp started a large rail-rolling mill, which took almost all of the Bessemer steel.

Krupp was also one of the principal German participants in the next great innovation that transformed steelmaking, the use of regenerative heat in what became known as the Siemens-Martin process. In a technique pioneered by William Siemens, a member of one of the most innovative German families, in Birmingham, waste gases were used to superheat incoming air and gaseous fuel in a honeycomb of bricks at the base of the furnace. In 1863 Krupp made contact with Friedrich Siemens, the brother of William, and from 1864 started experiments with regeneration in two carefully concealed laboratories in the Gussstahlfabrik. But the technique really took off only after two French experimenters, Emile and Pierre-Emile Martin, in 1864 added scrap iron to the molten metal and developed a means of burning off carbon from the mixture. By 1868 William Siemens had developed a new furnace, and Krupp commented: "This news is most interesting—this can lead to a tremendous revolution in fabrication . . . we must follow this chance, and not let it escape—we must be the first, if it is good."[12] In 1869 Krupp built the first Siemens-Martin furnace in Germany. In 1871 Krupp constructed, south of the Gussstahlfabrik, a new Martin works with twelve furnaces. The Martin furnace was operated with an initial charge of pig iron and then additions of large quantities of scrap metal. A scrap shortage induced Siemens in 1875 to introduce a new process in which particular high-grade iron ores could be used directly in the furnace. In the 1870s high-quality Martin steel could be used for casting very large pieces of steel in molds: ship propellers, gear shafts, locomotive parts. Krupp technology could now easily be scaled up.

The construction of axles and particularly of cranks evidently required much bigger hammers for the working of the giant steel forms. In 1852 a hammer with a 5,000-kilogram weight began operations in the Gussstahlfabrik, and by 1856 Krupp had a hammer of 7,000 kilograms. But this was not enough to overshadow the English and French competition in Low Moor in West Yorkshire and Le Creusot in central France, where superhammers were already the norm. Beating its foreign rivals was a significant step to Krupp's ascendancy as the symbol of a new technically dynamic Germany. Alfred Krupp instructed his managers to find out the weight of the biggest hammer in the Schneider works at Le Creusot, in order to know how "small they were."[13] He then devoted a great deal of attention to the construction of a massive hammer, "Fritz," for the working of cast steel, at a cost of 600,000 thalers, with a weight of 30,000 kilograms, capable of making steel blocks weighing up to 25,000 kilograms. It entered production in 1861 and made steel blocks for fifty years.

In 1854 Krupp sent a heavy ship shaft to the Munich commercial exhibition and in 1855 constructed the first shaft for driving ship propellers for the yacht of the viceroy of Egypt, Said Pasha, and in 1854 sent a heavy ship shaft to the Munich commercial exhibition. Such shafts were soon used for the transatlantic steamers of the Hamburg-Amerikanische Paketfahrt-Aktien-Gesellschaft (or HAPAG), and only rather later, from 1875, did the focus of innovation in the use of the giant steel shafts shift to German naval orders. By 1859, however, the Prussian military began ordering artillery—a significant breakthrough for the enterprise.

In the 1860s Krupp also started a process of vertical integration, as a response to the new possibilities of producing Bessemer steel, with the acquisitions of the Sayner Hütte and the Mülhofener Hütte in Sayn (both 1865), the Hermannshütte in Neuwied (1871), and the Johanneshütte in Duisburg and the Hannover mine in Bochum (1872). At first, Krupp had used Swedish and English ores for Bessemer steel production, but then he turned to German producers. There were acquisitions of ore producers on the Lahn and in the Westerwald, and a participation in the Spanish Orconera Iron Ore Co. Ltd., which stood out as an exceptional source of nonphosphoric iron ore and was the only non-German asset of the company in the nineteenth century. In 1872 alone, Krupp bought over three hundred ore fields.[14] The application of the Bessemer process really held out the possibility of conquering a mass market in plate and rails, while simultaneously Martin steel made possible giant cast-steel products.

By 1874, 12,000 workers were employed on an area of thirty-five hectares (almost three times as big as in 1865). There followed another sharp business setback, in which prices collapsed and the future looked uncertain. By Alfred Krupp's death in 1887, however, growth had resumed, and 13,000 were employed in Essen and 20,000 in the whole company. This was now definitively a very big business, the largest private company not only in the German Empire but in Europe. But even as a small firm, Krupp had evolved a distinctive business model, which—like the technology of cast steel—could eventually be scaled up. It had become a highly innovative enterprise: in the period 1877–1880, it was awarded thirteen "valuable" patents, the highest number of any German company except for Siemens.[15]

We have a unique view of Krupp's technical achievement in large part because of his innovative concern with documenting his accomplishments and products, largely for marketing purposes. In 1861 a photographic department was created, initially based in the Stammhaus, the old supervisor's hut that had been the final residence of Friedrich Krupp. The task of the new department initially lay in the creation of gigantic panoramas, composed of multiple photographs, that could be used in advertising to create an impression of the gigantic size of the enterprise

Figure 2.3 Print for the 1867 Paris World Exhibition. Courtesy of Historical Archives Krupp.

Figure 2.4 Krupp worker Wilhelm Engels, employed 1841–78. Courtesy of Historical Archives Krupp.

(and hence of its capacity to produce). The first of these panoramas was produced right away in 1861. Alfred Krupp took an intense personal interest: he specified, for instance, precisely how the photographs prepared in 1867 for the world exhibition should look. In the 1870s photographs of armor and armored artillery, as well as of the Krupp experimental firing range, were used in advertising.[16] But Alfred Krupp also quickly saw new possibilities for the new imaging technologies, in particular in the use of photographs to control the workforce. By 1871 he was explaining: "I wish to introduce forever the practice of photographing workers, and a much stricter control of the workforce, of their past, their impulses, their life. We must have a private police that is better informed than the municipal service."[17] The private police force remained an unrealized fantasy. But photography was used to monitor the workforce, and to allow the managers of an increasingly large enterprise to be able to identify individual workers and deal with troublemakers. For advertising, for documentation, and for control, Krupp built up a quite unique photographic record of industrial life. Every part of the business model was documented.

THE BUSINESS MODEL

What distinguished Alfred Krupp from his father, and constituted the core of his "luck," was his ability to work out a business model that involved, not simply adopting and adapting particular technologies, but also four other equally vital ingredients of commercial success: the discovery of new markets for new products or modes of production made possible by the new technologies; the cultivation of the state; an answer to the question of how to finance the costly process of expansion; and finally the establishment of an organizational structure that fostered a sufficient degree of loyalty and trust so as to allow the maintenance of consistent quality, even when production expanded and was scaled up to gigantic proportions.

The model began with a basic technology that was initially dependent on high-quality but low-volume production. The basic achievement lay in the scaling up of the crucible process, with the use of powerful hammers to make very large cast-steel products that were essential to the transport innovations that drove economic development in the mid-nineteenth century: railways and oceanic navigation. The commercial logic of this expansion required the maintenance of the high prices that had characterized the initial phase of high-quality production. But what happened when those prices were attacked as a result of competition, from other processes (as in the case of the formed steel products of the Bochumer Verein), from other producers, and also from those in foreign countries?

Krupp's answer to the question of price maintenance in a competitive and globalized economy was particularly German. That German answer oscillated between two varieties: first, a movement to control prices by restricting competition through cartels. But cartels depended on agreements with competitors, and required a high degree of trust. Such trust was quite foreign to Alfred Krupp's character, hammered out as it had been on the anvil of Friedrich Krupp's failures and humiliations. As he explained: "I hate the idea of fraternization with our competitors, since nobody will do anything for us, and everyone just wants to derive some benefits from such fraternization."[18] In consequence, not just Alfred Krupp but also the Krupp tradition was rather unsympathetic to the idea of cartels as a way of securing the elimination of competition. In the 1920s, for instance, Gustav Krupp von Bohlen und Halbach resisted pressure from his managers, who wanted him to bring the Krupp enterprise into the gigantic new steel concern Vereinigte Stahlwerke.

There was in Krupp's view a second and better way of managing competition. That alternative depended on cultivating markets in which the number of consumers was quite limited, and long-term guarantees and contracts could be negotiated. It pushed Krupp (and the Krupp tradition) away from a mass market, in which the firm would need to compete solely on the basis of price. This meant in the nineteenth century providing railway equipment, and then material for ships and for the military. Krupp's increasing military focus in the nineteenth century arose out of a choice of business model. Alfred Krupp laid out his commercial philosophy with great clarity: "It is not our purpose to ruin our competitors, but rather to make as much money as possible. In our interest, we must keep the prices sufficiently high, that the product remains priceworthy and that sales and profit are in an adequate relationship."[19]

GLOBALIZATION

From the very beginning, the managers of the Krupp enterprise were aware that they were operating in a framework that transcended national markets and national operations. England represented *the* challenge to every continental European entrepreneur: this was the most innovative and prosperous country in Europe. Friedrich Krupp had based his business model on the idea

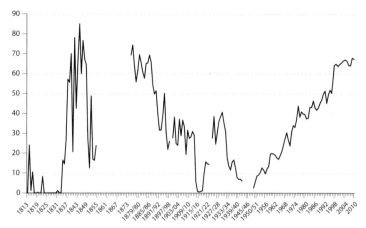

Figure 2.5 Export share of Krupp production (%), 1813–2010.

of producing products that could compete with those of England. At an early stage, Alfred Krupp explained that the technical superiority of his cast-steel minting stamps was such that they were in demand not only in France and Russia but also in America and England.[20] By the mid-1830s, he was selling his coin stamps to the Dutch and Turin mints as well as to Greece. The Austrian market was a key to developing the spoon-milling process that led to the establishment of the Berndorf plant. As late as the 1870s, Krupp was still trying to identify the best metallurgical engineer in Prussia, so as to be able to obtain quick and reliable reports on the experiences and successes of foreign countries, of England, France, Belgium, Russia, and the United States.[21] Success on the world market provided an essential argument in opening up domestic markets.

The most obvious step for Krupp was to anglicize himself as much as possible. He was baptized with the name "Alfried," but in preparing to go to England started to spell his name as "Alfred," and it is remembered only in this anglicized form. (In a similar move, Wilhelm Siemens had become William Siemens). Alfred Krupp's visit to England in 1838/39 became a decisive and formative moment in his business education. The visit was prepared with enormous care. Before and after the English trip, Krupp stayed in France visiting customers, mostly in the artisan communities of gold- and silversmiths. He took great care to study both the English and the French languages, and to make sure that he would make a good impression on his hosts. Unlike in the Ruhr, where his appearance was often workmanlike, he dressed very carefully, with proper boots and elegant silver spurs so as to appear as an English gentleman, in order to inspect and learn from the factories of the most innovative English businesses.[22] He also made sure that he traveled incognito, using the name "Schropp." Another German who lived in England called him "Baron," thought he was "quite a gentleman," and introduced him to his industrial friends. Since Krupp, who had written large quantities of letters from Paris, hardly corresponded at all from England, all kinds of stories later circulated: that he worked in a factory to learn the secrets of the coking process, even that he fell in love with one or more of two sisters in Liverpool.[23] In 1843 Krupp undertook another, this time shorter, trip to England. For his whole lifetime, he was fascinated by developments in other countries, and particularly took care to inform himself of the latest British factory designs. In 1867, for instance, his agents found inspiration in the Clydeside armor-plating works of John Brown.[24]

Krupp also built up a network of high-quality representatives in foreign markets: Russia was developed by Moritz Thies, whose early death temporarily halted

Krupp's business expansion in the east. The Paris representatives of Krupp, Richter & Hagdorn and later Heinrich Haass, in fact built up contacts throughout the world. In England, Alfred Longsdon became one of Krupp's most trusted confidants. And Krupp products were widely distributed, with deliveries to Mexico from 1841, to India from 1845, and to the United States from 1847. From 1851, there was also a New York agent, Th. Prosser & Son.

Later, Krupp regarded the company's products as the equivalent of ambassadors. In 1849 Krupp sent two cast-steel axles to the Pennsylvania Railroad. He also in 1851 sent cast-steel axles to the London world exhibition; and in 1856 the Paris-Orleans railway started to be enthusiastic about the superior durability of the cast-steel axle.

The major business breakthrough came in 1851 in the world exhibition in London at the Crystal Palace. The Great Exhibition had been planned as a demonstration of the principles of a pacifist internationalism, driven by the spirit of commerce. Richard Cobden, the main proponent of this view, argued that "it will witness a triumph of industry, instead of a triumph of arms." A guidebook prepared by John Tallis stated that "the Palace of Industry was the Temple of Peace."[25] In the light of these high-minded goals, one of Krupp's most eye-catching exhibits served as a distinct shock. "The English will have their eyes opened," he wrote to the "Collegium" or "directory board" in 1851.[26] Krupp displayed a highly polished and exceedingly shiny cannon, set next to an officer's armor with an elegant orange-yellow silk lining. The *Illustrated London News* referred to "the beautiful steel cannon."[27] Many comments focused in a similar vein on the aesthetics rather than the technical characteristics of the cannon.

Figure 2.6 The Krupp cannon at the 1851 London Great Exhibition. Courtesy of Historical Archives Krupp.

But the biggest Krupp triumph was the cast-iron block that demonstrated quite how effectively the crucible process could be scaled up. English producers exhibited a cast-iron piece of 2,400 pounds, and Krupp retorted that he made pieces like that every day, and that he would send the grandfather of such a cast-iron block.[28] The key to this gigantic undertaking was the simultaneous casting of steel from multiple crucibles. Between 1849 and 1851 two new factory halls with twenty furnaces, each containing four crucibles, were built. Krupp's cousin and work manager, Adalbert Ascherfeld, began drilling the Krupp workers in the simultaneous casting of steel, and in April 1851 managed to orchestrate thirty-one crucibles. For the 4,300-pound block for the Crystal Palace, *all* the Gussstahlfabrik's crucibles needed to be operated. The block won one of the coveted Council Medals. The German inventor and manufacturer Friedrich Harkort announced that "this thing will become one of the most remarkable milestones in the industrial history of Germany."[29]

Russia represented another marketing challenge. In the early days of the Gussstahlfabrik, Friedrich Krupp had already been fascinated by the possibility of actually producing steel in Russia. In the 1830s Alfred had sold his coining mills to Russia, and by 1839 was selling more in Russia than in France. In 1841 he even proposed to set up production sites in Russia, but the plans were not realized. But it was above all military products that promised to open up the Russian market. In 1856, at the conclusion of the Crimean War, Krupp sold artillery pieces; a few years later Krupp also turned to Egypt (where he had supplied a yacht in 1855). In 1859 he offered to provide shafts for forty Russian frigates, but the Russian ministry did not agree to a contract.

In a rather quiet period for the factory, the early 1860s, Krupp won a major Russian order in 1863. By 1864 Krupp was writing to Lieutenant General von Todtleben, a tsarist officer, about the growth of his establishment, which was now employing seven thousand workers, "of which a large part are now working for Russia."[30] A decisive part of the advance in artillery technology in the 1860s, the development of barrels constructed by means of nested rings of tubes, which greatly enhanced the strength and resilience of the cannon bore, came at the insistence of Russian military procurement.[31] The distinguished Russian scientist Ivan Vyshnegradsky also delivered a major impetus to Krupp's research on powder and explosives by sending Krupp a powder press. The resulting experiments with prismatic powder brought Krupp into the manufacture of steel grenades.

When one of Krupp's engineers expressed concern that the Russians had been allowed to stay too long in Essen and were going to copy the Krupp processes, Krupp replied: "in Petersburg they will never be able to build a rival factory using iron ore from the Urals and English coal without incurring huge losses." He also added that he was not interested in operating a factory in Russia, as "nobody would be able to stand the climate and the religious pressure for long, and we would have had to take valuable workers away from Essen, where we do not ourselves have enough."[32] On similar grounds, he later argued against setting up a subsidiary in Japan.[33]

In the middle of the severe business downturn of the 1870s, Krupp developed an even more grandiose view of globalization and its potential. He wrote to his son, who was staying (in part for health reasons) in Cairo, about his plans to provide railroad equipment for the whole world. During the German business depression, small foreign orders of less than ten thousand tons would not be sufficient to occupy the factory. Instead Krupp wanted to find orders in advance to keep the works running at capacity for at least two years, and saw railway lines "linking and crossing the great continents of Africa, America and Asia so that they will come to the status of civilized countries and with connecting and branch lines will keep industry busy until the end of the world—as long as some windbag does not destroy this expectation by developing air transport." He proposed specifically to link East Asia to Europe with a railway.[34] In the mid-1880s, Krupp concluded major contracts with the Leopoldina, Pian, Bahia, Minas, and Sorocabana railways in Brazil for the supply of large quantities of rails and iron bridges, as well as telegraphic equipment.

He was especially captivated by the idea that China would be the next economic and military superpower. In 1866 the first diplomatic mission of the Chinese government to Europe visited the Essen Krupp works, and in 1870 Krupp appointed a representative for China and Japan, the Cologne merchant Friedrich Peil. By the next year, China had already ordered 328 artillery pieces.[35] Alfred Krupp had a correspondence with the German traveler and scientist Ferdinand von Richthofen, who worked on the development of Chinese coal reserves. Krupp was enormously impressed by Li Hongzhang, the general and official who had engineered the coup of 1875, whom he thought of as "the Bismarck of China." Li in fact was a great admirer of both Bismarck and Krupp: he kept a photograph of Bismarck in his study, and depended on Krupp not just as a supplier of munitions and railroad goods but also as a model for a strategy of how to industrialize China.[36]

The profile of Krupp in Japan was equally prominent. Even before the appearance of Commodore Perry's black ships, Friedrich Graf zu Eulenburg had brought a Krupp rolling machine to Japan as a present and a statement of European technical prowess. In 1873, as part of a Japanese fact-finding expedition to Europe, a fifteen-man delegation visited the Krupp works. And Germany became very much the model for Japan's modernization as well.

THE STATE

At least part of the motivation for pursuing contacts with foreign governments so persistently was the hope that such orders would demonstrate irrefutably to the leadership of Prussia/Germany the value of Krupp products. From a very early stage, because of its beginning in the manufacture of coining equipment, Krupp had seen the state as a major consumer of its products. But state procurers are not subject to a purely commercial logic, and all kinds of extraneous arguments are often needed to convince public-sector purchasers of the virtues of a product and of an enterprise. The fear of being outstripped or humiliated by foreign powers is quite a powerful motor in shaping official decisions. Another is the impact of state orders on employment and social stability. Some of the first letters Alfred Krupp wrote after the death of his father were addressed to the director of the Berlin mint. Five years later, in 1831, at the age of nineteen, he wrote again to say that he had a stock of the best steel for stamping coins, and to ask that the mint not supply itself from England but rather create employment in the Rhineland.[37]

But the state appeared initially to the Essen manufacturer vital not just as a consumer of the company's products but also as a source of financial support. Krupp's mother had demanded a 10,000-thaler interest-free advance from the Prussian state as a compensation for the damage done by Friedrich Nicolai, who had had a Prussian patent for the fabrication of cast steel and had proved to be a swindler who would not share whatever knowledge he had. Krupp's own repetitions of the demand were accompanied by the claim that state support would mean more independence from England, and would ensure the feeding of "several hundred families."[38] In 1830 the widow Krupp asked the Prussian state again, this time for a 15,000-thaler interest-free credit, in order to equip the hammer and rolling mills with steam power. All the requests were rejected.

The Prussian state had its own logic and its own traditions, and indisputably the best way to capture the imagination of the Prussian state and its agents was to supply military equipment. In 1843 Krupp sent a cast-iron rifle barrel to Lieutenant von Donat, explicitly arguing that the success of the rifle amounted to "a demonstration in miniature of the suitability of this material for the manufacture of cannons."[39] By 1844 he was addressing Minister of War von Boyen with an appeal to replace wrought iron in rifle barrels and bronze cannons with cast iron. The ministry sent a drawing for a new cannon, and in 1846 Krupp produced a model. By August 1847 he was sending a 7.5 cm piece, but it seems to have excited little interest, and it was not tested by the Prussian military. In consequence, Krupp seriously contemplated sending the artillery piece to Paris in the summer of 1848, where street fighting meant that there was an obvious need for military equipment.[40] The revolutions of 1848 doubtless heightened the appreciation of the state authorities for military production. After all, social order now seemed to depend on the bayonet. In June 1848, Krupp wrote laconically to a former representative of the firm about the poor state of business: "My brother in Vienna is making not spoons—but weapons." In fact the Berndorf factory had converted itself from spoons to sabers.[41] At the Crystal Palace in London, the real engineering feat lay in the gigantic Krupp cast-steel block, but Krupp attracted almost as much attention with an elegantly presented and draped cannon. A Krupp cannon was set up in the marble room of the Potsdam Stadtschloss in order to impress the emperor of Russia in 1852.[42]

The early dabbling in weapons, from Krupp's viewpoint, was mostly an exercise in advertising the skills of his factory, conducted in the same spirit as the display of the polished steel cannon at the London Crystal

Palace. The main object of Krupp's interest lay in the Prussian state railways. Soon after the display of the cannon, Krupp sent Minister von der Heydt a picture of the Krupp steelworks and an appeal for orders for axles and tires for the new railway system.[43] But Krupp then also took the opportunity to explain that in order to supply such equipment, he would need guarantees of continuing orders.[44] Krupp was rewarded with a patent for eight years for the weldless railroad tires. The Krupp process was problematic, in that the Bochumer Verein soon developed the rival and cheaper means of using steel casts instead of worked steel. Krupp asked for an extension of his patent but was turned down in 1860 by the liberal ministry. The centenary history of Krupp in 1912 commented on this decision, which it claimed was motivated by the Prussian government's dogmatic obsession with the credo of economic liberalism: "Only later did the conviction gain hold, that excessive competition did not drive entrepreneurial risk-taking but on the contrary limited it."[45] Turned down by the ministry, Krupp sent an appeal to the prince regent, who had been impressed by Krupp's artillery pieces, and the Prussian state in the end agreed to a seven-year extension of the patent.

Crown Prince Wilhelm had been impressed quite early, and was the most obvious target for Alfred Krupp's astute advertising. He was passionately devoted to Prussia's military inheritance and interested in military equipment. In 1859 this *Kartätschenprinz* (grapeshot prince) became prince regent and in 1861 king of Prussia.[46] He visited the Gussstahlfabrik on October 9, 1861. Even to Wilhelm, Krupp made it clear that he regarded the production of artillery cannons primarily as a way of advertising the strength of the cast steel that the firm produced for

Figure 2.7 King Wilhelm I visits the Krupp works, 1861. Courtesy of Historical Archives Krupp.

railways and for industrial machinery.[47] After the Crystal Palace, Krupp presented a six-pound cannon mounted on a mobile gun carriage to King Friedrich Wilhelm IV. It was set up in the Neues Palais in Potsdam, but the king remained indecisive about whether or not to accept the gift. By contrast, when Prince Wilhelm saw this impressive product in the Deutz artillery workshop, he allegedly told his entourage: "I must meet this genius, Herr Krupp."[48] Krupp's old friend Friedrich Sölling told him in 1852: "You have fluttered around for so long in the exquisite air that you must smell of the court, and I am anxious to exercise my olfactory nerves on you."[49]

By the 1850s Krupp was already receiving visits from other German princes, such as Prince Wilhelm of Baden, and needed to ensure that he had suitable lodgings.[50] Hospitality, advertisement, and site visits to an increasingly impressive Gussstahlfabrik all became part of a marketing strategy in which potential customers were drawn into a network of trust and confidence. The first serious orders for steel cannons came not from Prussia but from Egypt, and democratic Switzerland also constituted an important market. France in 1857 tested the cannon very successfully (in contrast to the British experience of 1855, when the test cannon had been unconventionally loaded and exploded on firing at the Woolwich arsenal). Nationalism was already beginning to intrude on the business, and in 1859, with war in North Italy between Austria and France, Krupp instructed his French representative to withdraw offers of arms supplies. By 1865 Crown Princess Isabella of Brazil was visiting the Essen works, and Krupp was offering cannons to Brazil on an experimental basis. A few months later he was decorated with a Brazilian officer's cross, which he accepted, although he never wanted any German honors or titles.

Securing patents was crucial; and in order to negotiate effectively, Krupp tried to play off one state against another. At the same time as Krupp was trying to interest the Prussian state in his patents, he was making the same case in France. He promised Napoleon III's Minister Achille Fould that he would establish a factory in France, but only if the validity of his patents was recognized, and without any publicity that might allow competitors to copy Krupp's products.[51] When applying for a contract with the Prussian state railways, Krupp wrote that he would under no circumstances allow the contract to depend on the revelation of production techniques. The letter expresses a very characteristic nineteenth-century attitude in which constructive industrial zeal is contrasted with destructive and speculative financial activity, as well as in the casual use of stereotypes about financial activity being "Jewish." Krupp wrote: "The secrets are our capital, and that capital is squandered as soon as the knowledge is released to others. Industry today has become a field for speculators, Jews of the bourse, stock swindlers and similar parasites, who sit on their comfortable upholstered chairs and want to use what they can grab to exploit through joint-stock companies to pour money into their own sacks."[52]

Alfred Krupp was ferocious in defense of his business secrets. He had been outraged in 1854 when a skilled technician called Nesselrode, who had accompanied Krupp on visits to London and Birmingham and had been placed in charge of the department for railway springs, suddenly left the company and set up his own rival enterprise in Saxony. As a result of this incident, Krupp began to insist on much more precise contractual arrangements with his employees.[53] He also instructed his Berlin representative Carl Meyer not to reveal the nature of the orders for the Prussian military, pointing out that no lithographs were allowed of Prussian artillery in order to keep the secrets of the state.[54] He also wrote to the Prussian war minister Albrecht von Roon to point out that British military patents were a carefully guarded state secret.[55] Military orders were not only an advertising strategy for Krupp; they were also a way of convincing bureaucrats of the importance of secrets, of discretion, and of official guarantees of secrecy for Prussian patents.

Krupp liked to emphasize how "production for war" and "production for peace" had the same fundamental requirements: innovation and quality. At the beginning of 1858, in the midst of a business-cycle downturn, Krupp wrote to Alexander von Humboldt: "Here we are mostly concerned with the production of axles and wheels for railways and steamships. Besides these instruments for the traffic of peace, we also make weapons of war. Our task is indestructibility: for the former applications, in order to safeguard property and human life, for the latter to increase the capacity for destruction. The former takes the more important role and must feed us. I cultivate the latter with great sacrifices in the interest of progress, and it will only have a value for me if I can serve the fatherland at the time of need. But I gladly forgo such a moment, in which I can proudly prove what patriotic industry can do, for the blessings of peace."[56]

In 1852 the artillery pieces sent to the Prussian military had been built in the general Mechanical Workshop I. The year 1859, when Austria was humiliated on the battle-fields of northern Italy, constituted a breakthrough both for the Prussian army's approach to the issue of technical modernization and for Krupp's relationship with military procurement. In that year, Krupp won an order for three hundred artillery barrels for the Prussian military. In 1859 the company started to experiment with breech-loading mechanisms. Krupp could now create special-ized cannon-making equipment and workshops, and in 1861/62 moved production to a new, specially dedicated factory hall. In 1864 there was a second hall for cannons, by 1866 a third and 1870 a fourth. Cannon production expanded dramatically with the German wars of unifica-tion. Each production hall in the Essen factory, it seemed, was inaugurated to mark another victory of Prussian arms. After the battle of Königgrätz, General von Voigts-Rhetz wrote to Krupp: "You had a particular interest—apart from your patriotism—because of your cannons, which helped us most effectively. For long hot hours, your chil-dren conversed with their Austrian cousins."[57]

But for Krupp it was still vital to emphasize the competition between states. Once Wilhelm became king of
Prussia in 1861, Krupp turned his attention to the new
crown prince, Wilhelm's son Friedrich, and explained
that he was traveling to England to come into business
with the English War and Naval ministries, "an affair of
national interest," and to demonstrate that his breech-
loading mechanism was superior to those produced by
Armstrong.[58] At the same time, Krupp was demonstrat-
ing the artillery made for Russia to Prussian war minister
Albrecht von Roon.[59] In 1866, in the weeks before the
Austro-Prussian War, there was a major clash with von
Roon, as Krupp had artillery contracts not only from
Prussia but also from Austria and the southern German
states, and von Roon insisted that Krupp not fulfill this
order. Krupp protested vigorously and argued that he
knew nothing about politics and just wanted to work,
"and if I cannot do that without disturbing the balance
between patriotism and honor I will sell my factory and
become a rich man." But he did agree not to send artillery
against the wish of the Prussian government.[60]

In 1867 Krupp explained to King Wilhelm that as well
as presenting a thousand-pound cannon to the Prussian
government, he proposed to offer a similar artillery piece
to the Russian tsar.[61] In 1871, at the end of the Franco-
Prussian War, Krupp wrote to Wilhelm (now German
emperor): "In the interest of truth it is necessary to point
out that thanks for the perfection of the artillery are due
above all to the Russian government, and the Russian
army and navy, and for its support and confidence. Russia
has given Germany the example of how to appreciate the
product of its own country and of the Gussstahlfabrik."
Krupp was still at this time complaining of the excessive

attachment of the Prussian military to the idea of bronze artillery, which he regarded as a waste of material and of manpower. "We are now living in the age of steel. Railways, Germany's greatness, France's ruin, are in the steel age, the bronze age is over. Steel has finished being the material of war, it now has a milder destiny, it should be used for the first monument of victory, for monuments of great deeds and great men, as the expression of external and domestic peace, it should ring in church bells, be used for ornaments and commercial purposes, and in coinage."[62] This theme remained a lifelong concern. In his last address to the Krupp workers, in February 1887, he said: "In peace we are moving into a great future, and I was full of hope. But what is the use of all our orders, if work and transport are destroyed by war?"[63]

Krupp first met Otto von Bismarck in October 1864, when Bismarck was returning from his meetings with Napoleon III in Paris and Biarritz and visited Essen en route. The Prussian minister-president was immensely impressed, and called on the Essen manufacturer during Krupp's next visit to Berlin. The two men thought in parallel ways. Bismarck explained his philosophy during that first visit to Essen, setting out a view of the world that might as well have belonged to an entrepreneur: "If I see something as right and possible to achieve, I will try to accomplish it, even if the most skilled and intelligent people tell me it is impossible."[64] Bismarck also saw how a new politics could be built on business support, and in 1865 intervened personally to ensure that Krupp won the battle against the rival Bochumer Verein to take over the Sayner Hütte ironworks (which were needed in order to secure an adequate supply of pig iron as Krupp stepped up the Bessemer process). The whole incident is a fine example of the way in which lobbying was beginning to work in German politics. In 1864 Krupp had started negotiations with the Prussian trade minister von Itzenplitz for the purchase of the Sayner Hütte for 400,000 thalers, thought that he had a deal, and had even donated 5,000 thalers to von Itzenplitz to be distributed to needy and deserving miners. But the Bochumer Verein protested, and so did liberal deputies in the Prussian parliament, and Krupp needed to increase his offer. But King Wilhelm in the end decided in his favor, even though the Bochumer Verein had matched Krupp's bid.[65]

After the unification of Germany, Krupp expressed his pleasure that the new navy would be under federal control, and believed that Bismarck would push the new strategy. He saw a need for steel plates for ship construction and resolved to acquire a shipyard, perhaps on the Rhine, perhaps in the Netherlands or on the German coast.[66] He devised and presented to the crown prince a plan for a ship that "must in the future rule the seas."[67] At the same time, such orders were important in that industry had recovered, but he thought that the business recovery would not be of long duration.

Artillery was widely credited with the German victory of 1870–71 against France, in just the same way as the fast-loading needle rifle was said to explain Prussia's triumph over Austria at the Battle of Sadowa (Königgrätz) in 1866. From then until the First World War, generals in every European army were obsessed with artillery, and with every more powerful cannon that might be directed against the massive fortresses that constituted a preponderant element of European strategic thinking.

On June 13, 1871, Krupp sent the Artillery Inspection Commission a new field artillery piece with a ring-constructed barrel. From 1873 to 1874 the German artillery was reequipped with 7.85 cm and 8.8 cm artillery according to the specifications of Field Artillery Manual C 73. Krupp was immensely pleased with the result, but he wanted to show that the cannon was the result of his firm's engineering skill, and not of the foresight of the Prussian military (with the exception of General von Voigts-Rhetz, who had been a consistent supporter of Krupp). In consequence, he ordered a history of the cannon to be written in order to assert that the ring cannon was the intellectual property of Krupp. He also envisaged distributing the history widely in Asia, in North and South America, and in the Ottoman Empire and Egypt. The Prussian War Ministry reacted sharply, demanding that the pamphlet should not circulate abroad. But in practice Krupp seems to have ignored the instruction, and his representatives Longsdon in London and Meyer in Berlin always had copies at hand.[68]

Krupp also acquired a site for testing artillery, at first in Dülmen from 1873, and then a larger site in Meppen. The idea that states were competing entities still continued to be an essential part of Krupp's vision and his marketing strategy. He organized an international artillery festival to raise the military and technical consciousness of the participating dignitaries, generals, and officials. In 1879 representatives of eighteen states were present at what was termed the "Shooting Festival of the Peoples" (*Völkerschiessen*) in Meppen: Austrians, Belgians, Brazilians, Chinese, Englishmen, Italians, Romanians, Russians, Serbians, Spaniards, Swiss, Swedes, and Ottoman Turks. Only France was not invited. Alfred Krupp was particularly glad that he could have Turks at his festival once the 1878 Congress of Berlin had concluded the Russo-Turkish War.

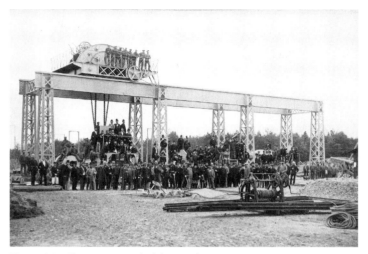

Figure 2.8 "Shooting Festival of the Peoples," Meppen, August 1879. Courtesy of Historical Archives Krupp.

He instructed that "particular attention should be given to the Turks, because they will certainly have another war and they will need cannons and even the poorest country has money for that!" The shooting stand was decorated with the colors of the new German Empire, while the two observation towers flew the flags of the observers.[69]

In 1879 an Irish member of Parliament told the British House of Commons that Krupp had circulated leaflets among British parliamentarians "in which he said that his 6¾-inch gun had been tried against an English 9-inch gun, and his gun had given far better results." But even before the Prussian military successes of 1866 and 1870, there had been a long stream of parliamentarians in Britain who were convinced that Krupp weapons were superior to those being bought by the British army and navy. In 1865 a Scottish Conservative MP complained about British procurement officials, who "knew nothing of the American gun, they knew nothing of the French gun, they knew nothing of the admirable guns used by the Prussians in the war against Denmark, and they knew nothing of Krupp's gun, which had been adopted in the Russian service." And in 1881 the former First Lord of the Admiralty, W. H. Smith, told the House of Commons: "At this moment, however good our Woolwich gun may be, there can be no doubt that our naval guns are inferior to the new naval guns found on board the German, the French, and the Russian ships. The later Krupp gun is decidedly superior to anything we possess at this moment on board any of our ships."[70]

It was not just a question of a race between countries. There was also a race in each country between defensive and offensive capabilities. Advances in one area required counterbalancing advances in the other, with the result that the arms race meant not just more powerful artillery but also a need for fortresses, armor, and devices that could protect artillery, both on land and in the water. Krupp contributed to both sides of this race. In 1879 the Essen works constructed a 15 cm L/6.4 siege mortar. The repeating cannon of 1879 was an important step in the direction of automatic firing. At the 1879 Meppen shooting, the new artillery shot through all the available armored plates, and the *Essener Zeitung* concluded that the event marked a "new great triumph of the German artillery industry."[71] In 1881 Krupp began experiments with the use of shrapnel. There were also advances in naval gunnery. In 1871 a new and powerful ship gun carriage was introduced. In 1878 swivel pivots made the artillery more flexible. In 1884 ball bearings were set to work in the targeting mechanisms for coastal armored ships of the Siegfried class.

The Franco-Prussian War also brought lessons in the need to protect artillery with armor. For ships at sea, heavily armored gun turrets were developed. As navies became more powerful, coastal defenses needed to be improved. Krupp sought Italian orders and in 1882 sold four 40 cm cannons with a 14 m barrel for the defense of the harbor of La Spezia.

Krupp turned in the direction of military orders at the time when this became the focus of intense competition. Armaments remained, as they had been when Alfred Krupp started his experiments on cuirasses and cold-worked rifle barrels in the 1840s, a way of proving himself as an entrepreneur, of enhancing his reputation not just nationally but internationally.

THE BANKS

The attraction of the state also lay in its ability to provide an alternative and perhaps more secure source of finance than could private individuals for a rapidly growing enterprise. Some of Krupp's earliest letters to Prussian administrative officials asking for government support were accompanied by the claim that the Rhineland "capitalists" were only interested on lending against the security of land, and that they were not interested in financing entrepreneurial initiative.[72] The Prussian minister with whom he had the most strained relationship was originally an Elberfeld banker, August von der Heydt. In 1859, when von der Heydt refused to renew the railroad tire patent, Krupp wrote indignantly to the Prussian authorities. He denounced the Trade Ministry's practices to the head of the General War Department, General von Voigts-Rhetz: "The state railways are circumventing my factory, against their own interests, because von der Heydt never wanted my establishment to flourish and had probably determined my ruin."[73]

When the Krupp enterprise was still just a craft workshop, it could be financed by relatively simple methods, above all by credit from relatives. The rise of Krupp was parallel, not simply to the political unification of Germany, but also to a process of industrial development in Germany, in which a new approach to financing emerged in the shape of the universal bank.

Most of the Krupp capital originally came from relatives and business acquaintances, notably from the brother-in-law of Friedrich Krupp, Johann Christian Friedrich von Müller, and his son, a farmer and a friend of Alfred's, Carl Friedrich von Müller. There was also some credit extended by Krupp's suppliers, in particular the brothers Brüninghaus, as well as the firm of Jacobi, Haniel & Huyssen. These early years of Krupp's business were highly precarious, and until the middle of the 1830s the enterprise probably incurred losses. It was the younger Müller who insisted on proper accounting as a condition of extending credit. In the later 1830s there was a turn to profitability, but larger credits were required as a result of the move into making complicated machinery and factory parts with long production and delivery times, and also as a result of market uncertainty.[74] Sales were very slow, especially of the expensive silverware-making equipment; and some purchasers, above all the Austrian mint, paid only slowly and reluctantly. In 1842 Alfred Krupp complained that he had lost twenty thousand guilders by "neglect of the business."[75] By 1846 he was worried about his debts to the Cologne bank of Herstatt, from which he had borrowed since the mid-1830s (on the security of Carl Friedrich von Müller), although he added that within forty-eight hours he could always marry a rich girl and get out of the financial difficulties.[76] In 1847/48 Herstatt indeed cut back the credit it would extend to Krupp, partly because of general business conditions but also partly out of worry about problems that were peculiar to Krupp.[77]

In 1855 Friedrich Sölling, a childhood friend of Alfred Krupp's who after 1844 had put 55,000 thalers of his money into the enterprise, wrote to Krupp: "You believe the credit of the firm is as great as its reputation, but that is not the case, and for the simple reason that we ruin it by drawing too much credit just at the moment when we seem secure."[78] Sölling at this time suggested turning Krupp into a joint-stock company (Aktiengesellschaft)— just as the Hörder Verein (1852), the Bochumer Verein (1854), or the Stettin Vulkanwerft (1857) had done. For the entrepreneurs concerned, forming a joint-stock company was usually regarded as a sign of defeat and vulnerability in a financial crisis. Krupp (like another great Ruhr entrepreneur, Franz Haniel) was consistently suspicious of joint-stock corporations. Instead, he concluded personal partnership agreements, which brought in a new capital of 250,000 thalers: with F. L. Niemann in 1856, and with the brothers Ernst and Julius Waldthausen in 1857. Ernst had been a friend of Krupp's since childhood. What particularly attracted Krupp to the Waldthausens was not that they were bankers but that they were friends, who could be tied by noncommercial bonds of amity and loyalty. In 1857 he wrote to Ernst Waldthausen that "by preference, we should avoid the assistance of banks—systematically!"[79]

The grounds for Krupp's worry about banks—whether private bankers such as Herstatt or the new joint-stock banks on the French model that were beginning to appear in the 1850s—were comprehensible. Each time a business crisis broke out, banks became nervous and vulnerable, at exactly the time when businesses were most in need of financial support. The small banking houses of the mid-nineteenth century were especially fragile, and in the crisis of 1848 the venerable Cologne bank of A. Schaaffhausen had gone under. The new and larger French-style joint-stock banks were fundamentally untested. In 1859 Krupp noted that in the war scare produced by Austrian fighting in Italy (the crisis that secured Krupp's position as a military supplier) the Cologne banks had panicked once more. He thus, quite logically, wanted to secure financial support from the state.[80]

One business crisis followed another, and each seemed to demonstrate the fickleness of banking. In 1864 the senior director of the bank Deichmann & Co. in Cologne, Wilhelm Deichmann, complained in a letter to Alfred Krupp that the banks in Amsterdam, Frankfurt, Paris, and London were daily rejecting large quantities of bills: "we do not mind a high discount, as long as we can be sure that the money can be obtained."[81] But in 1865 he concluded a substantial loan agreement (four million francs) with the Paris bank of F. A. Seillière, which had long-held connections with the iron industry in Lorraine.[82] The German banks did not really trust Krupp, though in 1849 another Cologne bank, Oppenheim, had been willing to step into the shoes of Herstatt and extend credit to the company as it embarked on railway-driven expansion. But in 1856 when the Disconto Gesellschaft, one of the new joint-stock banks, was asked about Krupp, its director gave the reply: "as much as K. is a genius as a manufacturer, I have had until now no cause to admire his financial skill."[83]

The financial crises of 1859 or 1864 were mild compared with the big crash at the end of the *Gründer* boom
of the early 1870s. In July 1873, in the middle of a major
crisis for the company, Krupp set out his life philosophy
again: "Not speculation or gambling, but rather the deliberate nonobservance of the principles of a commercial
entrepreneur, who is always trying to draw the highest
dividend from his capital, and the creation of a work
which in a certain measure is inseparable from the idea
of the development and importance of the state."[84]

The 1873 crisis represented an "existential challenge,"
as Lothar Gall has termed it. At one point Krupp hoped it
would be a purgative crisis that would drive his competitors out of business, and indeed two bankers on the board
of the steel firm Dortmunder Union told Krupp managers
that they thought "the rest of the competition would soon
pack it in." But in fact Krupp was also near the abyss. Gert
von Klass describes the outcome as "humiliation," and
Richard Tilly sees the drama as marking the ascendancy of
the new powerhouse of German economic development:
the German universal bank. The Dortmunder Union was
strong only because it was in the hands of the Disconto
Gesellschaft. A more recent and largely persuasive revi-
sionist account explains that in reality the banks never
had a significant influence over the Krupp enterprise, and
that Krupp had orchestrated a highly skillful financial
power-play. Debtors, if they are large enough, can exercise
a substantial leverage over their creditors.[85]

Even before the crisis that followed the Vienna stock
market panic of May 9, 1873, the company was badly
overextended with short-term debt, and already in July
1872 Krupp had been trying to obtain a credit from the
government to cover the costs of the breakneck expansion.

But in the course of 1873 the debt burden rose dramatically, from 13.5 million marks to 32 million by July 1873 (and to 64 million one year later). Krupp's major strategy lay in presenting the firm as a national institution, "even though headed by a private citizen,"[86] and even though in parallel initiatives Krupp was trying to raise money on the British capital market. He encouraged his negotiators "not to appear worried, but rather proud and bold," but it was hard to hide the extent of the firm's difficulties. Carl Meyer, the accountant who represented the firm in Berlin, reported after an initial discussion with the Iron Chancellor that Bismarck was surprised to learn that the company produced more railway goods than artillery pieces.[87] On March 30, Meyer had an audience with the kaiser but warned Krupp that he was unlikely to obtain the full 10 million thalers or 30 million marks credit that the company wanted. At this time, Krupp tried to emphasize to the government and the emperor that "no other state had the resources that Germany has in the shape of my factory." The state, Alfred Krupp said, cannot do without the performance of his big factory complex. A joint-stock company, driven by short-term profit considerations, would not be able to supply the same high level of quality.[88]

Ernst Eichhoff, the older brother of Krupp's wife, who had been a member of the board of the Austrian Lloyd shipping company in Trieste and who had joined Krupp in 1871 as a member of the *Prokura*, or management board, wrote to Krupp: "We need money, a lot of money and soon, that is the naked fact; with the slackness on the bourse and the fear of a credit crisis the bankers have become fearful."[89] Krupp replied to Eichhoff by insisting that he would get the money in Berlin, and sought a personal audience with the kaiser; but in the end, all that

Krupp managed to obtain was a bank package negotiated in part by Bismarck's banker Bleichroeder. The Prussian State Bank, the Seehandlung, led a bank consortium that lent 10 million thalers, at 5 percent but with an issue price of 90 and redemption at 110, repayable after nine years, so that the effective interest rate was around 7.5 percent. In addition, the banks appeared to insist that their agent should be taken into the company's management board (Prokura). The severity of this control was significantly reduced by the fact that the banks chose Krupp's agent and confidant Carl Meyer for this role. Meyer indeed presented his new role precisely as avoiding a tutelage of the banks: "While preserving all their rights, the banks will refrain from deputing a Controller on the condition that I explicitly commit myself to exercise this function in the interest of the consortium."[90] The banks may have realized that there was a chance of Krupp recovering, and in that case they needed to preserve some basis for future and profitable transactions.

One element of Krupp's fear in the traumatic moments of the early 1870s was that financiers wanted to destroy him because they were engaged in a kind of competition. He saw financiers as potential rivals. In 1875 Krupp started to worry about the expansion of Bethel Strousberg, perhaps the most flamboyant figure of the German *Gründer* boom, into Austrian railways, and about the likelihood that Strousberg would buy up factories for the production of railway equipment and also steelworks.[91]

Industrial expansion was best financed in the initial stages through family and friends such as Sölling and the Waldthausens, and in the later stages through the internal accumulation of profits. Banks, however they developed, in Krupp's eyes constituted a constant threat to entrepreneurial dynamism but also to patriotic engagement.

THE WORKERS AND THE MANAGEMENT

In the early days of Krupp, the factory, even when it expanded from the four employees of 1826, was more like a skilled craftsmen's workshop. As it expanded, there was necessarily a transition to more formal practices of management.

In the mid-1830s, Alfred's younger brother Hermann joined the management of the enterprise. In the 1840s, the management of the Gussstahlfabrik was enhanced with the entrance of Adalbert Ascherfeld and of the third brother, Friedrich Krupp. In 1849, after the departure of Friedrich Krupp, Carl Gantesweiler, who from 1845 to 1855 directed the commercial activity of the business, was given power of attorney (*Prokura*).

In 1862 a collective *Prokura* was instituted as a kind of management board. A few years later there were more formal structures, and in 1865 the works were divided into twenty groups (*Ressorts*) with separate managers. The pattern that evolved in the 1860s for a long time remained the basic model for an expanding enterprise: it had a strong element of centralized control, especially since Alfred Krupp exercised a substantial micromanagement, intervening even in quite small decisions. He also insisted again and again that effective control was necessary to the success of the enterprise.[92] "Apart from goodness and justice as a fundamental principle of our action, firmness is needed . . . we must not be afraid to punish shamefulness and dishonor."[93] There was a need for regulations to ensure that "work is controlled to such an extent that laziness and time-wasting is impossible."[94] In the 1870s, he was still preparing amazingly detailed missives about the appropriate clothing of workers, and especially the importance of good shoes and dry feet: the possession of good and waterproof shoes, he insisted, should be made a condition for inclusion in the enterprise's health insurance scheme.[95]

This concern reflected the deep paternalism that long remained a characteristic of the Krupp enterprise. Krupp believed that German workers were better educated than their English, French, or American equivalents, and if they were inferior it could only be because they had bad leadership or management.[96] The application of management principles to the question of caring for employees and establishing employee loyalty appears very early in the history of the enterprise: in 1836 Krupp established a scheme for health insurance, with voluntary membership. This scheme was transformed in 1853 into a general health and life insurance fund, and shortly afterward a pension scheme was added.

As early as 1844, Krupp argued that by paying a small premium relative to other factories, he could create a skilled and loyal workforce.[97] The processes required for making steel in crucibles demanded great skill, and were hard to supervise, and expensive products could easily be wrecked by carelessness: so workers needed to be highly motivated.[98] The logic of the work process, as well as Krupp's social philosophy, made the company a pioneer in the provision of services and facilities for its employees. In 1856 a hostel for single workers was built, and in the 1860s Krupp began to construct housing for workers, in order to allow part of the workforce to live close to the factory. But the really large-scale building activity

Figure 2.9 Workers' dwellings in Westend settlement (built in the 1870s), 1914. Courtesy of Historical Archives Krupp.

took place in the *Gründer* boom of the early 1870s, when the firm was desperate to attract and retain a qualified workforce. The major workers' "colonies" were next to the factory—Nordhof, Westend, and Schederhof—and Cronenberg was on the west side of the factory. About half of the workers' residences were two-room apartments, with a living room/kitchen and a sleeping area; the rest were three- or sometimes four-room dwellings. In 1868 Krupp established the "Konsumanstalt" (company store) to supply basic foods and clothing needs; there had already been a factory bakery since 1858. In 1870, during the Franco-Prussian War, a hospital was constructed at first to serve the needs of wounded soldiers, but which then became the basis of a company hospital.

The business model relied on the creation of long-term loyalties within a *Verband*, or association, as Alfred Krupp often called his enterprise. But business-cycle fluctuations, with the pressure they brought to rationalize and downsize, necessarily constituted a threat to solidarity and community. In 1867 Krupp advised the firm against laying off a large number of workers, and against dramatic announcements of dismissals. "Reductions can be made gradually, but a sudden change would produce revolt. It is not necessary to hurry, since no shareholders are waiting for their dividends, and because this is not the case, we are less interested in annual profits than in a solid and content workforce, for this reason all of our employees, workers and officials are better placed than those whose industry simply depends on greed."[99]

Alfred Krupp had a powerful view of how hard, industrious work had an educating or uplifting role if it occurred in a general context of improvement or development. He perfectly enunciated the Protestant work ethic, in which work and renunciation build godly communities: "The purpose of work should be the common good, then work is a blessing, work is prayer."[100]

Krupp's obsession with the general good, as well as a more practical concern with how skilled workers could be retained, had a counterpart: extreme hostility to organization or political activity on the part of the workforce. "I hope that in secret there is a permanent observation of the spirit of the workforce, so that we never miss the beginning of an agitation or fermenting. I demand that the best and most skilled worker or master is removed as soon as possible if he even appears to incite opposition or to belong to an association." Krupp referred to political agitation in the Ruhr mines and warned against an "epidemic" that would appear "whenever we show weakness."[101] In old age, Alfred Krupp sounded more and more cranky and extreme when he reflected on this subject. In 1872 he wrote: "The matter is so clear in dealing with men: I must treat them and tread them down as if they were willful children and that is now becoming repellent to me."[102]

The company statute or *Generalregulativ* of that year, however, remained for a long time the basic constitution of the company: it was indeed still echoed in post-1945 documents.[103] Alfred Krupp drew it up at a substantial distance from the Essen works: he composed the document in the mild seaside resort climate of Torquay in England. It aimed at providing for "these and coming times a secure order and a harmonious cooperation in order to secure the prospering of the whole and the welfare of the individual." As Krupp put it: "I must be sure that in 25 or 50 years time no disorder as a consequence of any kind of bad will is possible. The regulation must be designed for every case and every procedure, and define each individual's duty and rights." The Prokura would represent the owners of the company. The group heads had the responsibility of informing the Prokura. In each group there were individual administrative and productive units, each with a leader who reported to the group head.[104] In paragraphs 20 to 23, the document spelled out that "in order to give relief to the workers and officials, the firm will continue to build family residences, shops for food and clothing, halls of residence, savings banks and other similar institutions. It will be a particular concern to create schools for the education and formation of children, and to give adults the opportunity for further education and entertainment. Sickness insurance, support and pension insurance, hospitals and care homes shall if at all possible protect those belonging to the association from worries over illness, disability and old age for themselves and their dependents." In addition the factory promised to assist families burdened by the requirements of military service, and advised its employees to conclude life insurance policies.[105] A biconfessional school with instruction for both Catholics and Protestants was established near the Cronenberg settlement in the early 1870s.

During the business downturn of 1873, the company's finances were severely strained. Krupp at first tried to apply his business philosophy and resolved not to dismiss workers, as other companies were doing, but rather to retain the workforce in the certainty that better times would come again.[106] Then he realized that the downturn could be used to enforce control. "The situation and the mood must be used. We must immediately introduce the strictest control of work forever, and dismiss everyone who resists . . ."[107] Wages should be reduced, but first the workers should be prepared for this by the threat of dismissals. Krupp did lay off workers, though fewer than his competitors: from 1873 to 1879 the Gussstahlfabrik cut its workforce by 3,600 (or 30 percent), while the Bochumer Verein lost 40 percent, the Hoerder Verein 44 percent, and Borsig 47 percent.[108]

In the late 1870s a recovery began. It was largely the result of continued globalization, with a big expansion of railway orders from the United States in the early 1880s and major orders for military products. The new growth seemed an endorsement of Krupp's very personal management philosophy, although there was a new head of the Prokura, in effect the chief executive: Hanns Jencke, who came from the Saxon state railroad administration. Thus a new managerial style began in the company, although Alfred Krupp was in any case becoming more and more distant from the enterprise. In the end he commented: "I do not want to do anything, I am a nothing."[109] He talked of giving up all the "small-scale writing": "everything must be finished without me."[110]

THE FAMILY

Until 1848, Fried. Krupp had been a family business, whose principal owner was the founder's widow, Therese Krupp, and whose management lay in a rather undefined way in the hands of her three sons, Alfred, Hermann, and Friedrich. Alfred was simply the most dynamic as well as being the eldest, and in 1829 he was already being described as "Herr Gussstahlfabrikant Alfred Krupp."[111] In the later 1840s, when business was hit by a sustained downturn, this ownership model appeared problematic. The downturn also reduced the value of the enterprise and made a buyout possible. Hermann Krupp was paid off with the Essen Gussstahlfabrik's stake in the Berndorfer Metallwarenfabrik and disappeared to Austria. Alfred Krupp was especially unhappy with his youngest brother, Friedrich, and later complained: "My brother, who had once worked very hard and faithfully for me, let himself be seduced to think of himself as superior, he regarded himself as a superman and took no notice of me."[112] On the advice of Carl Schulz, an Essen businessman and the brother-in-law of Therese Krupp, the widow Krupp removed Friedrich from the business and on February 24, 1848, in the midst of recession, sold the whole enterprise to Alfred for forty thousand thalers, a price substantially lower than it would have been during the heady business expansion of the early part of the decade. She was dying, and a few days later drew up her will, in which she threatened to reduce her son Friedrich's share to the legal minimum if he were to give away the secrets of the firm or start a rival enterprise.[113] Shortly after that the 1848 revolution swept over Germany. Krupp was so short of money that he literally sold the family silver in order to keep paying workers their wages, as well as to make other payments coming due. This gesture—much celebrated in subsequent tellings of the Krupp story—cemented the relationship of Alfred Krupp and his *Verband*.

Alfred Krupp was a solitary figure, who—as he sometimes ironically put it—was married to the factory. From an early age, his correspondence is filled with complaints about ill health. He became ever more of a hypochondriac. In 1855 he had the first of a number of long nervous breakdowns, which obliged him to take a long cure in Bad Pyrmont.

A marriage might be a way, not just of gaining some human support, but also of securing the financial position of the firm: of marrying into a network of potential investors and lenders. Indeed Krupp's business partner Sölling urged him to marry, explaining that marriage was like a lottery, in which there might be a good or a bad ticket.[114] It was not clear whether Sölling meant this from the personal or the financial side. Indeed in 1853 Krupp married Bertha Eichhoff, the daughter of a pensioned customs inspector, after a very rapid courtship. Bertha was attractive and lively but not very wealthy. She soon found life in Essen in the middle of the hammers and furnaces intolerable, and stayed away for medical treatments in Berlin or a variety of spa towns. Alfred and Bertha's only child was born in 1854.

The marriage furnished a new set of relatives who could be brought into the factory. Family relations offered the best solution to the problem of trust. Alfred Krupp put the very secret puddling process under the management of Richard Eichhoff, a relative of Bertha's, rather than a technical expert from his own enterprise because he worried about the possibility of defection. In 1856 the foreman Freitag indeed moved over to the rival enterprise Bochumer Verein, and Krupp's fear about the loss of business secrets became even more acute.[115]

The loneliness remained. Bertha wrote to Alfred Krupp that she was worried by his solitude and that he needed someone he could trust: "sometimes it is useful and necessary that you do not intervene so much in material interests, but let a third person act for you."[116] She wanted him to be more of a family man, but in essence Krupp always remained wedded to an enterprise and an idea and not to a person.

This reality was powerfully expressed in the family residence. Long after the firm had begun to flourish, Alfred Krupp stayed in the small and rather makeshift supervisor's hut (which was later called the Stammhaus) that his father had fled to in the years of poverty and crisis. The hut was simply extended a little in order to provide additional living accommodation and a guest room. Only in 1861 did Krupp leave the small house in the middle of the now gigantic production site and move into a new and much more representational "Garden House." It was surrounded by gardens and a pond, and flanked by greenhouses; but it was still in the middle of the large steelworks. A few years later, in 1864, Krupp bought and rebuilt a large farmhouse, the Klosterbuschhof, on the *Hügel*, or hill, overlooking the Ruhr Valley and at quite a distance (about eight kilometers) from the Krupp plant.

In 1870 Krupp started to build on that site a much more grandiose construction, the Villa Hügel. He was skeptical about architects, whom he regarded as prone to waste money, and wanted a solid construction that was "as cheap as possible."[117] He provided the basic sketches himself and merely had them refined by a building supervisor, Barchewitz. In particular, the house would be an advertisement for iron and steel. It had an iron frame, and many details were made of iron as well. One of the engineers involved with the project, Ludwig Klasen, published in 1876 a "Handbook on the Construction of Big Houses with Iron," using examples from the Villa Hügel. In particular, the gigantic upper hall was originally designed in a clinical white with its iron support structure showing, and with iron railings and a glass roof.[118]

The house was technically well connected, with a telegraph link to the factory, and by 1887 there also existed a telephone connection. By 1890 the villa had its own railway station. In 1871 Alfred Krupp decided that the chronometer in the porter's lodge of the villa should be the central timekeeper of the Essen factory, and at nine o'clock each morning the correctness of the clocks was checked.

The main function of the house was representational, rather than the provision of domestic comfort. It was an advertisement for modernity, with sophisticated heating and ventilation systems as well as new methods of communication. But as a house it did not work very well. It was too big, too insistent in its use of iron for construction, and in consequence—like every grand palace—drafty and uncomfortable. In the first years, it was plagued with problems relating to heating and ventilation. The Villa Hügel was clearly an extension of the factory, adjusted in the light of the changing market. Krupp's international business in particular required a constant through-flow

Figure 2.10 Villa Hügel shortly after completion, 1873. Courtesy of Historical Archives Krupp.

of dealers, diplomats, as well as princes and potentates, who were usually placed in a smaller villa (*Kleines Haus*) connected to the main villa.

Brazilian emperor Dom Pedro II visited the Krupp works in August 1871, when he was presented with a complete Prussian artillery piece of the type that had been so effective in the recent war with France; and he returned repeatedly. He was followed by the shah of Persia, by exotic figures such as Kalakaua, king of the Sandwich Islands; Marquis Tseng of China; princes of Sweden and Spain; and Gazi Muhtar Pasha of the Ottoman Empire. The visitors needed elaborate entertainment: for a time in 1885, Alfred Krupp even employed the composer Engelbert Humperdinck to tinkle on the grand piano. Ostentation was crucial for business success.

As Alfred Krupp put it, "The commercial manufacturer must be a waster of money in the eyes of the world."[119] Hospitality was simply a business practice, an analogy to the practice of presenting guns, models, or other presents to ministers. (Sometimes there were surprises here. Krupp was extremely irritated when his gifts were reciprocated, for instance when Sultan Abdul Hamid II was sent a cannon and then sent back a jewel estimated to cost 461,000 marks. Alfred Krupp noted that he had never received any presents in return when he had given equipment to Russians.)[120]

Alfred Krupp's will clearly stated that the Villa Hügel was not personal property but was an integral part of the operation of the factory. The costs of running the Hügel amounted to almost 15 percent of net profits (*Reingewinn*) between 1878 and 1887, and rather more than that under Alfred Krupp's son and successor.[121] At the same time as the villa was completed, Krupp also began to insist that the Stammhaus, the original supervisor's hut in which Friedrich Krupp had spent his last dismal years, should be returned to its original condition and reequipped with appropriate furniture. The company required both houses: one for representation, the other for depiction of the dramatic history of a rags-to-riches story.

One of the incidental functions of the grand house was that it kept visitors away from the factory, so that the secrets of its operation could be shielded from prying eyes. Krupp wrote to his managers explaining that he could not agree to a royal request to receive visitors in the Gussstahlfabrik: "If at the request of the Crown Princess we let foreigners (Italians and others) visit the factory, then we would also have to take all Englishmen and other visitors that she sends. This would thus be a good opportunity to express the reasons why it is impossible to show the factory. Whether this news is taken badly or not is irrelevant."[122]

The family moved into Villa Hügel at the beginning of 1873, but they quickly found the new and vast house uncomfortable, not just physically (because of drafts) but above all psychologically. The major cause of the growing alienation of Alfred and Bertha had been concern over the fragile health and precarious development of their only child, Friedrich Alfred, who was born in 1854. The boy's asthma was undoubtedly to a substantial extent the consequence of the bad air in the environment of the original dwelling. But then conflicts developed over education: Friedrich Alfred wanted to study; his father hated the idea. The son was attracted to Margarethe von Ende, the educated and highly intelligent daughter of a Prussian aristocrat and government official who in 1872 had been sent as the district director of the Rhineland (*Regierungspräsident*). Alfred Krupp took an instant dislike to the father, while Bertha was sympathetic, and was captivated by the daughter and frequently invited her to the Hügel. When the Krupp heir eventually married Margarethe, in 1882, the ceremony was attended by Bertha Krupp but not by her husband.

Alfred Krupp was increasingly disillusioned and suspicious. He wrote to his son that he should be very careful in the choice of his friends and that "not everyone whom I trusted proved himself as my friend when he realized that I was absent and could no longer check up on his activity."[123] "The more promising the future of the enterprise is, the more the traps that will be set for you."[124] But he was equally distrustful of his own son, and for a time in 1880 contemplated leaving the company instead to his Austrian nephew Arthur, a man with a ruinously power-ful urge to expand the Austrian Krupp works.

When Krupp in 1845 employed his cousin Adalbert Ascherfeld as a manager in the Gussstahlfabrik, he warned Ascherfeld that he would have no time for reading or for politics. "Apart from a blessing from above for the success of our enterprises, your agreeable and worry-free future depends entirely on your own energy and activity."[125] He appeared to himself as the embodiment of the Protestant and Prussian work ethic. "A simple attitude is required, with no thought about anything else (except one's own house), and with no distraction by the pursuit of studies, art or other passions, with a view of work not as a burden or an unpleasant but necessary condition for existence, but rather as supreme pleasure."[126]

In 1872 Krupp was thinking of withdrawing from busi-ness. He wrote to Ernst Eichhoff from Torquay, England, that he still wished to keep the factory "for all times" in the hands of his family, but that this would require dramatic alterations in working practices. "Everyone according to his ability and value will be placed or moved, honored or cast aside. I want to see order brought in, and an end to calls for patience and yet more patience."[127] Mines were bought for a ninety-nine-year period in the belief that the enterprise would always be in the hands of the family.[128]

The lack of trust that emanated from Alfred Krupp began to poison the whole enterprise. In modern man-agement jargon, it would be claimed that "Krupp could not let go." The company became more rigid and less

innovative in the last years of Alfred Krupp's life. Carl
Meyer wrote in 1877 about Krupp's capacity for quar-
reling with his managers but noted that "he is at the
same time of such a childlike amiability that one cannot
be cross with him. I am sorry for him to the depth of my
soul, since he is heading toward a moral and material
ruin if he does not stop."[129] By 1882 Krupp was separated from his wife and leading an increasingly solitary
existence in the Villa Hügel. Like Storm's *Schimmelreiter*,
this charismatic entrepreneur was increasingly cut off
from his family and from the enterprise he had created.
But like Theodor Storm's fictional character, Krupp also
built a powerful legend, an idea of what business was
about, that survived him.

THE LEGACY

By the end of his life, Krupp had already become a legend. The company history produced on the first centenary
put it like this: "The life of Alfred Krupp was work, from
childhood to the edge of the grave."[130] Kaiser Wilhelm I
wrote on the death of Alfred Krupp to his son Friedrich
Alfred: "You know how highly I estimated him who with
his art gained a European reputation and for our own
fatherland has been of inestimable importance."[131] The
kaiser was right to emphasize both the national importance and the global reputation. Competition between
states had become a process that depended closely on the
management of business competition within the setting
of a national context.

In 1889 a severe statue of Alfred Krupp was erected at
the main entrance of the Gussstahlfabrik. On the front
side of the base were the words: "The purpose of work

should be the common good." A clunky celebratory poem was recited:

Let us raise our glasses
Drinking to the firm's good state,
Which for all its working masses
Helps in every blow of fate.
The firm is our father,
I would want to add,
We are all Kruppianer rather
And that's not too bad![132]

The idea of "Kruppianer" became a model for social relations in the new German Empire. There was an autonomous world created for but also by the employees and their families, in which the enterprise and its mission established a privileged identity. Skilled workers were tied to the factory, not only by strict discipline, but also by bonds of loyalty: the discipline was a mechanism for achieving social integration. That complex identity focused on the name "Krupp."

In 1902 the economic historian Richard Ehrenberg ended a study of great historic dynasties, in which he looked at the story of the Fuggers and the Rothschilds, with an account of Alfred Krupp. He concluded that "the biggest private industrial company in Germany, perhaps in the world, was the creation not of a joint stock company but of the genius of a single man."[133]

Alfred Krupp perfectly fits the mold of the heroic entrepreneur. Profoundly skeptical of joint-stock companies, banks, and capitalism in general, but also of big-scale science and modern research methods, he was a genius at extending to its utmost limits the possibilities of the craft entrepreneur. He developed an extraordinarily successful business model that allowed the principles of the small workshop to be extended on a gigantic and global scale. But in order to survive, that model required adaptation and compromise with the world of joint-stock companies and banks, as well as the harnessing of big science. That was the task that fell on his son and heir.

THREE

SCIENCE

Friedrich Alfred Krupp

The Manns of Lübeck reproduced many of the features
of family enterprises, in both a good and a bad sense.
Thomas Mann's older brother Heinrich was a rival and a
competitor, but ultimately also a much less accomplished
novelist. He has, however, often been regarded as a better caricaturist of the behavior of the upper bourgeoisie
in imperial Germany. From 1906 to 1914 he worked on
a novel, *Der Untertan* (*The Loyal Subject*), in which he
depicted the weakness and at the same time arrogance
and duplicity of the new German industrial leadership:
the personality of the main figure of the novel, the industrialist Diederich Hessling, bears a striking resemblance
to that of Kaiser Wilhelm II.

Heinrich Mann's novel was not just a satire on the
commercial classes under the empire but also a veiled
attack on the kaiser himself. The dramatic high point of
the novel comes when Hessling prostrates himself and
sinks into unconsciousness in the imperial presence.
Some of Friedrich Alfred Krupp's comments sound as if
they might have come from the lips of the odiously obse-
quious Hessling. In 1896, for instance, he commented
adoringly on Wilhelm II, "He is a very important person,
and it moved me greatly how he begins to be more measured in his expressions and opinions."[1] There was never

Figure 3.1 Friedrich Alfred Krupp and Margarethe von Ende, 1882 (Teich Hanfstaengl studio). Courtesy of Historical Archives Krupp.

any doubt about Krupp's dedication to the kaiser or his patriotism, but he was clearly also not Diederich Hessling. Hessling is servile to superiors and brutal to inferiors, while Friedrich Alfred Krupp was a rather kind and gentle person who tried to improve relations with the workforce. Photographs show a withdrawn figure with a slightly stooped posture that is quite different from the proud bearing of Alfred Krupp. Friedrich Alfred also—in stark contrast to Mann's Hessling—reflected endlessly about the problems of his age, and tried to find answers based on modern science.

Otto von Bismarck had commented on the particular character of Alfred Krupp's enterprise: "Such establishments as for instance that of Krupp would not be conceivable under anything other than a monarchical constitution as for instance in a republic."[2] In just the same way as the regime of Alfred Krupp had seemed to mirror the establishment of the German Empire and the Bismarckian political settlement, Friedrich Alfred's world corresponded to that of Wilhelmine Germany. Alfred advised his son in 1885: "You must be to the future kaiser what I am to the present one, then no swindler can damage the factory."[3]

Friedrich Alfred Krupp indeed had many parallels with Kaiser Wilhelm II, who admired and respected him, and continued to protect him when he became mired in scandal. Lothar Gall regards him as the embodiment of "Wilhelminism."[4] Volker Wellhöner describes the critical historiography of Krupp as having ingested a "tubelike conglomeration of all the negative characteristics of German imperialism."[5] But seeing in the kaiser or in Friedrich Alfred Krupp only the bad sides of megalomania and byzantinism misses the peculiar way in which these men were caught in a trap between the needs of modernity and the claims of traditionalism. Wilhelm was above all an enthusiastic and ecstatic modernizer. He argued in 1902 that "the new century will be dominated by science, including technology, and not like the previous century by philosophy. The German is great in his scientific research, great in his capacity for organization and discipline."[6] For "German," the kaiser could easily have said "Kruppianer."

Both Krupp and the kaiser had contended with rather fragile health as children. The kaiser had a withered arm. Friedrich Alfred had a bad asthmatic condition, doubtless a consequence of growing up in the middle of the Gussstahlfabrik, continually breathing in the toxic and sulfuric gases. Both men had distant and aloof fathers. Both seemed to compensate for their missed childhood in later life, when they exhibited childlike and embarrassing behavior. In their personal lives, they both wanted to be freer, more informal, more modern, in a world dominated by strict rituals—in court or in the Villa Hügel. They both found that the search for more modern social forms was dangerous and would be misinterpreted by their opponents.

On inheriting the enterprise, F. A. Krupp surprised his managers by the vigor with which he asserted himself. Twelve days after his father's death he wrote a stern letter to the *Berliner Börsenzeitung* to protest against an article that had called Hanns Jencke the "general director" of Krupp, and to point out that the "management of the firm has passed to me and it is my task to manage it in the spirit of my late father."[7] In 1893, when Jencke demanded measures to make the company more financially secure, Krupp reminded him that "according to the testament only one person can be the owner of the factory, and this person will remain the head of the administration." "It must not be forgotten," Krupp went on, "that the owner of the company and the company are a unity. What is decided by the management is decided in the name of and on the responsibility of the owner. The person of the owner of the factory is not to be separated from the person of the owner of the private family wealth."[8] Jencke in practice withdrew more and more from the enterprise, engaging first in the new and powerful interest organizations of German business, above all in the Centralverband deutscher Industrieller (CdI) and the Verband deutscher Eisen- und Stahlindustrieller. He was on the executive board of the CdI from 1885 and was its chairman from 1901 to 1905. In 1902 he left Krupp and in 1903 became chairman of the supervisory board of the Dresdner Bank.

The company began to develop a new corporate culture. Its employees learned to speak and think "Kruppsch."[9] The liberal social thinker Friedrich Naumann talked at this time in a different context of the evolution of a "patriotism of the company." Friedrich Alfred Krupp paid a great deal of attention to his attempt to modernize labor relations. In 1899 he set up a cultural and educational association, the Kruppsche Bildungsverein, which provided technical and scientific courses but also uplifting concerts and theatrical events. It was a conscious attempt to transcend class limits and appeal to both factory workers and white-collar employees; and in the years before the First World War, the proportion of factory workers in the membership rose from 30 percent to 50 percent.[10] Krupp also intervened personally in labor relations. In the smitheries dispute of 1902, when the management wanted to introduce new operating rules and procedures and a director of the craft workshops producing smaller cast-steel products started to escalate the conflict by dismissing twenty-five workers, Krupp managed the clash quite skillfully. A delegation of workers was invited to present their grievances at the Villa Hügel, and Krupp spoke tactfully and directly, insisting on some but not all of the changes (such as the shortening of the lunch break). As a consequence, an incipient strike was prevented. The British *Evening Telegraph* wrote admiringly that "if other employers cultivated the methods of Herr Krupp . . . industrial disputes between labour and capital would quickly become things of the past."[11] Krupp's attitude in this dispute reflected his efforts at a more general reorientation of social relations. Krupp developed and expanded the provision of workers' housing that had begun under his father, and added to the medical facilities for sick employees. But he also thought that a general social reform should be a national imperative. Krupp self-consciously wanted to manage affairs differently than had his father, who increasingly seemed like a figure from a quite different world of long ago. Alfred Krupp had frequently expressed his skepticism about formal studies and university education, at a time when Germany was establishing a global scientific and intellectual preeminence. Friedrich Alfred was a Wilhelminian in that he saw that only a superior knowledge of science would produce business prosperity. He had initially blossomed under the influence of the family doctor and natural scientist, Dr. Emil Ludwig Schmidt.[12] He was enormously impressed in 1874 by a visit to the new zoological station in Naples, and started a lifelong fascination with marine biology and its implications for the process of evolution.

Later, he studied chemistry at Braunschweig University and worked on the use of carbonic acid in the late 1870s to improve the homogeneity of cast steel.

But science for Friedrich Alfred Krupp had a much broader mission. It was a new religion, a substitute for the traditional gods. "There is no loving God of the Christians and no strict and vengeful God of the Jews," he is reported to have told his wife. "God is too high and powerful for us to be able to have an idea of him. It is as if a protozoan or an amoeba would try to develop an idea of man. . . . But this is certain, that every scientific progress is a building block for the discovery of the nature of God."[13] It is not surprising that he became an admirer and follower of the massively popular and influential philosopher and zoologist Ernst Haeckel, the author of *The Riddle of the Universe*. Krupp's secretary later termed Haeckel "the intellectual originator of all the activity of Herr Krupp." And in 1900 Krupp donated thirty thousand marks as prize money for an essay competition initiated by himself and supported by Haeckel, on the theme of the implications of the theory of evolution for the development of politics and legislation. The winning essays called for the subordination of individuals to the state and for the institution of eugenics and racial science. It would be ahistorical to conclude that these terms meant the same as they later did for National Socialists, but Krupp and Haeckel were undoubtedly using Darwinism to react against the liberal political philosophies of the nineteenth century as well as against reactionary conservatism. To both men, the older political philosophies seemed antiquated and superficial, and in need of replacement by the ideas of science.[14]

Business also became more scientific. In 1887, of the directors of Krupp, two were technically trained and the other four came from an administrative, commercial, or financial background. Fifteen years later, in 1902, of thirteen directors, six were scientifically trained. Krupp created what was first simply called "Laboratory II" and later became the Chemical-Physical Experimental Institute, where the nonrusting steels that were patented in 1912 were developed. One indication of the new orientation is the number of analyses conducted in the chemical laboratory of the Gussstahlfabrik. In 1889 it carried out an impressive 12,000; but by 1911 that figure was 500,000. The company became once again one of the most technically innovative German corporations. In terms of the number of patents awarded between 1897 and 1900, it ranked third in Germany, after the chemical companies Bayer and Hoechst.[15]

Figure 3.2 Research Department, 1912. Courtesy of Historical Archives Krupp.

BUSINESS EXPANSION

Wilhelminism was above all about size and power. Friedrich Alfred Krupp immediately presided over a rapid expansion of the business. From 1887 to 1893 the area of the Gussstahlfabrik increased from forty-two to fifty-one hectares, and the number of employees rose from 13,000 to 17,500. By 1899 there were 25,000 employees. The smelting workshop from the 1870s, with its old crucibles, was rebuilt to use gas furnaces developed by Siemens. In 1888 a second Siemens-Martin Works was opened, and the process was eminently suited to the mass production of steel. By 1900 the fifth Martin Works was being built. There was technical innovation in the use of nickel for artillery barrels, and in steel armored plates through a patented technique known as "gas cementing."

The large-scale development of the production of pig iron seemed a necessary response to the increasing demand for steel. Krupp had to become a more "normal" iron and steel producer. Originally, Krupp had thought about building such a plant in Lorraine, near the major ore source; eventually he chose a site in the Rhine-Ruhr area, but with better access to water transport. It may also have been important that Lorraine was obviously vulnerable in the case of war with France. In addition, there were already skilled Krupp workers on the lower Rhine, who could provide an initial core for the new workforce. From 1895 Krupp embarked on the construction of a large steelworks in a site favorable for transportation opposite Duisburg on the Rhine, at Rheinhausen. The new plant was initially planned to comprise five large blast furnaces, a Thomas steelwork with three converters, and a rolling mill for rails and ties.

Figure 3.3 Friedrich-Alfred-Hütte in Rheinhausen, c. 1910. Courtesy of Historical Archives Krupp.

In Essen, additional halls were constructed for steel processing, culminating in 1900/1901 with the construction of the Mechanical Workshop VIII, which was designed to produce heavy steel parts for ships and machinery. It included a turning lathe twenty-four meters in length and weighing three hundred tons. The old hammering technique was increasingly outdated, and the first hydraulic press was introduced in 1890. In 1888 electricity generation made for the much easier transmission of power to individual manufacturing processes, and in 1893 came the first electric crane.

The most dramatic developments, however, occurred in military production. In 1890 came the naval gun with a cradle carriage. Barrels were breaking in consequence of the use of picric acid in shells, compelling the introduction of nickel steel for artillery-barrel construction from 1890. The application of nickel to steelmaking was initially difficult, and raised major technical problems in terms of the consistency of the steel. There were also major advances in firing speed, with the use of electrical detonation mechanisms. In 1902 Krupp began to produce antitorpedo cannons with breech mechanisms that opened with the recoil of the gun, though Krupp had initially lagged significantly behind Rheinmetall in designing recoil mechanisms. Also in 1902 came the first mobile howitzer with a recoil mechanism.

Naval armor, for which malleability and sufficient plasticity to cushion impact was at a premium, also increasingly required the use of compound steel and in particular the use of nickel. From 1890 Krupp began the production of nickel-based armored plate. By the turn of the century, in part because of the new naval program, Krupp became identified as above all a producer of plate armor.

One innovation that Krupp initially flirted with, but then dropped, would have taken the company in a completely different direction. In 1893 Rudolf Diesel concluded an agreement with both Krupp and Maschinenfabrik Augsburg (which later became part of MAN) for the production of the first diesel engines. Krupp built a total of eight stationary engines but in 1899 ended this experiment, which seemed small-scale compared with the growing importance of large naval orders.

Above all Friedrich Alfred resumed the expansion of the family business through mergers and acquisitions. In the last year of his life, Alfred had acquired the Annen works, which specialized in cast forms and had made railway and shipping material as well as artillery and rifle steel. But after 1887 the pace of expansion quickened, with the acquisition of minette (phosphoric) ore fields in Lorraine as well as of mines on the Lahn later in the 1890s. In 1889 Krupp bought a majority stake in the Sälzer und Neuack coal mine in Essen. After the creation of the Rhenish-Westphalian Coal Syndicate in 1893, the need for independent access to coal became more urgent.

This expansion was very much a personal initiative of Friedrich Alfred Krupp. Hanns Jencke was skeptical about many of the proposed acquisitions, and argued that it would be better to focus on Krupp's core competence. The contrast between an owner pressing for high-speed growth and a management that wanted to apply brakes is quite unusual for a family firm, where it is often the management that wants increased prestige, power, and remuneration as a result of growth, while the family owners are worried about financial drain. Behind the difference in attitudes in the case of Krupp lay an argument about the appropriate form of the company. Some German companies, notably August Thyssen's steelworks as well as Siemens, were already beginning to reject complete centralization and to experiment with the multidivision form (or M-Form) later celebrated by Alfred Chandler as the characteristic business organization of modernity. Jencke indeed pointed out that a single centralized directorate was inappropriate for a more widespread and diffuse corporation, but such a transformation would have meant a loss of control by the owner. For that reason, it was inconceivable.

The Gruson works of Magdeburg (established in 1855) had long been a competitor to Krupp. It had developed the case-hardened castings used in railway switches and tram wheels, but its main competitive advantage lay in the production of armored plates for the defense of artillery pieces in fortresses. In 1882 it had provided a dramatic practical demonstration of the power of its armor plate to resist artillery fire. Gruson was also developing as a major competitor for rapid-fire artillery after 1887, and then in the manufacture of shells. The Krupp director Fritz Asthöwer, who had already in 1886 sold his own steel company in Annen to Krupp, played a central role in initiating the merger negotiations.[16] In December 1892 the competitors reached an agreement that was subsequently approved by Wilhelm II, and which gave Krupp two seats on the executive board and two on the supervisory board of the Grusonwerk, and also gave Krupp the right to buy Gruson at a fixed price. This option was exercised quite soon, in the next spring, and Krupp took a big syndicated bank loan to make the 24-million-mark purchase. Unlike in 1873, when they had hesitated to support business, the banks were competing ferociously to manage this issue: both Bankhaus Delbrück and the Dresdner Bank wanted to take the lead.[17] Banks had now become convinced of the permanent place of Krupp in German business life. In the subsequent period, Krupp expanded the civilian production of the Grusonwerk, mostly for export. It became a major producer of mills and presses for the production of vegetable oils as well as machinery to process sugar and coffee.

Another acquisition proved to be more problematic. Friedrich Alfred Krupp believed that German economic success would depend more and more on the development not only of maritime commerce but also of the German navy. In that regard too, he was a true contemporary of Wilhelm II. Providing naval artillery, and armored carriages, seemed to lead the company logically to ship construction. There was the outstanding British model of Vickers. But the acquisition of a shipyard proved to be a highly precarious commercial undertaking. The Kiel

Germaniawerft had been founded in 1863 but had always been commercially quite precarious. It collapsed financially in 1878, and again—under new ownership, based in Berlin Tegel—in 1882. It was the banks that pressed for a better solution in the shape of a takeover by Krupp, who was attracted by the prospect of large-scale naval orders but worried about the financial implications. Wilhelm II also encouraged Krupp to embark on this new field of activity, and in 1896 Krupp concluded a contract with an option to buy the Germaniawerft. After the deal, the kaiser telegraphed his approval. As in the case of the purchase of Gruson, this further expansion of Krupp had the highest imperial sanction. Krupp personally engaged himself in the push for acquiring the shipyard, organized a large (20 million marks) bond issue, and eventually in 1902 exercised his option and took over the Germaniawerft. Again this required a large syndicated bank credit, and again the banks competed with one another for the privilege of dealing with Krupp. Even at a time when the market had substantially weakened, and some major bankruptcies occurred, Krupp was able to insist that a large number of banks should be involved, so as to avoid dependency on the Dresdner Bank as the leader of the financial syndicate. In 1908, when the Dresdner Bank and the Disconto Gesellschaft insisted on a 4.5 percent coupon in the aftermath of the abrupt market panic of 1907, Krupp, with a new 50-million-mark credit provided by those banks, managed to fan the competitive instincts of Deutsche Bank and obtained an interest rate of 4 percent.[18]

Krupp oversaw a radical transformation of the shipyard. Between 1896 and 1914 the number of employees rose threefold; the area of the yard increased from 6 to

22.5 hectares, with slipways that were in part protected by glass roofs. Before the First World War, the yards supplied nine battleships, five small cruisers, thirty-three torpedo boats, and ten submarines, as well as more than three hundred commercial steamers and also some yachts. But the Germania shipyards also had orders from the Austro-Hungarian, Norwegian, Russian, Brazilian, Argentine, Italian, Ottoman, and Chinese navies. On August 4, 1906, the Germaniawerft finished the construction of the first German submarine. Submarines were built not only for Germany but also for the Habsburg Empire, Italy, and Norway.

Despite all this, the Germaniawerft was never very profitable, and was never very secure about its naval order book. On some of the big ships of the line, Germania incurred substantial losses (700,000 marks, for instance, on the construction of the *Prinzregent Luitpold*). In 1903 Krupp began secretly to buy up shares of the rival Stettin Vulcan shipyard, not initially so much in order to mount a takeover bid but to block capital increases and hence increases in capacity at a rival shipyard. A year later, when there was discussion of a possible merger of the two yards, Krupp was worried that it might fan the intense political discussion that had broken out over his alleged monopoly position in the supply of armaments and in particular of armor plate.

PROFITS AND COMPETITION

Armaments in general (but not naval equipment) were easily the most profitable part of the Krupp business, though they generally represented well under half of the total business revenues and profits. For the period from 1887/88 to 1901/2, the gross profit margin in the peacetime production amounted to 14.9 percent, while for armored plates the figure reached an extraordinary (and politically controversial) 52.0 percent, and for other "war materiel" the margin was 29.1 percent.[19] Most of Krupp sales were domestic.

On international markets Krupp performed relatively badly. Up to the end of the 1880s, the overwhelming part of military sales were made abroad. After Friedrich Alfred took over the works, however, the proportion of foreign sales decreased. The enterprise looked as if it was becoming less globalized during the Wilhelmine era (see fig. 2.5).[20] Foreign sales were still important, and Krupp liked to cultivate some foreign markets, such as China or the Ottoman Empire. Friedrich Alfred Krupp continued his father's excellent relations with the Chinese viceroy Li Hongzhang, and in the 1890s the Krupp works even made a cast-iron statue of Li as a gift that was eventually erected in Shanghai. One reporter for the *Shanghai Mercury* complained in 1893 that "'Made in Germany' on every article is now the motto of the day in Tientsin, and unless things bear these magic words the Viceroy. . . . will have none of them." But Krupp firmly resisted pressure from the German government to participate in the development of a steelworks in Hanyang, arguing that there was no adequate supply of coking coal.[21]

In part, of course, the appearance of deglobalization was due to the exceptional vigor of the German market after the mid-1890s and also to the dramatic new naval expansion program, as well as increasing international tensions and a gathering arms race in which technical developments in artillery and armor were regarded as vital to national defense. National strategic objectives in the more conflictual international environment meant that the Krupp company could not easily cultivate global

Figure 3.4 Otto Lang's statue of Li Hongzhang, in Villa Hügel park, 1896.
Courtesy of Historical Archives Krupp.

markets as it had done in the mid-nineteenth century. Initiatives from Britain for closer cooperation were turned down by Krupp. There was no cooperation with Vickers on the production of armored plates. In 1898 British business interests approached Krupp in vain in a quest for a joint venture in artillery production; Krupp explicitly and demonstratively asserted his patriotism as a ground for his refusal. The German government also pressed the company to limit arms sales to countries that might be hostile to Germany: not just France, Russia, or Britain, but even Denmark.[22] But nevertheless, Krupp supplied the powerful defense artillery for the Belgian fortress of Antwerp and continued to win Belgian munitions orders until the outbreak of the First World War, although the orders were actually fulfilled by Cockerill in Belgium according to Krupp specifications.[23]

Deglobalization reflected a strange reality that should not simply be ascribed (as it often has been) to progressive entrepreneurial failure. In the 1880s few doubted that Krupp was (or maybe Krupp and its French rival Schneider-Creusot were) the world's preeminent manufacturers of arms. But two decades later, Krupp was losing market share to competitors such as the British firms Armstrong and Vickers, as well as to Schneider. Of twenty-nine large warships sold to the big and ambitious "new" countries, Argentina, Brazil, and Mexico; the Ottoman Empire and Egypt in the eastern Mediterranean; and Japan and China in the Far East between 1900 and 1914, Vickers and Armstrong together provided eighteen. A compilation of armament sales in these seven markets shows Britain as having a market share of 63.2 percent, with French (9.4 percent), Italian (9.0 percent), and U.S. (8.9 percent) exporters ahead of the very feeble 7.6 percent share achieved by Germany. Vickers squeezed the Germans out of Spain in 1908, and in 1911 it was endangering Krupp's firmly entrenched position in the Ottoman Empire.[24] At the same time, German non-military steel products were continuing their apparently inexorable conquest of world markets, at the expense of the British competition.

Perhaps there is some plausibility in the entrepreneurial explanation. The British firms did very keen cost calculations, and also went to great lengths to offer very special products: the *Rio de Janeiro* was the largest prewar battleship in the world, eliciting a personal protest from Kaiser Wilhelm that even Germany did not need ships of that size. Krupp, which had started to supply battleships to Brazil even before the big German naval expansion began (the cruisers *Camamurée* and *Tupy* had been completed by the Germaniawerft in 1896), in consequence needed to resort to claims that it could "make battleships exactly like the English designs of the best type in both ships and ordnance."[25]

In Germany, the steel industry was—despite attempts to form syndicates to eliminate wasteful competition—highly competitive. There were two firms, Thyssen and Phoenix, that were bigger steel producers than Krupp in the middle of the first decade of the twentieth century, as well as some smaller businesses barking at the heels of the big three.[26] But in armaments, this kind of competition (so notable in Great Britain, where Vickers and Armstrong eyed each other with great suspicion) was lacking. The German government in repeated instances intervened to stop competition between German firms, although Rheinmetall as well as state armories remained active in the munitions business. The result of the imperial government's concerns in the early 1890s about Gruson and Krupp getting in each other's way in the end diminished the German competitive edge in the global market. Later, the kaiser intervened personally to stop the Ottoman Empire buying arms from Rheinmetall rather than Krupp. The anticompetitive stance of the imperial government produced high profits, especially in domestic orders, for the new quasi monopolist. But it did not provide a powerful international competition, and instead offers a fine lesson in some of the difficulties involved in the concept of building up a national champion.

POLITICS

Under Alfred Krupp, the factory had maintained a fine balance between cultivating official contacts—above all with the royal household—and a self-conscious disdain for politics. Alfred had again and again warned against involvement in political life, though he had lobbied energetically and made his passionate hostility to socialism a principle of the workplace philosophy. The older Krupp was a fine instance of the figure that Thomas Mann later identified as the "unpolitical German." He had tried to minimize any contact with the press or with political parties. But this was precisely one of the aspects that made him appear so antiquated to his son and to a new generation of managers. By the end of the nineteenth century, the explosion of the public sphere made the traditional stance untenable.

Some features of the Krupp *Weltanschauung* nevertheless remained constant: above all the insistence on close contact with the ruling house. Wilhelm II visited the Gussstahlfabrik in the summer of 1890, and then returned in a biannual pilgrimage. When the kaiser visited Essen in October 1900, he appointed Krupp as "Secret Councillor" with the title of "Excellency." He thought that Krupp was "part of the state," and others inside and outside Germany shared this impression, as for instance did the Ottoman sultan when he asked the kaiser to "order" Krupp to reduce his prices.[27]

Friedrich Alfred Krupp became much more engaged in politics, with eventually deleterious consequences for the business. Political activity became more necessary because of the increased importance of the state as a customer, and also because of the heightened importance of public opinion and the press. But it was full of pitfalls. Krupp's first experience was an unhappy one, and from that initial point matters deteriorated. Krupp as well as his general manager Hanns Jencke, with two other industrialists, Carl Ferdinand von Stumm-Halberg and Count Hugo Sholto von Douglas, had been invited to join the State Council for a meeting in February 1890 that was a decisive moment in the escalating tension between Bismarck and Wilhelm II. Krupp and Jencke made quite opposite impressions: Krupp appeared as rambling and indecisive, and incapable of taking a firm viewpoint, while Jencke eloquently set out the Bismarckian position in opposition to the extension of labor-protection measures.

F. A. Krupp had been induced to be a candidate for the Reichstag for the Essen constituency in 1887, but was defeated by a member of the Catholic Center party. In 1889, asked to stand again, he had refused. But in 1893, when there was substantial tension over the military budget, he was urged by a newly forming "national" movement to pursue his candidacy, even though he was still reluctant. The efforts of 1892 to form a National Party had been self-consciously distinct from the efforts of the existing political groupings: the vision was of a broad antisocialist-rallying movement that would transcend all the older distinctions of the right. Krupp saw in this movement a new political opportunity, and grasped the chance to be modern. He was elected for the Essen constituency with a small majority and never joined a conventional political party, although he was counted as a "guest" (*Hospitant*) of the Free Conservatives, the former Bismarckian party. His political interventions were limited. He never spoke in the Reichstag, although he did go so far as to prepare a speech in favor of lifting the ban on the Jesuit order. Another political initiative turned into a fiasco when, in 1894, Krupp wanted to enlist Bismarck's support in lifting some of the agricultural tariffs and expanding the possibilities for German export orders in Russia and elsewhere. Bismarck did not want to be drawn into a clash of industrialists and agrarians, and informed Krupp by letter of his reluctance to take a stance. But Count Dönhoff spread the notion that Bismarck was warning of the dangers of war with Russia if the tariff reform proposals were not accepted, and at an evening event in the presence of Wilhelm II, Krupp added that this was indeed the view of the former chancellor. Bismarck was outraged, and Krupp was obliged to apologize. But the incident was highly publicized and weakened Krupp's political standing still further.[28]

Wilhelmine politics was characterized by a proclivity for scandal. Friedrich Alfred Krupp unintentionally contributed richly to the provision of material for the periodic eruption of outrage. He started his own reign in the Essen enterprise on a sour note. In 1887 a speech that he had made in Constantinople was widely criticized as being sycophantic to Sultan Abdul Hamid II. The left-wing *Volks-Zeitung* claimed that he had begun his address to the tyrant in a truly oriental way: "Sire, the generosity and goodness of Your Majesty have become legendary in all of Europe, they are the subject of praise and prayers all over the world." Krupp denied that the quotation was authentic. But the *Berliner-Zeitung* described the atmosphere of this encounter with the word that would later be used over and over again to describe the atmosphere of Wilhelm II's Germany: "byzantinism."[29]

In 1892 an old scandal was dug up again in the aftermath of criticism of the engineering entrepreneur Ludwig Loewe for having negotiated in 1868 to supply weapons to France. The attacks on Loewe were heavily anti-Semitic, and the whole scandal became known as the *Judenflintenhetze*, the campaign against Jewish guns. In this context, the liberal and left press pointed out that Alfred Krupp had behaved in exactly the same way in 1868, in the run-up to the Franco-Prussian War, even though the letter of Krupp's was from 1858, not 1868, and the scandal and the question of the dating of the letter had already been ventilated in 1873.

But the major accusation that developed in the course of the 1890s concerned the pricing of Krupp's military contracts, and was a direct outcome of Krupp's turn to new and much more aggressive methods of publicity, public relations, and the shaping of public opinion. In 1890, as part of the move to an era in which mass politics and the news media were becoming crucial, the company established a so-called News Office at the instigation of the former foreign representative of Krupp, Carl Menshausen, with the goal of collecting information from newspapers and other sources, and also of channeling information to the media. Krupp soon became a major enthusiast of the new era of *Weltpolitik* and *Flottenpolitik*. He helped to create the *Süddeutsche Reichskorrepondenz* as an organ of imperial and naval propaganda. The new paper's guiding hand was a journalist who had long been close to the Foreign Office and the making of German foreign policy. Victor Schweinburg from 1896 conducted a regular correspondence with Krupp and supplied him with internal details from government circles in Berlin. Schweinburg also published articles in the *Berliner Neueste Nachrichten* that were sympathetic to the Krupp interests.[30] Alfred Tirpitz, the new state secretary in the Naval Office, in 1897 turned to the Centralverband deutscher Industriellen, as well as to Krupp personally, in order to launch a publicity offensive in favor of naval rearmament. Krupp was initially very reluctant, explaining when he met Tirpitz that he was prepared to support the campaign but not to engage himself personally, as "every indiscretion regarding such an effort might prove damaging."[31] Schweinburg was a decisive figure in organizing the Navy League, which was conceived at a meeting in the Berlin Hotel Kaiserhof in January 1898 and launched in April 1898. Within a year it had 247,000 members. But Tirpitz and Krupp had stepped into a hornet's nest, because Schweinburg's efforts seemed to be in competition with a more genuinely populist initiative launched by someone regarded in government circles as a nobody, an obscure Berlin manufacturer of cod-liver oil named J. E. Stroschein, who had attempted to found his own alternative naval pressure group a few months before Schweinburg's initiative. The radical populists saw the Navy League as an attempt, masterminded by Krupp, to exclude nonestablishment voices from the debate about

German armaments. Stroschein started to attack "business patriotism" and the "clique of businessmen."[32]

The political cunning of this attack lay in the way it brought together radical-right populists from the Pan-German League with socialist and Catholic critics of the imperial establishment. The official Catholic Center party newspaper, *Germania*, attacked Schweinburg for his Jewish descent and for being a "paid hack in the service of others without his own opinion."[33] Critics argued that Schweinburg had been engaged in the illegitimate acquisition of official documents, and that he had been involved in a brawl. The debate rapidly turned into an attack on Krupp, who had initially tried to defend Schweinburg.

Indeed the linkage seemed obvious to the critics: it appeared that Krupp was passionate about pushing naval propaganda because he, the richest capitalist in Germany, stood to benefit from naval orders. Under the pressure of the attacks, Schweinburg resigned from the Navy League. In the autumn of 1900, Krupp too left the executive board of the league. The league was deeply embarrassed about its commercial ties, and in 1900 announced that since December 1899 it had no longer accepted contributions from "industrialists and businessmen who want to make money out of the naval expansion."[34] Dietrich Schäfer, a historian and passionate promoter of the league, made it clear that the credibility of the initiative depended on rejecting any contribution from those who might benefit from the shipbuilding program.

But it was the socialists, rather than the populist right, who could present the best arguments when they took up this theme. In the 1899 budget debate the socialist leader August Bebel attacked Krupp explicitly. The big military suppliers, he said, formed a "giant ring, which has its headquarters in Berlin, where the prices are dictated that exploit the German people, where these gentlemen make millions and millions at the cost of the people, without the army and navy administrations being able to do anything because they are in the hands of these men."[35]

In 1900 the Reichstag Budget Commission concluded that as the only suppliers of armored plate, Krupp and Stumm had reached a price convention, and argued that of a proposed expenditure by the German government of 260 million marks over the next sixteen years, 130 million was pure profit. The *Frankfurter Zeitung* attacked the *Berliner Neueste Nachrichten* as being in the hands of Krupp. The kaiser himself sent a telegram of complaint to the Krupp directorate after the Boxer Uprising in China: "It is not appropriate, at a moment when I am calling my soldiers out to fight against the yellow beasts, to try to make money out of the seriousness of the situation; and it will be taken badly by the people."[36] Barbara Wolbring argues that the figures on profits were not a grotesque misrepresentation, and that Krupp did indeed make margins of some 60 percent on armored plate (although the Germaniawerft incurred major losses).[37]

Tirpitz responded to the critique by putting pressure on Krupp to reduce prices. On February 27, 1900, Tirpitz outraged the Krupp management by sending a cable asking for information on the level of Krupp's profits. Krupp began to feel that Tirpitz was actually behind the political attacks, and demanded an audience with the kaiser. There Krupp tried to defend his business practices, pointing out that "the engagement in armored plate had not been a result of Fried. Krupp's own initiative but had been carried out most unwillingly and only after continual insistence and persuasion by the Reich Navy Office." He argued that the superior strength of the nickel armor plate was saving the navy money. And he pointed out, not only that his firm had engaged in colossally costly research, but also that the insistence of the navy on secrecy concerning its equipment was damaging Krupp's competitive chances in foreign markets. Finally, he unleashed a polemic against joint-stock companies. "My hands are tied, I cannot defend myself, and I am damaged on every side. Competition against the joint-stock companies is almost impossible. If a private individual buys a firm, he needs to put gold on the table, but a joint-stock company simply issues shares at a high price." He threatened that if the attacks continued, he would transform Krupp into a joint-stock company. "A joint stock-company would alter the mood at one stroke, because then all circles would have a material interest in the prospering of the enterprise."[38]

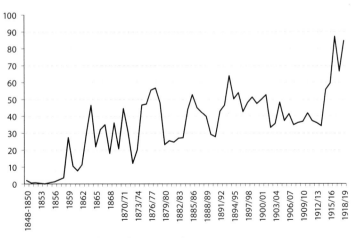

Figure 3.5 Military share of Krupp production (%), 1848–1919.

But Krupp was fundamentally helpless. Tirpitz's predecessor as secretary of state for the navy, Admiral Friedrich Hollmann, wrote sympathetically to remind Krupp: "You must never forget that you live in a glass house; acknowledging the precariousness of your situation, you should not put stones into the hands of your opponents. If other people take advantage of commercial opportunities, irrespective of what they are, without encountering the least objection, your position has become so extraordinary, that you are not allowed to make a monetary demand. You are not allowed to act commercially."[39] Tirpitz on the other hand repeatedly tried, with rather little success, to encourage other firms to compete with Krupp. In 1901 he tried to interest the rival Rheinmetall company, a formidable manufacturer of artillery, in the production of armor plate.[40] Meanwhile Friedrich Alfred Krupp became disillusioned with politics, and began to think about a complete withdrawal from business life.

In 1901 the debate was renewed when the Reichstag Budget Commission accused Krupp and the Saarland steel producer Stumm of having supplied armored plate to the United States at lower prices than to Germany. But this new wave of accusations became enmeshed in an even more extraordinary drama.

PERSONAL DISASTER

Friedrich Alfred Krupp in these years of naval expansion became an increasingly lonely and remote figure. Once again, the Villa Hügel seemed to become a steely and impersonal prison of solitude. In Essen Krupp appeared shy and remote, and seemed increasingly strained by the continual demands of being a highly public figure. On the other hand, in Capri, under the Mediterranean sun, he let himself be inspired by the models of classical antiquity and slid into a mixture of scientific investigation (in cooperation with a marine zoological institute in Naples) and playfulness.

Since the late 1890s, an appreciable distance had been growing between Friedrich Alfred Krupp and his wife Margarethe. Both increasingly used doctors and psychologists in their attempts to undermine each other. The leading neurologist Oskar Vogt treated both Friedrich Alfred and Margarethe. The most regular correspondence of the couple was with Dr. Ernst Schweninger, who had achieved fame as Bismarck's physician. Friedrich Alfred showed the doctors his wife's letters, and complained to them that he could only sleep if they arranged for his wife to be away from him. Margarethe too wrote regularly to Schweninger complaining that her husband did not discuss his travel plans with her.[41]

In fact, Friedrich Alfred's visits to the island of Capri soon proved to be a disaster. He rapidly established himself as a munificent patron, building a road hewn into the rock face from the town of Capri to the harbor, an engineering triumph that cost forty thousand lire. Krupp's beneficence on the island was attacked by German liberal and socialist newspapers, who contrasted Krupp's exploitative factories in the Ruhr with his Mediterranean role as a rich patron who threw his fortune around. The satirical periodical *Wahre Jakob* in 1902 presented a cartoon in which lean Krupp workers in Essen were juxtaposed with fat and greedy priests and nuns on Capri bathing in the gold coins that came out of the mouth of a cannon.[42] Krupp was one of the founders of a brotherhood dedicated to "artistic and pasta-istic meetings," the Congrega di Fra Felice, whose members called each other by their first names, and which met in a grotto that had once been inhabited by a hermit. The amusements seemed quite innocent, but those excluded from Krupp's generosity were quickly envious and hostile.

Italian politics decisively contributed to the eruption of the scandal. Krupp's main beneficiaries in Capri were clericalists, organized around the mayor (*sindaco*) and proprietor of the hotel in which Krupp stayed, the Quisisana. The mayor's rivals from the socialist party saw an opportunity to use Krupp to discredit the local bigwig. The Neapolitan newspaper *Propaganda* on September 18, 1902, published an article claiming that Krupp had engaged in homosexual orgies at which minors had been present, and that he had been expelled from Italy. On October 15, a further article, "Capri Sodoma," spoke of a "circle of degenerates created under the protection of a rich sexual degenerate," and of a "pig who threw around money by the thousand lire."[43] Krupp's staff in Essen initially ignored the Italian attacks, although a copy of the article was also sent to Margarethe Krupp, who by now was increasingly resentful of her husband and was close to a mental breakdown.

The Italian news gradually filtered into the German press. On November 15, the affair exploded when the main German socialist newspaper *Vorwärts* carried a report about "Krupp on Capri." It presented Krupp's corruption of the natives of Capri as a "terrible picture of the influence of capitalism," and it argued that since Krupp's sodomy constituted a violation of paragraph 175 of the Civil Code, he should be prosecuted in Germany. "Herr Krupp, who is visited by foreign princes and statesmen when they come to Germany, is one of those natures for whom Paragraph 175 constitutes a continual torment and threat. . . . The pity that a victim of a fateful mistake of nature deserves must be suspended if that sickness requires the employment of millions for its service. In this sense there is no adequate excuse for the man."[44]

The newspaper was confiscated, and Chancellor von Bülow urged Krupp to sue for libel. Friedrich Dernburg in the *Berliner Tageblatt* explained that "Krupp has become the victim of his gold."[45] Newspapers close to Krupp quoted the Italian foreign minister denying the rumor that Krupp had been expelled from Italy. Even the liberal *Frankfurter Zeitung*, which had been a harsh critic of Krupp in the armaments question, came to the conclusion that Krupp was innocent. More immediately and extraordinarily, the crisis provoked a dramatic breakdown in marital relations between Krupp and his wife. Both tried to psychologize the response of the other. Friedrich Alfred wrote to Schweninger that "physically I am fine, but psychologically it is hard, because my better half is always giving way to eruptions of passion and jealousy." One of his final letters complained that "my wife has not yet had the depressive stage that was predicted. She stands on the same view as at the beginning: that everything is misunderstanding and misinterpretation."[46] Krupp and his advisers consigned Margarethe Krupp to psychiatric care in the university town of Jena. But on November 22, 1902, Krupp died—probably as a result of a stroke. Because of the Capri scandal, there were inevitably rumors of suicide. Margarethe in her written memoirs later simply claimed that her husband's last words were, "I forgive my persecutors."[47]

Figure 3.6 Cortege of Friedrich Alfred Krupp with Kaiser Wilhelm II, 1902. Courtesy of Historical Archives Krupp.

In the aftermath of the catastrophe, the kaiser defended Friedrich Alfred Krupp in an extraordinary way. He, but not Margarethe Krupp and her daughters, followed the coffin through the streets of Essen. Before leaving Essen, he gave a speech at the railway station in which he blamed socialists for Krupp's death. The accusations constituted nothing more or less than a charge of murder, "as there is no difference between someone who mixes and holds out poison and someone who from the security of an editorial office destroys with poisoned arrows the reputation of a fellow human being and kills them by mental torture." In his peroration, the emperor called out: "Whoever does not separate themselves completely from these people, carries the moral guilt on their head."[48]

The Krupp management handled the aftermath of these speeches very badly. They prepared addresses to the emperor, to be signed exclusively by Krupp workers, distancing themselves from the socialists. In the Magdeburg Gruson works, two longtime employees were dismissed for refusing to sign, though the director responsible was later reprimanded. In one of Bebel's greatest speeches, while not mentioning the name of Krupp, he explained that "we fight the German bourgeoisie to the utmost" and attacked the kaiser's breaches of the principle of neutrality toward political parties. The kaiser was "irresponsible from a legal point of view, indeed even criminally irresponsible." The Social Democratic Party (SPD) could not respond to the imperial attacks. But Bebel estimated that every speech of the kaiser's meant a gain of another 100,000 votes for the SPD.

Indeed, in the 1903 elections, the SPD had a massive breakthrough in the Ruhr area, and in particular in Essen. Anxious Krupp company statisticians calculated that a quarter of the Kruppianer had voted for the SPD. By contrast, in the Saar, where there was no scandal, patriarchal politics continued, even though the accusations about armaments contracts also involved the Stumm works. In Stumm's electoral circle, only 170 out of a total of 34,363 votes were cast for the SPD.[49]

Friedrich Alfred Krupp's attempt to combine personal capitalism with the modern world had ended disastrously. Political engagement had proved to be a booby trap. He was clearly not merely a real-life incarnation of the fictional Diederich Hessling, but the position of his enterprise and its role in the politically sensitive armaments economy made him a symbol of the imperial state. Krupp was an easier target for the opposition to attack than the kaiser: in that sense, like Hessling, he was a substitute for the kaiser. In the end, he was highly vulnerable in the face of a sustained and vicious attack that used all the instruments of the new politics of scandal and sensation. But the enterprise that he had so rapidly expanded went on to spectacular success along the business course he had set.

F O U R
D I P L O M A C Y
Gustav Krupp von Bohlen und Halbach I

Heinrich Mann's *Der Untertan* was only the first part of a trilogy of novels on imperial Germany, the third part of which, *Der Kopf*, was published in 1925 and has a character, Geheimrat von Knack, who dominates the town of Knackstadt, based on Krupp and Essen. It was a marked contrast to the celebratory and anti-British novel based very literally on the Krupp story and published by the nationalist writer Rudolf Herzog in 1917, "*Die Stolten-kamps und ihre Frauen*" (The Stoltenkamps and Their Women). Herzog's version of Friedrich Krupp tells his son at the beginning of the novel, "We will rule the world, because we own steel"; and the son replies, "No, father, we will belong to steel. That is our life responsibility. We will die and it will stay and grow, until the whole world is steel." And at the end of the novel, with the World War, Germany is "now freed of slurry and turned into steel in the furnace of destiny."[1]

Heinrich Mann by contrast used a surreal story to set out the basic lines of the black legend around Krupp. "The whole intelligence of a great country, its will is concentrated in Knackstadt. A smoking, thundering will, a will served by capital. Armaments capital, it pushes out from Knackstadt ignoring frontiers and oceans to all countries of the earth. It meets other armaments capital and makes

Figure 4.1 Gustav Krupp von Bohlen und Halbach, 1906 (Kessler studio). Courtesy of Historical Archives Krupp.

friends, despite the enmity of countries." The kaiser tells Knack: "You are my friend, the shield of the German kaiser protects your house." The hero, an idealistic and high-minded pacifist named Claudius Terra, is engaged in an idealistic struggle against the death penalty, becomes temporarily corrupted in the employment of Knack, where he directs a bureau for espionage and sabotage, and explains that Knack owns part of the rival French armaments firm Putois-Lalouche (loosely translatable as Whoremongers Sleazy & Co.). "War means that both these firms profit, they are both reinsured. Both peoples can perish so that the firms will flourish." The chancellor explains to Terra, "We want the fleet to extend our power. You build it because it is good for business." The core of the accusation is not only that armaments producers such as Krupp (or Vickers or Skoda or Schneider-Creusot) profited from conflict but also that they fanned it. They sold arms to all sides in a conflict—and far from being patriotic, the Krupp figure also sells weapons to Germany's adversaries. The only way for the states to fight this sinister power would be to create a state-owned coal and steel monopoly.

The story of a pacifist who moves from the Foreign Office to become a senior manager of Germany's leading armament supplier seems so outrageously implausible that Heinrich Mann's novel is easily dismissed (the action is also so fast paced as to be extremely hard to follow). But in historical fact, a young man with pacifist leanings from the German Auswärtiges Amt (Foreign Office) was indeed sent on secondment in 1908 to Krupp as an assistant to one of the directors, and was so successful that he stayed on, was given power of attorney in 1911 and became a deputy director, and in 1913 at the age of thirty-four joined the board. Wilhelm Muehlon was not happy, and he tried to leave Krupp in the spring of 1914. After the outbreak of the World War he finally took his departure on health grounds, worked on some diplomatic missions to Romania, and increasingly came to be at odds with the German political leadership and his superiors in the Auswärtiges Amt. He moved to Switzerland and started to build an international pacifist network. He created a sensation in 1918 when he published in his memoirs some accounts of conversations in Berlin in July 1914, above all with the very well-connected Karl Helfferich of Deutsche Bank, which seemed to show that Germany in July 1914 had been actively pushing Austria into the war.[2]

One of the oddities of the memoirs, written sometime before the early 1930s but only published in 1989, is the positive picture they offer of Gustav Krupp von Bohlen und Halbach, the new representative of the family, someone whom Muehlon saw as his patron and who was increasingly at odds with the nationalist management of the company.

After the death of Friedrich Alfred Krupp, and in precise accordance with his will, the company was transformed into that legal form which Alfred Krupp and his son had detested and despised so much, a joint-stock company. But it was not quite a normal joint-stock company, in that the overwhelming majority of the shares were held by Bertha Krupp, the elder daughter of Friedrich Alfred and Margarethe. Of 160,000 shares, the young Bertha Krupp, who was designated "owner and director of the family firm," held 159,996; the remaining four were owned by Gustav Hartmann of the Dresdner Bank, a longtime confidant of Friedrich Alfred, who became chairman of the new supervisory board, Ernst Haux and Ludwig Klüpfel, members of the directory board, and Felix von Ende, a painter and a brother of Margarethe Krupp. Later, the ownership was slightly reshaped, so that small shares were in addition held by Friedrich Alfred's widow, Margarethe, and by Bertha's sister, Barbara von Wilmowsky. But the principle of single ownership had only been modified in conformity with the stock exchange law, which specified that a joint-stock company should have at least four owners. The fundamental reality was that the company belonged to a single heir.

But it was also clear that the heir, who was sixteen years old at the time of her father's death, would not take an active part in the management of the company, even when she reached the age of twenty-one. She was not going to be another Helene Amalie or Petronella or Therese Krupp, or one of those many dynamic women from an earlier era who frequently played central roles in the development of the continental European iron industry. The early twentieth century had a different conception of the suitability of women in business life than did the early nineteenth century (or the early twenty-first century). Margarethe Krupp had told the finance director of the Krupp enterprise, Ernst Haux, using the famous phrase of Toni Buddenbrook, that she found business accounts incomprehensible and that in such matters she "was a goose."[3]

About two years before he died, Friedrich Alfred Krupp had directed a missive to his wife in which he explained: "I think, in view of the extent of the tasks that the operation of the enterprise requires of the leading director, that it would be impossible that this task can be taken on and accomplished by a woman, even if she has all of your conscientiousness, circumspection and energy.

I think that the feeling of an impossible responsibility would rob you of the restful enjoyment of life, which I wish to you."[4] After Friedrich Alfred died, the sentiment was also reflected in a poem by Margarethe, who liked to poetize as well as paint:

> In the house the head is the man
> The wife the heart that is true
> The sunshine is the man
> The wife the deep sky blue.[5]

The only person who gave a dissenting perspective was the kaiser, who had written an oddly emotional condolence letter to the young Bertha Krupp: "Since God has denied you, my dear young lady, a brother, so the whole work with its thousands of souls is placed in your hands and on your youthful shoulders. A task for which a man would need all his power and knowledge and skill should be carried out by such a young girl! Isn't that unheard of? Unthinkable? No! Because if it were so, then God would never have decreed it. . . . It will come into your consciousness that God has given these men and their work and their future over to you, and that it is your <u>duty</u> to take on this great task, without timidity or anxiety, because it is <u>decreed</u> thus and thus <u>must</u> be."[6]

The historian Klaus Tenfelde concludes that "in a certain sense Krupp until 1924/25 was not a capitalist enterprise, in which prices and profits were calculated on the basis of a market estimation of costs and competitors' prices."[7] The verdict is correct in the sense that Krupp specialized in products in which competition was very limited. But it was at the beginning of the twentieth century a very successful enterprise, which expanded at breakneck speed and with record profits, which surged from less than

8 million marks in 1901/2 to almost 25 million marks in 1906/7. Over the same period, the number of employ-ees in the Gussstahlfabrik rose from 26,692 to 31,539, and in the whole of the Krupp enterprise from 47,129 to 64,354. It is hard on the basis of these figures to see why subsequent authors diagnose an entrepreneurial failure in the post–Friedrich Alfred era.[8] If anything, the opposite is the case.

There was also a dramatic technical transformation, and Krupp moved into some quite competitive areas. In January 1905 a Thomas works for the cheap mass pro-duction of steel started operating in Rheinhausen, with five 25-ton converters supplied with molten pig iron from a mixer that held 900 tons. Rail production was moved from Essen to Rheinhausen, so that mass production was removed from the Gussstahlfabrik and it could resume its traditional emphasis on finished products made by highly skilled workers. In 1911 the production of steel in an electric furnace began. From 1909 Krupp scientists led by Benno Strauss experimented on the development of noncorroding and acid resistant steel based on a chrome and nickel alloy. It received a German patent in 1912 and over the next hundred years became, under the trade-mark NIROSTA, a major Krupp product. It was used extensively in appliances made for the chemical industry, which provided the bulk of the initial demand, and then in equipment for foodstuff processing, in medical equip-ment, and even in architecture. The top of the New York Chrysler building of 1929, an icon of skyscraper elegance, was clad in 4,500 plates of Krupp nonrusting steel.

Equally significantly, some of the oldest and most vener-able production techniques were abandoned. In 1910 the long history of puddle steel came to an end. The enormous steel hammer "Fritz" was demolished in 1911 and replaced by a more modern and efficient forming mechanism. It is thus wrong to think of the new interest in history signaled by the creation of a historical archive in 1905, or by the collection of family documents, or by the establishment of a company newspaper in 1910, *Kruppsche Mitteilungen*, or by the elaborate rituals and medieval jousting displays of the celebrations planned to mark one hundred years of activity in 1912, as being fundamentally nostalgic, atavistic, or backward looking. On the eve of the First World War, Krupp had become a highly successful and innovative enterprise, with a management that had liberated itself from close dependence on the owners of the company.

The fast pace of Krupp's expansion, and its coincidence with the naval rearmament program, indeed convinced many foreign observers that the pace of Krupp expansion should be interpreted primarily as an act of German government policy. The British conservative statesman A. J. Balfour for instance in 1909 castigated the Liberal government for being blind to the dangers posed by Krupp's dynamism. "They became conscious as far back as 1906 that there was a development going on in Krupps. They must have known before that the connection between Krupps and the Government was very close, and that the development which began in 1906 in Krupps, and which has been going on rapidly ever since, they must have been aware that that development was one closely connected with Governmental policy, and could not be disassociated from the accumulated strength of the German Navy. And that was the moment they began to diminish the number of capital ships which they were asking this country to build."[9] In reality the volume of business and the number of Krupp workers had fallen between 1906 and 1909, but the myth of the ever-onward growth of German naval militarism lived on. There was also a surge of military exports in the decade before the First World War, with a spike in 1907/8 reflecting the increase in international tensions around the Bosnian crisis as well as the aftermath of the Russo-Japanese conflict.[10]

The reality is that there were very high expectations of the company, and that in consequence any problem was interpreted as a flaw in the basic business model. There was also considerable upheaval in the management. When Friedrich Alfred Krupp was the owner, he had tried to inject fresh talent from the outside. Of the Krupp directorate in 1902, five came from the outside and only five from within the company. In addition, in accordance with Friedrich Alfred's emphasis on science, seven were scientists or engineers. The new general manager, the successor to the capable Hanns Jencke whom the kaiser had admired so much, was appointed in his early forties, in October 1902, as the Capri scandal was unfolding, and as the kaiser blocked the proposal to appoint the progressive mayor of Danzig, Clemens Delbrück, as the director of Krupp.[11] The new man was another outsider, like Jencke, with a civil service background, who had been a medium-level Prussian administrative official in Essen. Max Rötger was far from being incapable, but he was ineffective, and he complained of being frozen out of decisions by the traditionalist Krupp directors. He had no special area of competence of his own, and he was brought in mostly to manage the meetings of the directorate and to manage conflicts as a colleague but not as a superior.[12] His fate was sealed by the concatenation of two events.

First, Germany (and hence Krupp's order book) was hit by the financial crisis of 1906/7, and profits dipped appreciably. Second, on October 15, 1906, Bertha Krupp, who had still not reached the age of majority, married a German diplomat to whom she had been introduced in Rome, Gustav von Bohlen und Halbach. Under the terms of a royal patent of October 15, 1906, he was permitted to call himself Gustav Krupp von Bohlen und Halbach. The bridegroom was intended to take part in the running of the company, and he had experience in some important markets (as well as an American mother): he had worked in the German embassy in Washington as well as in the mission in Beijing before he took the posting in the Prussian legation to the Vatican. Initially, he had contemplated taking a position as a Krupp director; in the event, he started as deputy chair of the supervisory board, and then in 1909, after the ousting of Max Rötger, took over the chairmanship of the supervisory board.

Like his late father-in-law, Gustav Krupp was also treated with some initial reserve by the Krupp directors. He showed up at the factory every day at nine and asked for explanations, but he felt isolated. One of the Krupp directors explained to Muehlon that he should not let himself be used by the owner, and that he would do better sticking with the directorate. But Muehlon did not hesitate in indicating his admiration for Gustav Krupp, especially when the industrialist told the kaiser that he was very much in favor of a yearlong halt to the naval arms race with Britain; Muehlon felt obliged to comment that "I don't know anyone else in Germany who could be relied on to have a similar attitude."[13]

Margarethe Krupp, the widow, had indicated that she wanted to reduce the company's imperial and court connections, although the firm clearly continued to need good relations with its most important customer, the German state. The continuing political links were clear in the choice in October 1909 of another outsider, Alfred Hugenberg, as chairman of the executive board, and in practice the firm's general manager. Hugenberg had started a political career as an agitator with the Pan-German League, after writing a dissertation with the étatist economist Georg Friedrich Knapp, which concluded with an appeal for imperial expansion. He regarded social democracy as a major threat and in 1912 drafted a memorandum, which Gustav Krupp von Bohlen und Halbach sent to the government, on the necessary protection that the state should offer to strikebreakers. At the centenary celebration in 1912, Hugenberg made a highly political speech in which he condemned the move for extending the principle of universal suffrage as constituting the imposition of class rule. In 1912 Hugenberg also took a step that would shape his subsequent career. As chairman of the Ruhr Coal Mining Association, he created a press organization with the goal of coordinating industrial influence on the media.

The conflict with socialists fanned the ongoing political controversy. In the course of Germany's rapid rearmament, the political clashes about the pricing of armaments, which had formed the real background to the Friedrich Alfred Krupp scandal, continued. The fiery young socialist Karl Liebknecht in April 1913 denounced "agents" of Krupp for having bribed imperial officials in order to gain access to the price calculations on armaments orders. In the subsequent investigation, one Krupp craftsman who had been seconded to Berlin was sentenced to three months in prison, and the Krupp director in charge of war materiel sales ("KM"), Otto Eccius, was fined the relatively trivial sum of three hundred marks.

Eccius was depicted by Muehlon as a corrupt and extravagant specialist in bribery and corruption. A larger-than-life character who loved to use his expense account and luxuriate in fine hotels, he had been painted as a shadowy background figure (standing in the back right-hand corner) in the monumental centenary portrait of the Krupp *Direktorium* and supervisory board painted by the German-British academician and portraitist Sir Hubert von Herkomer in 1912. As the controversy dragged on, the Reichstag created a Commission on Armaments Supplies, which seemed to the military authorities a step toward democratization, and to the major suppliers as a move toward socialism and the creation of a state monopoly supplier. In particular the Center party deputy Matthias Erzberger, the commission's rapporteur for naval artillery and someone who had been liberally supplied with material against Krupp by the rival steel producer August Thyssen, took up the baton from Liebknecht in the fight against the Ruhr barons and formulated a demand for a "mixed public-private enterprise." Hugenberg provided a passionate counterargument, emphasizing the importance of foreign markets that would be lost by a state munitions producer, and stating that Krupp's independence was a precondition for its effectiveness and thus also a "requirement of national honor in the light of its responsibility to the nation and its position in German industry."[14]

The issue was not resolved in peacetime, but the outbreak of war in August 1914 clearly transformed the terms not just of the armaments debate but of the conduct of business in general. In December 1914, Hugenberg wrote of his fear that the war would "mean the definitive end of the era of economic individualism."[15]

Figure 4.2 Hubert von Herkomer painting of Krupp directorate, 1912: Gustav Krupp von Bohlen und Halbach standing at center, Alfred Hugenberg to the left behind him (directly in front of painting of Alfred Krupp), and Otto Eccius third from right. Courtesy of Historical Archives Krupp.

WAR

The fundamental logistical problem for Germany after August 1914—as well as for the other belligerents—lay in the absence of substantial planning for a long war. Strategies for steel and munitions production had been shaped by the assumption that any possible war would necessarily be short. The basic prewar mobilization program envisaged that Krupp would produce 200 cannons and mobile artillery pieces in the case of hostilities, as well as 144 torpedo weapons. But in 1914/15 alone Krupp needed to increase production to over 1,000 artillery pieces. In the course of the war, in fact, Krupp produced a total of 10,843 complete artillery pieces, and 9,439 barrels.

In addition, the first months of the war showed that Germany had developed the wrong products, and that the German army was outgunned. In 1908 the War Ministry had stopped development of a 15 cm artillery piece with barrel recoil. Although the surprise Japanese use of heavy coastal defense guns in the siege of Port Arthur had showed the offensive power of heavy artillery, there were only two Krupp 42 cm cannons ("Big Berta") ready for action in 1914. They were used to spectacular effect in the siege of Liège, as well as against the fortifications of Namur, Antwerp, and Maubeuge. In all, twelve were built during the whole of the conflict. Krupp's pride, a very heavy artillery piece named the Paris Gun or Paris Geschütz (sometimes it was also known as the Wilhelm-Geschütz), was much too big and unmaneuverable to be of much military effectiveness. It fired a ninety-four-kilogram shell from a barrel thirty-four meters long, at such an altitude that the shell was the first man-made object to enter the stratosphere. It was used only from March 1918, in the last months of the war, to bombard Paris from a distance of 120 kilometers, and was fired a total of 452 times and caused some 250 deaths. The Big Berta and the Paris Geschütz were psychologically impressive, but they were not weapons that fundamentally changed the course of the war.

Germany improvised in a highly effective way, but in a way that transformed the informal defense procurement system and its reliance on Krupp's near monopoly in heavy artillery into a centralized planning system. The War Raw Materials Office of Walther Rathenau and Wichard von Moellendorf was so successful that it persuaded Vladimir Lenin that socialism, in the sense of planned and centrally directed mass production on the basis of limited resources, was a quite practical proposition.

The expansion in the production of artillery pieces was less dramatic than the increase in the output of shells and grenades: from 4.5 million in 1914/15 to almost 24

Figure 4.3 "Big Berta": the 42 cm Krupp cannon. Courtesy of Historical Archives Krupp.

million in 1917/18.[16] The armaments producers were required to expand production at a rate that would have been inconceivable even in the summer of 1914. And in the same way as the military planners had not really thought about what fighting a sustained war would mean before 1914, after 1914 they were not inclined to give much thought to how industry would deal with peace.

Such calculations were left to a few increasingly uneasy industrial managers. Richard Foerster, the director responsible for Krupp's mining activities, was looking ahead toward the postwar economy as early as the autumn of 1915. He argued that it would be unlikely that there would be "a lasting and general boom after the conclusion of peace," and that the tax burden would rise, since it was unlikely that Germany could keep the occupied areas, regain the lost colonies, and get reparation payments.[17] The immediate problem he faced, however, was major shortages in the supplies of fuel and coking coal. At first, coal output in Germany was severely affected by the mobilization of miners. But more generally, the coal shortage could not really be resolved by resources in Germany; it seemed to require the acquisition of additional resources, in Belgium or northern France. At the end of 1917, Krupp took over one-third of the French shareholding of the Friedrich Heinrich mine in Lintfort.

The war also posed a logistical challenge to Krupp. The model for much of Krupp's military production—as opposed to the standardized manufacture of railway parts and equipment—had involved essentially scaling up a shop of skilled craftsmen. The Gussstahlfabrik was in practice a concatenation of many separate production sites. Sometimes Krupp just needed to produce high-quality steel—which required the use of a multiplicity of alloys. Large quantities of steel plate were used for the conning towers of submarines (441 were ordered and 301 actually supplied during the course of the conflict). But the actual engineering of military products on a large scale required a conceptual revolution, which Krupp never fully implemented, in large part because of worries that there would be no permanent peacetime demand for the products of a new, expanded, and Americanized business operation. Only in the course of the war did Krupp shift over to the production of interchangeable parts in artillery.

One alternative was to begin again from scratch, by starting up on new (green field) sites or buying up other plants. That was a favorite suggestion of the banks, who pushed for industrial concentration and rationalization. At the initiative of Emil Georg von Stauss of Deutsche Bank, Krupp in 1916 established Bayerische Geschütz-werke in Munich.

The Germaniawerft concentrated increasingly on submarine production. It had developed its first submarine in 1902, and built two submarines for the Russian navy before the German navy started to demonstrate any interest. The yard completed thirty-six boats by the time of the German declaration of unconditional submarine warfare in April 1917, including the *U-Deutschland*, launched in 1916, which embarked on spectacular transatlantic voyages to buy otherwise unobtainable raw rubber from the United States. After April 1917, the Germaniawerft was overwhelmed by submarine orders.

The turning point in terms of planning for sustained business expansion was the political response to the stalemates after the great offensives of 1916: the German siege of Verdun, the British offensive on the Somme, and the Russian Brusilov offensive. On September 9, 1916, Gustav Krupp traveled to Hanover, meeting Hindenburg and Ludendorff, and started discussions on a gigantic expansion of Germany's military potential. Hindenburg proposed a tripling of industrial output, of shells from 2.5 million to 9 million a month, and artillery barrels from 800 to 3,000. The resulting government arms plan was known as the "Hindenburg Program."

The agreements concluded on January 29, 1917, were highly favorable for Krupp. There was a direct subsidy of 55 million marks, as well as regular payments of up to 19 million marks for the armaments expansion. The company had become in practice part of the German state. By the end of the war, Krupp was producing steel at annual rate of 1.6 million tons, twice its prewar capacity. The Krupp directors pointed out in discussions with other steel companies that the plants had not been paid for, and that the company would need to make claims for government support.[18]

In this novel wartime situation, the firm did not behave like a conventional profit-maximizing enterprise. For 1914/15, the figures would have justified a 24 percent dividend, but instead the company paid the prewar dividend and put 20 million marks into a foundation for the support of dependents of those killed in the Great War; an additional amount was paid for the furthering of German colonization in the East. In 1915/16 too there was no extraordinary dividend, and the extra profits were used to finance the extension of buildings. The overall profits fell to 66.7 million marks that year, from the 1914/15 level of 81.9 million. In 1917/18, the most profitable war year with a sum of 125.1 million marks, a 10 percent dividend was paid; for 1918 a 4 percent dividend was calculated but not paid, because of the changed political circumstances and very substantial uncertainty in December 1918. The profits were largely plowed back into the business.[19]

At first, it seemed easier to handle the logistical and organizational sides of the challenge of expanded production than to think out the engineering or the financial consequences of a transition to mass production. Krupp started to expand the original Gussstahlfabrik site very dramatically. The company even provided new accommodations and canteens for around 40,000 workers. After the initial uncertainties of war and the setback of the first battle of the Marne, while at the same time the company's ranks of skilled workers were decimated by conscription, expanded production required a very dramatic rise in the workforce. Over 6,000 employees were called up in August 1914 alone. At the beginning of the war, there had been 83,030; by the middle of 1918, at the peak of the wartime expansion, that figure had more than doubled, to 168,892. As Germany collapsed militarily and politically in November 1918, there were still 166,213.

The requirements of expanded production as well as the gaps left by military conscription were filled mostly with women workers. By May 1918, the Gussstahlfabrik employed some 25,000. Women took over a great deal of the clerical work but also worked on lathes and in the assembly of shells. From 1916, Krupp also started to recruit workers in the neutral states, whose economies had been hit badly by the outbreak of war: first Switzerland, then the Netherlands. In 1917 and especially in 1918, the firm also more or less forcibly recruited workers in enemy countries, in Belgium and in the formerly Russian Polish territories. By the end of the war, there were around 7,600 foreign workers, or 4.5 percent of the total workforce, mostly from Belgium.[20] They were employed separately, away from the main production sites, and often in construction; a special police unit was formed to supervise their activity. By international law, prisoners of war could not be used in munitions and war-related production, but around 200 were set to work in the Krupp-owned Sälzer & Neuack mine.

There were substantial wage increases during the war, especially for unskilled workers. But there were also major price increases, and shortages of food. In consequence, the organization of factory canteens and their supply became increasingly vital. The company started to organize food supply where the market and the state failed. As part of the Hindenburg Program, four enormous refectories were created. In November 1917 the company constructed food storage facilities to ensure adequate supplies during the critical winter months.

In the summer of 1916 there were some strikes, above all in Kiel at the Germaniawerft and also in the Krupp-owned Emscher-Lippe mine, though not in the Gussstahlfabrik, the traditional core of the Krupp ethos. The company started to react to workers' complaints.

In early 1917 all the Krupp works, including the Gussstahlfabrik, were hit by a new wave of labor radicalism. In Essen, workers demanded pay increases of 30 percent to compensate for high food prices on the black market. Gustav Krupp wrote to Chancellor Bethmann Hollweg to complain about the failures of official food supplies, and noted that even old Krupp workers from the prewar period were taking part in the new political mobilization. The management had to start negotiating directly with workers' representatives. From March 1917, in line with the provisions of the Patriotic Auxiliary Service Law, there was an official elected representation of workers in the factory; and Krupp also created "committees of consumers" to address the substantial grievances about food supply and quality. The gigantic canteens that were built to benefit the workers actually proved to be powerful focal points of increasingly radicalized protest. In May 1917 Gustav Krupp visited the imperial headquarters and reported to the kaiser that "we are going to have serious difficulties on the home front . . . our workers know quite well that they already now have full power in their hands. For a time they will still go along, but when the inevitable food crisis comes, everything will be over."[21] A month earlier he had written to Ernst Haux that "the sliding of our monarchical and state authority

Figure 4.4 Kaiser Wilhelm II with a worker in the Krupp factory, September 1918. Courtesy of Historical Archives Krupp.

down the slippery road to democracy is something that I have worried about for a long time, since 1910. . . . In consequence, I have long wished for a sensible and not too distant end of the war." He also expressed his unease about the opening of unrestricted submarine warfare, which had brought the United States into the war.[22]

In the early months of 1918, the major focus of workers' protest in Essen concerned long hours of work: Krupp workers were still working sixty hours a week, while in some big cities, notably Berlin, the hours had been reduced. Some of the workers campaigning for reform made the point that the General Staff supported their demand for reduced hours.[23] In Kiel, by contrast, the demands were preeminently political, and concerned the negotiation of a peace settlement.

The visit of the kaiser on September 9 and 10, 1918, marked the beginning of the end of many Krupp traditions.

The kaiser seems to have let himself be convinced that his aura would be enough to pacify the protesters and restore social peace to the most conspicuously national of German enterprises. He tried to engage in conversations with individuals and small groups of workers. One of the women workers said, "Our kaiser is really a dear fellow." But the tone at times was also disrespectful and even dangerous. On the second day of his visit, the kaiser spoke to a large group of around a thousand workers. He began on the basis of a text that had been prepared by the chief of the civil cabinet, Friedrich von Berg, but he then became carried away and extemporized in an extraordinary peroration that appalled Berg and other observers, calling on God's protection and remembering the Lutheran hymn "Ein feste Burg ist unser Gott" (A Mighty Fortress Is Our God): "Every one of us receives their task allocated from on high. You at your hammer, you at your lathe, and Me on My throne. But all of us must build with the help of God. . . . We must now unite, here the words are most appropriate, and become as hard as steel! The German people's block, forged by steel, will show its power to the enemy. Whoever is resolved to hear this appeal, whoever has his heart in the right place, whoever will keep faith, should now stand and promise me in the name of the whole German working class: we wish to fight to the last! May God help us! And whoever wants that, should shout yes!" The Krupp works newspaper, as well as the official government-authorized press account, records a loud "yes" shouted by those present.[24] But it was clear to everyone that the war was lost and that this appeal to loyalty, to company and to country, already belonged to a world that was going under.

FIVE

TRADITION

Gustav Krupp von Bohlen und Halbach II

The most famous industrial novel of the Weimar Republic was Erik Reger's *Union der festen Hand* (Union of the
Firm Hand), published in 1931, which immediately won
widespread acclaim and received the Kleist Prize. Its
author, whose real name was Hermann Dannenberger,
had worked in the Krupp business from 1920 to 1927 as
an employee in the statistical office; he aimed at report-
age rather than romanticization. The Krupp works, lightly
fictionalized presented as the firm of "Risch-Zander," is
the central location of the novel. Risch-Zander is highly
suspicious of banks and their influence, and maintains a
sentimental paternalism. An enormous influence is still
wielded by Risch-Zander's mother-in-law, the widow of
the "old Risch." Alfred Hugenberg is depicted as Alfons
Hachenpoot, a "pubertarian poet" who, after leaving the
company, goes on to run a newspaper and media empire.
Other major Ruhr industrialists, August and Fritz Thyssen, and Hugo Stinnes, also appear under pseudonyms,
as do the politicians Heinrich Brüning and Hjalmar
Schacht as well as the propagandist of the "Decline of
the West," Oswald Spengler. Risch-Zander's son more
and more comes to resemble the grandfather, the "old
Risch." The father himself, who like Gustav von Bohlen
married into the business, finds it hard to understand the

Figure 5.1 The Krupp family, 1923. Courtesy of Historical Archives Krupp.

new and rapidly changing politics, but knows that some-how the business has to adapt by paying more atten-tion to the psychology of the employees. Reger portrays him as a figure of inherent moderation and decency, who finds the methods of the modern business world bewildering. Risch-Zander believes that "indebtedness is a debacle which threatens even the old industrial fami-lies." Company magazines, the newspaper world, the cinema—all are used to manipulate minds and to make propaganda for business "rationalization." The Union of the Firm Hand is fundamentally a political organiza-tion, and its wealthy backers go on to launch an "Ida" or Institute der deutschen Arbeiterbeseelung (Institute to Restore the Soul of the Worker) as a means to create an awareness among the working classes of belonging to the larger entity of the German *Volk*. In the end, as Reger erroneously portrays it, these institutions created at the initiative of organized heavy industry will work with the Nazi movement.

The Union and the Ida may be loosely based on the establishment of a Renewal League (Erneuerungsbund) and the story of the DINTA (German Institute for Technical Labor Training or Deutsches Institut für technische Arbeitsschulung). But Gustav Krupp von Bohlen und Halbach in reality played a rather small role in these institutions. On the other hand, he was acutely aware that the conditions of business had changed, and one of the industrial slogans of the Reger novel might well have come from Krupp documents: "Now it is high time that the economy should think about economizing." So too does the exhortation "From the cannon to the locomotive!"[1]

REVOLUTION

One of Reger's great set-piece descriptions involves the chaotic and humiliating scene of the kaiser's last visit to the Essen works of Krupp. The bombastic, deluded emporer confronts a workforce seething with radical notions (personified by the novel's main character, a communist worker) and foreshadows the abrupt and utter collapse of imperial Germany: the naval mutiny, the Bolshevik-inspired soldiers' and workers' councils—in short the revolution that erupted within weeks of the kaiser's visit to Germany's industrial heartland. From the Essen industrialists' perspective, revolution appeared to come from the outside, brought above all by mutinous soldiers. Now all the traditions of the house of Krupp seemed to be at risk.

The company struggled to find a new role in a state that was reinventing itself dramatically. Alfred Hugenberg was pushed out of the directorate, probably because of his political radicalism. The new Krupp strategy involved as far as possible a return to basics, trying to re-create the company of the prewar days. The management, now led by a skillful negotiator, Otto Wiedfeldt, engaged a great deal of its attention toward removing as many of its nonlocal workers as possible. Calculations in October 1918 were based on the premise that Krupp could employ a maximum of 30,000 in the Gussstahlfabrik, which corresponded to an estimate of 21,000 existing workers who had been already employed at the beginning of 1914 plus 6,000 to 8,000 former employees who had been conscripted and could now be expected to return to the factory. Special trains were engaged to take the surplus workers, now deemed potentially dangerous, away from Essen. Already by November 19, 1918, 2,570 Belgians, 1,000 Poles, 4,800 Dutch citizens, and 50 Swiss had left Essen. But the foreign workers were not the heart of the problem. By the end of November, a total of 52,000 workers had left the Krupp factory alone. The dismissed employees were promised that pay arrears and retirement claims would be transferred quickly to their home addresses.

Wiedfeldt had been treasurer of the city of Essen and had worked in arbitrating prewar labor conflicts before going to Japan to work in the Railway Ministry and then returning to the German imperial administration, where he was responsible during the First World War for the introduction of the bread ration card. He had established a reputation as a social reformer; and even before the First World War he emphasized the importance for business of high wage levels, claiming that the great depression of the 1870s would not have been as severe if wages had been raised rather than forced down.[2]

At the same time, the regime of the new patriarch, in dealing with the core Kruppianer ethos, also reflected a back-to-the-roots philosophy. Gustav Krupp had been largely disengaged from the company in the heady days of expansion before the First World War. But a characteristic of cultures that revolve around the family business as a central ideal is that the family comes back in hard times, as a survival mechanism or as a source of resilience. Gustav Krupp drew up an announcement to the effect that "my wife and I have never considered our so-called private wealth as anything other than as a reserve for the Krupp works, which can be used to protect the existence of the works as well as for justified demands by the officials and workers."[3] This promise fits perfectly in the patriarchal tradition of Krupp, and indeed corresponds to the famous example of Alfred Krupp's willingness to sell the family silver during the revolutionary year of 1848. But it may have contributed to the long-term problems of the company, in that it encouraged managers (as well as workers) to think of the company rather in the same way they contemplated the Prussian-German state, as a cash cow that could be milked forever.

For those remaining in Essen, there were still many challenges. The food supply remained precarious and a potential source of radicalization. As in the war, the company needed to step in where the market failed and provide accommodations and meals. Krupp was still feeding eight thousand people in its large canteens in the middle of 1919. But the main issue was the management of political discontent. From mid-1919 a labor agreement was negotiated with the metal unions. In 1920 a Works Council with twenty-three workers' representatives was established, in line with the new labor legislation of the Weimar Republic. The Gussstahlfabrik was relatively peaceful, even during the March 1920 Kapp putsch and the subsequent general strike, when workers' organizations defending the Republic briefly took over the Ruhr Valley and civil war seemed imminent. Gustav Krupp had moved his family away from Essen, to the family's hunting lodge at Sayneck. Many of the leading managers hid or took additional security precautions.

Buying off labor did not solve the issue of what sort of production should follow the company's dramatic expansion and orientation toward military production for a state and a worldview that had ceased to exist. The initial response was rather helpless and improvised. In December 1918, the management called for ideas for new peacetime products. Some 1,300 suggestions were sent in. There were important initiatives in making agricultural equipment and also calculating machines and cash registers, as well as experiments such as the use of quality steels in dental work. Some of the innovations in new product lines, perhaps predictably, were dismal failures. In the mid-1920s, when monetary stabilization allowed for the first time an accurate assessment of profitability, the general level of profit on engineering equipment was 1.5 percent, but textile and paper machines were incurring losses of 34.4 percent, the cash registers were losing 14.7 percent, and cinematic equipment 14.4 percent.[4] A later critical assessment, from 1938, suggested that at this point the most rational strategy would have been to give up specialty production and concentrate instead on mass steel products in Essen and

Rheinhausen, as well as on the company's extensive coal mines.[5] But that would have been an unthinkable break with the Krupp tradition.

The immediate response was to go back to the beginnings of the firm in the early and mid-nineteenth century, when it was engaged in the manufacture of finished products and especially of railway articles. The publicly owned railway system became the major provider of employment in postwar Germany but also a powerful instrument of successive Weimar governments fighting to stabilize the economy. In April 1919 the factory won a major order from the Prussian State Railways. The Gun Carriage Workshops VI and VII were converted to the production of locomotives and railcars. The railway products were major successes on export markets. In the Weimar years, Krupp picked up the global orientation of the late nineteenth century once again. But there was also the constant sense that everything had been better in the days of empire.

It was this pervasive nostalgia for the prewar days that made the old strategy of using military products to build a link with the state seem relevant and attractive once more. But there was an obvious obstacle. The Versailles Treaty required the substantial demilitarization of Germany and restricted the production of military material. From 1920, a special unit of the Inter-Allied Military Control Commission, with six British and two French officers, was based in the Essen works. It required the destruction of an estimated ten thousand machines that had produced military goods. The evasion of such controls is one of the most famous stories of Weimar politics (and was a crucial point in the indictment of Gustav Krupp at Nuremberg in 1945). The army leadership was desperate not to lose

151

Germany's military capacity. In January 1922, the Reich-swehr signed a secret agreement with Krupp to develop weapons, and from the mid-1920s a group of seconded Krupp engineers worked in a Berlin engineering office on the development of new armaments. The army also discussed moving production away from Essen, which was in too exposed a position in the west of Germany and thus too vulnerable to French military incursions as well as to weapons inspections.

Krupp's most important initial contribution to hidden rearmament lay in a series of contracts with the Swedish armaments producer AB Bofors. By September 1919 Krupp had already transferred a Dutch order for 7.5 cm artillery to Bofors, and in September 1921 reached a general agreement under which Krupp transferred patents, designs, and production experience to the Swedes. Krupp engineers were sent to Stockholm. The technology transfers were accompanied from 1920 by stock ownership, via Swedish middlemen, so that by 1927 Krupp owned just under a third of the stock of Bofors.

Krupp U-boat plans were sold to Japan, and Krupp engineers sent to supervise production. From 1922 three German shipyards, including the Germaniawerft, took a share in a Dutch company, Ingenieurskantoor voor Scheepvaart N.V.

Later in the 1920s, Krupp developed firing and guidance mechanisms for ship-based rockets. From 1930, there were also experiments with the construction of 8.8 cm antiaircraft artillery (*Flak*). After 1926 the company developed an experimental tank, called "large tractor" in order to disguise its real purpose, which was equipped with a BMW engine and a gun turret made by Rheinmetall. This equipment was tested between 1929 and

1933 by the Soviet army. From 1930, a four-ton tractor with caterpillar traction was tested in the same way
(this construction entered serial production as a tank in
1934). In 1920 Krupp reached an agreement to produce
locomotives for the Soviet Union and later developed an
agricultural concession in Manych, which it hoped would
provide a basis for the modernization of Russian farming.
As in the German tradition, there was here a close inter-
relationship between production for the military and the
hope of access to a larger and perhaps in the longer term
more stable civilian source of demand.

By 1922 the question of relations with the new Soviet
state had become a crucial issue on the international
agenda. Wiedfeldt, one of the few German industrialists experienced and polished enough to be able to function on the international stage, explained to the British
prime minister David Lloyd George, in a long interview
in London in March 1922, his firm's policy of binding
Russia into the international system and civilizing the
Bolsheviks. Lloyd George seems to have been impressed;
he suggested that British and German firms should work
together in developing the Russian market. The British
Liberal leader also expressed the idea that business leaders were more likely than politicians to promote peace,
and he thought that Krupp should develop an increased
political influence over the government in Berlin. To that,
Wiedfeldt replied that Krupp had fully supported any
government that was not treasonous, and that he felt that
for the foreseeable future no stable government in Germany would be possible without the support of the social
democrats. But Wiedfeldt's fundamental tone was deeply
pessimistic: "if there is no radical action soon, we in Germany will drift toward collapse."[6]

INFLATION

It was not only the general economic circumstances that led to heightened uncertainty; the firm was also vulnerable because of the financial and monetary chaos of the early years of the Weimar Republic, which made orderly accounting an impossibility. The increased expenses involved in keeping employment levels up and in obtaining imported raw materials, as well as the increasing fiscal demands of the state, could initially be met by using the extensive reserves built up in the war years. The C-shares issued at the outbreak of the war in order to finance the expansion of the works were used to pay a special emergency tax (*Reichsnotopfer*).

Krupp was less inclined than other German companies, such as the Stinnes concern, Siemens, or Thyssen, to expand by buying up additional plants and engage in a flight into real assets. Otto Wiedfeldt produced a series of more and more critical memoranda urging a restructuring along the lines of the competition. In the first of these reform plans, in 1919, he cited Stinnes, Röchling, Phoenix, Bochumer Verein, AEG, and Siemens as examples of superior management. They had evolved into complex systems of interlocking holding companies.[7] In the summer of 1919, AEG had suggested closer cooperation with Krupp, perhaps also with the participation of Siemens, and in the next year the stock exchange was swept by takeover rumors. Walther Rathenau of AEG visited the Krupp works in Essen and spoke of the "impression of the greatest monument of German economic life," a rather ambiguous compliment.[8] There were also talks of closer cooperation between Krupp and Daimler. Wiedfeldt told a Stinnes manager that cartels were "an unsuitable means, which in the long run do more harm than good, and which do not foster honest business."[9] The comment seemed to echo the highly influential memorandum, also of 1919, of the general director of the Deutsch-Luxemburg steel company, Albert Vögler, which is often seen as the genesis of the movement to create a German equivalent of the U.S. Steel Company: "the time of the syndicates had passed."[10]

But the Krupp family was worried about the loss of family control that would be implied in such an expansion. The only exception to the family's reluctance to pursue acquisitions involved the acquisition of foreign stakes, above all in neutral countries such as Sweden and the Netherlands. Bertha Krupp's private holding bought a Dutch company founded in 1920 as a branch of Krupp, the Devon Ertsmaatschappij.

In the course of the increasingly rapid currency inflation, Krupp resorted to borrowing. In summer 1922 a syndicated bank credit was put together by Dresdner Bank of one billion marks (at that time worth 1,140,000 gold marks); when it was repaid in October 1923, the value of the credit amounted to merely 53,000 gold marks. At the time, however, Otto Wiedfeldt had worried that Krupp might not be able to afford the repayment of this credit. He started thinking about additional sources of capital. One innovation—and an indication that the World War had not destroyed globalization completely—was that the company approached foreign banks. In early 1923, Krupp started to borrow from Dutch and British banks. Only after the stabilization of the German currency did it approach the new and innovative giants of international finance, the New York investment banks.

One alternative that might have solved the problem of capital shortage during the inflation was a partial sale to a foreign company. The first attempt at an international takeover came in the late summer of 1920, when Schneider-Creusot wanted to build up a stake in Krupp in a dramatic and bold move that would have opened up the Ruhr to permanent French interest. In the summer of 1921, Wiedfeldt suggested the sale of a minority stake to U.S. Steel, but Gustav Krupp turned down the suggestion on patriotic grounds.[11]

Many analysts, including Klaus Tenfelde, conclude that there was an entrepreneurial failure at Krupp and that the Wiedfeldt strategy, which was modeled closely on that of Stinnes, would have been a better course to follow. According to this critique, Krupp retained much too long an excessively centralized form of management; it should have adopted the best practice that was clearly emerging (and already clearly successful at Thyssen) before the First World War. Wiedfeldt would have liked more decentralization, but his views were less and less influential.

The Krupp company instead thought of ways to extend its traditional patriarchy. In the era of inflation, Germans became obsessed with property and with the acquisition of real or inflation-proof assets, which were generally termed *Sachwerte*. It looked natural that Krupp should offer *Sachwerte* as well as monetary compensation to its workforce. In December 1921, the company agreed to introduce an experiment in which special shares ("D"-class shares) were created to be given to employees as a supplement to wages paid in the rapidly depreciating German currency. A total of 1,663 white-collar employees and 690 factory workers participated in this scheme.

Inflation made rational accounting impossible. In general, inflation makes for an overstatement of the return on equity, with increasing levels of inflation generating increasingly optimistic assessments of a company's performance. In that sense, inflation and the distortion it imparts to monetary values appears to give a reddish glow to the company's cheeks, but this reflects fever and pathology rather than ruddy health. The historian Gerald Feldman gives a fine example from the summer of 1923, when the Krupp Banking Section drew up a memorandum on its debt level: "our paper mark debts have remained the same [as last Saturday], namely about 80 billion. But the result in gold marks under a depreciation factor of 17,800 is only 4,445,000 over against the 6,046,000 of the previous week, thus giving an improvement of our status by 1,601,000 gold marks. . . . You can see herein a substantial improvement of our status which has simply developed through the depreciation of the paper mark."[12]

One of the principal political motivations behind the continuation of the government's inflationary policies was the preservation of high employment levels, and thus of social peace—a highly necessary action, given the strength of the threat of left-wing revolution. Steel production increased, as did the overall employment levels in the Krupp works. But there was something wrong in a situation where the company's printing works began to be referred to as the "most important" part of the business, because of the money-printing work that was contracted from the central bank, the Reichsbank, as well as because the presses also were critical in issuing the company's own substitute money or *Notgeld*.[13]

Only right at the end of the inflationary process did demand collapse. Workers were now laid off, and between October 1923 and October 1924 the workforce of the

Figure 5.2 Krupp inflation money: 500 million "Krupp marks" (company scrip printed at the factory), 1923. Courtesy of Historical Archives Krupp.

Gussstahlfabrik fell from 52,000 to 35,000 (and for the whole Krupp concern from 98,000 to 74,000). In the crisis at the end of the postwar inflation, the eight-hour workday was suspended too, and replaced by a 57.5-hour "provisionally normal" working week, imposed by means of an arbitration award from the Reich Labor Ministry.

The complete collapse of the currency in 1923 was also a regional crisis for the Rhineland and the Ruhr Valley. Krupp was inevitably badly affected by the political crisis that followed the French occupation of the Ruhr. On Easter Saturday 1923, French soldiers who were inside the Gussstahlfabrik shot at a protesting group of Krupp workers and killed thirteen. The company strongly supported the workers' protests and created a patriotic monument for them. The French authorities came to the conclusion that the resistance to occupation had been organized by the Krupp management. On May 1, Krupp and three of his directors were arrested by French troops and sentenced to prison (as well as having substantial fines imposed). Krupp's sentence was for fifteen years, though he was

Figure 5.3 The Ruhr struggle: demonstration in April 1923. Courtesy of Historical Archives Krupp.

released after seven months as Gustav Stresemann's foreign policy restored Franco-German relations.

The only move to rationalize the business, the creation of the holding company Aktiengesellschaft für Unternehmungen der Eisen- und Stahlindustrie (or Afes) in the summer of 1923, was motivated more or less exclusively by the need to deal with the problems following the French occupation, and to prevent France from operating the whole concern by seizing the Gussstahlfabrik. As in other Ruhr enterprises, the holding company was designed to separate the vulnerable and occupied core businesses in the Ruhr from subsidiaries in the other parts of Germany.

In 1923, no rational financial calculation of any kind was possible because of the political pressures and the monetary distortion. The end of the inflation provided a chilling sobriety. The first stable-currency balance sheets showed the extent of Krupp's losses, above all because the very substantial reserves held in nominal fixed-interest securities. For June 30, 1923, a gold mark accounting loss of 59 million was calculated; for September 30, 1924, an additional loss of 125 million. The extent of the loss was disguised only by revaluing the company's real estate holdings.

STABILIZATION

It was really only with currency stabilization that the full extent of the problems of Germany's major corporations, including all the large steel companies, became clear. The Stinnes concern had to be broken up after the death of Hugo Stinnes. Thyssen was in a deep crisis, traumatized by the aftermath of a succession dispute as August Thyssen struggled with two temperamentally quite different sons, the nationalist Fritz Thyssen and the cosmopolitan bon vivant Heinrich Thyssen-Bornemisza. Krupp too was hit by financial crisis but solved it in a rather different way than some of the other major steel companies, which saw the creation of a steel trust as the most promising way out of their difficulties. Much of the pressure to amalgamate came from the foreign banks. The most prominent of the new international New York investment banks, Dillon Read, started to negotiate a $100 million credit for the six major German steel companies to allow the financing of business rationalization. At the end of 1924 Wiedfeldt, now the German ambassador in Washington, helped negotiate a separate Krupp credit in parallel discussions. Krupp eventually concluded its own agreement for a five-year $10 million bond issue with Goldman Sachs & Co., on better terms than Thyssen had been able to reach in separate negotiations with Dillon Read.[14]

The terms of the American bond issue were nevertheless humiliating. The Dresdner Bank as agent for the American creditors imposed a trusteeship on the Krupp inventories, so that the Krupp warehouses carried legal notices that their contents were the property of the U.S. bondholders.

Krupp's losses continued to mount and produced an existential crisis for the company, just as in 1873. From October 1924 to August 1925, the Gussstahlfabrik incurred a loss of 16 million reichsmarks (RM), and the Germaniawerft an additional loss of RM 18 million; and the company as a whole faced a major liquidity shortage as its debts shot up from RM 70 million to RM 121 million.[15] It had piled up expensive inventories: thus, for instance, it had ten months' scrap requirements. In 1925 the discussion about the future of Krupp and its independence reached a crisis point. Krupp embarked on radical cost-cutting measures, including the closure of the Annen works, the Hermannshütte, the Saynerhütte, Martin Works II, III, V, VII, and the Casting Works II. The crisis was eventually resolved in exactly the same way as Alfred Krupp's 1873 trauma had been: through a mix of politics, bank credit, and the chance event of a general economic recovery. As in the 1870s, many Germany companies saw industrial organization, cartels or syndicates, and now also trusts as the best way of limiting the ravages of a hostile market; as in the 1870s, Krupp resisted that argument and preferred to stand alone.

On March 17, 1925, Gustav Krupp went to Berlin to speak with Chancellor Hans Luther. He suggested that the company had lost around RM 250 million over the past ten years and asked for a government credit of RM 60 million. Luther turned the request down, on the grounds that there was no legal basis for such assistance, and that anyway the government did not have this kind of money at hand. Ten days later Wiedfeldt sent a more detailed memorandum to the Finance Ministry. At the beginning of April the cabinet decided in favor of the demand, and on April 17 a formal agreement was signed. Krupp would receive RM 11 million as compensation for its disarmament costs, with some additional money in the form of prepayments for military orders (RM 2.8 million), tax postponement (RM 3.5 million), deferral of the turnover tax (RM 1.2 million), a subsidy from the Army Ministry (RM 1.8 million), and payments from funds reserved for productive unemployment relief (RM 2 million), in all a total of RM 22.3 million in grants. In addition, the state-owned bank Reichskreditgesellschaft would lend RM 12 million and the state insurance company Reichsversicherungsanstalt RM 3 million.[16] As a precondition for the state assistance, Krupp would need to find an additional RM 50 million in bank credit. But the German central bank refused to lend, the Dresdner Bank was unable to put together a syndicate, and Krupp needed to turn to the smaller Essen bank of Hirschland in order to obtain a rather smaller emergency liquidity support. The state had helped, but the banks were still hesitant.

Wiedfeldt, who had returned from his post in Washington in March 1925 and left the company in April 1925, remained as an adviser, although he was increasingly unwell and died of leukemia in July 1926. In a lengthy memorandum of September 1925, he argued strongly in favor of merging Krupp into the new giant

Vereinigte Stahlwerke. Only the mines and Rheinhausen were working profitably, as well as some parts of the steel products business, in particular wheel parts. Central products of the Gussstahlfabrik were loss making, and the company needed public subsidies to keep above water. After examining alternatives such as continuing state support, a radical reduction of the size of the firm with a concentration just on the mines and on the Rheinhausen steelworks, or massive capacity expansion in order to restore the prewar volumes of production, Wiedfeldt concluded that everything was hopeless: "each of these paths would lead to overindebtedness and collapse." Wiedfeldt made a passionate plea to break with the Krupp tradition: "Only one thing matters: saving the firm. All other considerations of a personal and material nature, all personal wishes, must be completely ignored. I know that goes against Krupp traditions, which tend to cautious procrastination and to compromise, and which with noble dignity always try to meet personal wishes."[17]

In particular, the Kiel Germaniawerft was a massive problem: "it cannot continue." But there was a more general management failure: "All officials, especially the top ones, must be removed if they are not needed, without any special considerations. That is necessary financially and because of the effect on labor morale. The continual chatter about the position and business of the company, which hurts us, comes from the discontent of the Essen officials. No position must be filled with double the number needed. We have no money for that."[18] Managers should be compensated for particular merits; but correspondingly, there should be a ruthless dismissal of the ineffective and incompetent.

If the Fried. Krupp AG did not join the steel trust, Wiedfeldt believed that it would have to reckon with the hostility of the banks that were promoting the concept. Any continued dependence on banks would mean "the end" of the firm; in consequence Krupp needed to avoid taking on new debt. "The talk about future bond issues must stop completely."[19]

The creation of a steel trust would increase the competitive pressure on Krupp. Joining the trust would create a reliable stream of income for the Krupp family, which would get just over a fifth of the shares in the new trust. Without such a step, the family fortune, which Wiedfeldt estimated at RM 120 million (compared with 450 million marks before the war), would be exhausted within a year or a year and a half. It might even—Wiedfeldt suggested—be possible for "Herr von Bohlen" (as he called Gustav Krupp) to chair the supervisory board. And the family might retain the Grusonwerk as a way of continuing the military tradition of the company, as well as retaining the stakes in Bofors and Rheinmetall. But Wiedfeldt watered these radical conclusions down in the version of his memorandum that was actually discussed by the supervisory board. In August and September 1925, Wiedfeldt conducted discussions in London about a possible sale of a large stake in the company to British steel interests, but Gustav Krupp rejected this alternative, with the same degree of patriotic resolve that had earlier led him to turn down a such a sale to a French or American corporation.

Other enterprises carried on similar discussions about the gains and losses to be obtained from affiliation to the steel trust. The Haniel family was polarized, with one member who saw himself as a modernizer arguing strongly in favor of trustification, and the traditional managers of the Gutehoffnungshütte arguing against that option. Heinrich Thyssen-Bornemisza complained that the "trust would shatter a broadly conceived and extensive family enterprise."[20] But financial exigency made family firms vulnerable.

Gustav Krupp at first tried to negotiate better terms for accession to the steel trust. He suggested that the distribution of shares in the new enterprise be based on revenues rather than on production capacities, and he tried to make a case that the headquarters should be in Essen rather than Düsseldorf (a move that in a sense did take place eighty-five years later, when ThyssenKrupp moved its headquarters from Düsseldorf back to the traditional Krupp base in Essen). On September 5, 1925, the Committee of the Krupp Supervisory Board discussed the possibility of joining the steel trust but took no clear position. It did, however, take a position on the need for further radical downsizing, including the closure of the locomotive and wagon works. On September 20, Gustav Krupp finally decided against joining the trust. At a Sunday morning meeting, he spoke with the metal dealer and major shareholder of Phoenix, Otto Wolff, who emphasized the future of the steel trust as a mass producer. Krupp by contrast saw the future of his company as remaining an independent family business. Later he argued that neither domestic nor foreign markets were ready for a large anonymous firm, and that the traditions of an old family firm would bring substantial commercial advantages. In addition, he thought that such decisions should not be made under financial pressure. In a letter to Albert Vögler, who would become the chief executive of the trust (Vereinigte Stahlwerke AG)), he stated that a family firm "despite restricted means was in a position to follow particular technical developments in a more individualized way."[21] This statement captures the heart of the Krupp philosophy, which was fundamentally skeptical of mass production. There was no room for a construction such as the Gussstahlfabrik in the new business view of Vögler and the banks. One year later, when Vereinigte Stahlwerke spun off the Thyssen engineering works as a separate company, Demag, Krupp believed that his position had been vindicated.

In June 1926, shortly before his death, Wiedfeldt was still warning that within one or two years Krupp would either collapse or be obliged to join the Vereinigte Stahlwerke. He pushed for a much more radical downsizing program. Instead Krupp opted for a much more modest commercial cooperation with the remaining large independent steelmakers, GHH and Hoesch. In 1927 these enterprises played a central role in the establishment of the Ruhrlade association, which was conceived as a behind-the-scenes mechanism for allowing the steel barons to influence the major industrial pressure groups, and which represented only the most token concession to the demand to give up the principles of family business.

RECOVERY

In fact, for a few years the gamble on independence paid off, and Krupp appeared to be successful once more. The company shared in the short-lived prosperity phase of the Weimar Republic, and followed an austere path of plowing profits back into the firm as investments. Steel production increased rapidly after 1924 and reached a peak in 1926/27, but then it began to fall once again, first because of labor problems, then because of the general economic downturn.

There was also some technical innovation. From 1926, Krupp started to produce a new hard metal it called "Widia." The concept—a tungsten carbide alloy—had originally been developed by the electric company OSRAM in the course of experimenting with filaments for lightbulbs. Krupp purchased the patent and began to market the carbide metal. The major use of this alloy, from Krupp's perspective, would be in tool-making. In 1928/29 General Electric concluded an agreement with Krupp for marketing a similar product in the United States, "Carboloy." But negotiations with British partners collapsed because of Gustav Krupp's resentment of the wartime campaigns of British steel industrialists against him.

As in the boom years of the 1900s, Krupp also engaged once more in the quest for mass steel production. Two new blast furnaces in Essen-Borbeck to produce large quantities of steel were complemented by the creation of the world's largest forging press. Krupp had initially tried to finance this through state credits but the government rejected the proposal, so Krupp then had to turn (in January 1927) to a 6 percent RM 60 million bond issue. The two new blast furnaces began working in May and September 1929, in other words just months before the Wall Street crash seemed to transform the prospects of the world economy. The result was that the Borbeck capacities could not be adequately used: for 1930/31 the capacity utilization was 56 percent. By 1931/32 that ratio had fallen to 41 percent.

For three years—1926/27 to 1928/29—Krupp made very modest profits. From September 1926, Krupp stopped reducing the workforce, and the number of white-collar workers started to rise in 1927.

In October 1928, Krupp participated in the Ruhr lockout, an attack by industry leaders on the state-imposed system of compulsory arbitration, which the employers increasingly blamed for their rising costs and decreasing profitability. The company announced the dismissal of workers. But Gustav Krupp was quite skeptical of the hard-liners among the Ruhr employers, and worried about the consequences of the conflict. Bertha Krupp was even more explicit, stating that "she was not prepared to gamble her paternal inheritance in a game designed to allow dashing cavalry officers to continue their legal hussar-rides indefinitely." In a repeated series of meetings with other industrialists at the Villa Hügel in November 1928, Krupp pressed more and more insistently for an end to the conflict. At the final meeting, on November 26, the principal hard-liner, Paul Reusch, was especially dismissive of Krupp's softness.[22] The lockout did not end until December 4, 1928.

After December 1928, both production and employment briefly recovered again, and in July 1929 employment reached a peak at 70,159. But then the depression started to hit Germany.

DEPRESSION

As in the 1870s, a company producing investment goods was very vulnerable to a general downturn. In the early 1930s, orders for machine tools and heavy equipment simply evaporated. There were high fixed costs, and the company needed to maintain its core of skilled workers. Labor costs thus inevitably rose as a proportion of the firm's commitments, despite pay cuts and the dismissal of employees. Wage cuts could not compensate for the decreasing labor productivity as utilization levels fell more and more below capacity. By September 1932, employment in Essen had fallen to 16,812 and in the enterprise as a whole to 46,107 (respectively a fall of 41 percent and 51 percent from the 1928 levels). On July 1, 1930, wage rates were cut throughout the Gussstahlfabrik. In March 1931, Krupp abrogated its agreement with white-collar workers and demanded a 15 percent cut; an arbitration agreement instead imposed 6 to 8 percent, with additional reductions for reduced hours of work.

Railway orders, traditionally a means by which public authorities had tried to stabilize demand, were generally ruled out because the Reichsbahn had been extensively modernized and reequipped. It had some of the most modern locomotives and rolling stock in the world. In March 1931, the Reichsbahn agreed to a seven-month program for rail construction but found the financing of this order very difficult.

The extent of Krupp's financial leverage made the crisis worse. The company's strategy of financial reconstruction and expansion after the 1925 crisis had involved an extensive amount of bank credit. But in the depression, German banks faced substantial pressure from the central bank, the Reichsbank, to reduce their debt levels and raise their capital ratios. They consequently obliged their business customers to reduce their debt. On September 30, 1931, Krupp had debts of RM 43.162 million to banks and RM 29.748 million to other creditors, who also faced the same compulsion to reduce debt exposure. One year later, in 1932, these figures were respectively RM 34.128 million and RM 9.025 million.

It was at this time, in October 1931, that Gustav Krupp, who had previously been politically quite reticent and had not wanted even to be identified in public as a member of the executive board of the steel industry's Gruppe Nordwest, took on a very prominent position as chairman of the major industrial federation Reichsverband der Deutschen Industrie.[23] Krupp's chief political concern was initially with the credit crunch, which Krupp blamed on the central bank and its president, Hans Luther. He denounced Luther's policy in meetings with Chancellor Brüning and suggested that Germany would be better off if Luther's controversial predecessor, Hjalmar Schacht, were recalled to the position.

But Krupp was decisively opposed to any suggestion of a transition to autarky, and it was clear that even in the global downturn export orders represented the only chance for continuing to produce. In particular, the major source of demand was the increased demand of the Soviet Union for equipment and machinery in the framework of the First Five Year Plan. In 1931 government provided almost RM 1,000 million in export credits for the Soviet orders. By 1932 three-quarters of German exports of metalworking equipment and three-fifths of rolled steel exports were going to the Soviet Union.[24]

The British devaluation of the pound in September 1931 put additional cost pressure on Krupp. The commercial director, Arthur Klotzbach, produced in October 1931 a memorandum in which he called for a new round of wage and salary cuts.

The situation appeared quite hopeless. Within six years of the severe financial crisis of 1925, there was a general economic collapse. The banks, which had been powerful exponents of the logic of amalgamation in the 1920s, were now quite powerless, themselves victims of the credit crisis. Foreign banks no longer displayed any interest in giving credit to companies in a country that had negotiated a standstill on debt payments, which blocked the transfer of the foreign exchange required for servicing debt. But the Krupp management appears not to have lost hope completely. In December 1932, presenting the accounts for the year 1931/32, Arthur Klotzbach boldly predicted: "if the signs do not deceive and if new political unrest does not disturb economic confidence, we have reached the bottom here and in the world."[25] Reaching a bottom, however, does not necessarily mean recovery. Germany, and Krupp, were at a turning point.

SIX

POWER AND
DEGLOBALIZATION

Gustav and Alfried Krupp von Bohlen und Halbach

The popular image of Gustav Krupp as the cannon king who benefited from rearmament and whose family slid into increasing moral and political degeneration was molded not just by a popular work of history, the American journalist William Manchester's *Arms of Krupp* (1964), but also by films such as Luchino Visconti's *The Damned (La caduta degli dei)* (1969), in which a wildly amoral, dysfunctional, and murderous family is presented as the "Essenbecks." Visconti, the last scion of a Milanese Renaissance family, was fascinated by the cultural dynamics of dynastic decline. The basis for his critical treatment was derived above all from the account presented as the prosecution case at the Nuremberg International Military Tribunal, but the image also came from the visions of corrupt cannon kings presented by George Bernard Shaw and Heinrich Mann. Could Thomas Mann have described the dynamics of the Krupp family? In the 1970s, Thomas's son Golo Mann tried, but failed, to write a biography of Alfried Krupp, the son of Gustav Krupp von Bohlen und Halbach. He did provide a cautiously ambiguous characterization of the father's relations with the Nazi state. "There are two conflicting views. One is that he cooperated in as much as he needed to hesitatingly and under

Figure 6.1 Nuremberg trial of Krupp directors, 1947. Courtesy of Historical Archives Krupp.

pressure, and occasionally resisting. The other is that he and his company cooperated willingly and with pleasure, much more intensively than they needed to. . . . I think the second thesis is incomparably more wrong than the first, but that too is not wholly true." And Alfried Krupp was described as thinking in the following terms: "a real fellow goes with power, especially when it is real power, as now, that is the only practical attitude."[1]

Alfried Krupp himself produced a bizarre addition to the fictional literature about business life when, in prison after the Second World War, he wrote a pained and painful persiflage of two business careers under the Nazis with the title of "The Life and Works of a German Economic Leader, as Depicted in Nuremberg Documents."[2] The first biography begins: "His life was shaped by greed for money, blood and power. His grandparents

173

on his father's side carried out the bloody business of butchery, on his mother's side his grandparents were greedy tax collectors. . . . Already as a child he screamed louder and longer than other children. . . . In him there was an untamable drive for everything concerned with technology, because even as a child, he felt or rather he knew, that a future war would be won by the side that was technically superior. Thus, even in the cradle, he used his rattle as artillery, his nightstand as a command position, and he used a bicycle that his parents gave him not just for locomotion but to bring danger to other peace-loving cyclists." The fictional business leader went on to rob foreign factories, kill his workers, and employ forced female labor—that he then refused to feed—in his household. He was given millions by the Nazi government, which he immediately transferred to Swiss banks. He was tried at Nuremberg but by mistake acquitted and restored to all his positions. The style of these fictional biographies seems to have been taken from the defense affidavit of the chief Krupp munitions engineer, Erich "Kanonen" Müller: "After a childhood full of hardship, an extraordinary technical talent, manifest at an early age, together with iron will launched him, after he had passed his examinations with highest honors, and had first proved his technical ability inside and outside of Germany, on a quick ascent in a promising civil service career with the German Reichsbahn. His change over to industry, to the Krupp firm, is not to be explained by the tasks he had carried out till then, nor was it caused by financial or political considerations. Only his technical talent is his recommendation and the impulse to prove himself in a field completely new to him. [. . .] There was, for him, no general economic, no

Figure 6.2 George Harcourt portrait of the Krupp family, 1930. Courtesy of Historical Archives Krupp.

commercial and financial, no military and tactical, but only technical problems."[3]

ROOM FOR MANEUVER

Recently, in the aftermath of international debates about restitution and the responsibility of business in totalitarian regimes, a great deal of historiographical debate has concentrated on the extent to which businessmen had choices or a freedom to maneuver in the Nazi era. Many modern interpretations of National Socialism have taken what is sometimes called a "voluntarist turn" in emphasizing that the functioning of dictatorship depended not so much on direction from above as on a myriad of individual acts of complicity, which were sometimes motivated by ideology and sometimes by opportunism. Such a view can clearly also be applied to business history. Property rights were largely preserved under the dictatorship, and it has in consequence been argued by some historians

175

that business decisions were not politically directed or determined. According to Christoph Buchheim and Jonas Scherner, for instance, state procurement authorities relied on conventional contracts, which provided market-based incentives in order to attempt to induce the cooperation of industry. There was thus little open compulsion and little attempt even to follow the example of Rathenau and Moellendorff in the First World War and use raw-material allocations as a planning instrument to redirect resources in the national economy, although some aspects of First World War planning such as "contractual guarantees of adequate returns" were adopted again in the 1930s.[4]

The modern debate is only a new round in a controversy that goes back to the postwar Nuremberg trials and to the cases brought by the U.S. military authorities against individual businessmen. The judges in the Flick case largely accepted the defense argument that business was subject to compulsion, in striking contrast to the Krupp trial, where the conviction of Alfried Krupp and the Krupp directors rested on the notion that the business leadership had had some room for maneuver. At the Krupp trial in Nuremberg, Alfried Krupp's attorney, Otto Kranzbühler, asked Albert Speer's former chief of staff, Karl Otto Saur: "did a firm have the possibility to refuse an order placed by the Armament Ministry on the ground that they would not make enough profit on it?" Saur replied, "No, they could never make that argument. . . . If, however, they could prove that with the arranged price or fixed price they could not work, then we had to find a new basis for that firm, or we would have to leave that firm out of our orders."[5] But the structures of the arguments presented in Nuremberg go back even further. In the late 1930s, Krupp executives took the example of the

First World War to show that at that time the company "had no longer been free in its investment policy."[6]

The "voluntarist" account misses something important: the market economy had not really worked well in the Weimar Republic, especially in the case of the heavy industries that were central to German rearmament and were at the core of the Nazi vision of a reordered economy. The steel industry in particular was plagued by massive overcapacity, and it was inevitable that the memory of near bankruptcy in the mid-1920s and again in the early 1930s shaped the outlook of companies when orders began to flow once again. They looked to nonmarket processes that would affect the outcome of the economic process, and which might provide a mechanism for absorbing heavy losses. Rather than being driven by the search for massive profits (on which the Nazi state placed limits in terms of ceilings on dividend payments), companies were driven by the experience of massive losses. Even before 1933, the market was highly political.

The steel industry was a vital case, central to the state's obsession with armaments, and the most obvious industry in which industrial power translated into military might. Buchheim and Scherner conclude that even in this case "Germany's private steel companies were not prepared to expand capacity to meet the rapid increase in demand arising from the state's rearmament program despite the high profits that they were earning."[7] Was there something more than profitability at stake? Was it the memory of bad experiences in the First World War, was it political reluctance, was it the outcome of a struggle between managers who used different business strategies as a tool to fight out their personal rivalries?

Historians, especially in dealing with the question of industry under National Socialism, have often naively assumed that business is simply driven by a quest for profit. The Marxist historian Tim Mason concluded: "It was easy for the huge armaments firms to prosecute their immediate material interests, but in the process the responsibility for the overall economic system was left . . . to the political leadership."[8] The accounts that see business as being driven by profit miss something vital to the German tradition, which distrusted profits. This long-standing skepticism was reinforced by the lessons of the depression. Capitalism became a target of general vilification. The Nazi propagandist Joseph Goebbels denounced it, explaining: "we are fighting not against capital, but against capitalism."[9] He defined capitalism as the *misuse* of productive goods and of money. But this view of capitalism was also that of, for instance, Alfred Krupp in the mid-nineteenth century. The Krupp enterprise was built on the foundation of twenty-five years of nonprofitability. By the early twentieth century, the company was a large bureaucratic institution, and bureaucracies are not driven by the profit motive. Already in the nineteenth century, commentators had often referred to the Krupp works as a "state within a state." In some bureaucratic enterprises, individual employees and especially senior employees could use political levers and influence to extend their power. Krupp, however, in large part because the ages of the principal family members were, by chance, conveniently spaced for succession, maintained itself very explicitly and self-consciously as a family company. The family became a carapace against the intrusions of the state, but within this particular family there was a clash of different generations that opened the way to increased state influence.

Already in the Weimar Republic, political decisions were crucial in affecting economic outcomes: in subsidies, wage levels, trade policy, access to credit, as well as military contracts. Gustav Krupp had become a central figure in industrial politics in 1931, at the most critical moment of the economic crisis.

In 1933 everything was still highly politicized, but everything also very obviously changed. The end of the depression, the resumption of military demand, the new political order: from the point of view of the management of the Fried. Krupp AG, it was not easy to separate the new developments. There were two obvious and immediate issues for the company and its management: first, the extent to which Krupp should engage with the new regime; and second, a deep concern about avoiding the mistakes made during the First World War, when rapid expansion and a complete orientation toward military production had created a crippling problem of overcapacity.

Hitler emphasized the remilitarization aspect of work-creation measures. On February 8, 1933, he told the cabinet that "the next five years must be dedicated to the rearmament of the German people. Every publicly supported work-creation scheme must be judged from this standpoint: is it necessary for the restoration of the military strength of the German people?" But, characteristically for the conflicted and confused character of much of Nazi economic planning and policy making, just one day later, on February 9, he apparently accepted the fiscal argument that the speed of rearmament could not be further increased.[10]

REARMAMENT

Rearmament was important for Krupp, but at first more for political and psychological reasons than for commercial ones. At a supervisory board meeting of January 1936, Gustav Krupp gave figures for direct military orders as being only 9.3 percent of Krupp sales, and indirect military orders 10.8 percent. This proportion was still well below the pre-1914 levels of armaments production. But as in the nineteenth century, armament orders had more than a purely quantitative significance for the company's management; they were a way of proving the company's worth and establishing an entrée with the government. The annual report for 1934/35 nevertheless stated: "For the first time after years of interruption we have carried out substantial contracts for the German Wehrmacht and with that have returned to the honorable tradition of our house."[11]

By 1933/34 Krupp had already returned to profitability, though not initially primarily as a result of military demand. Until 1935 the Gussstahlfabrik, which was the heart of the Krupp tradition, supplied relatively little in the way of armaments. The order book in March 1933 was slightly below that of September 1932, but then a substantial recovery began. Orders for trucks increased, in large part as a consequence of the new government's concern with motorization and its lifting of the heavy rates of taxes on automotive transportation. A large number of the trucks went to the military. Production for "KM," or war materiel, was 8.1 percent of the Gussstahlfabrik activity in 1932/33 but almost double that, 16.1 percent, in 1934/35; if semifinished products and trucks supplied to the military are included, those proportions go up to 12.7 and 25.0 percent.[12]

The company also took important symbolic steps in the direction of a new armaments economy. In 1934 Krupp participated as one of five large German firms in the establishment of the Metallurgische Forschungsgesellschaft mbH or Mefo (the others were Vereinigte Stahlwerke, GHH, Siemens-Schuckert, and the Deutsche Industriewerke Spandau AG). The aim was to create creditworthy signatures that would allow the Reichsbank to discount armament bills.

In the summer of 1934, the Army Procurement Office (Heereswaffenamt) gave the Gussstahlfabrik a relatively modest but symbolically important contract for eighty heavy howitzers and eighty-six 10 cm heavy artillery pieces. In 1935 Krupp obtained contracts worth RM 6.6 million from the Reichswehr and RM 8.2 million from the navy. As before and during the First World War, naval orders were especially important for the problematic Germaniawerft, which had long been the company's financial Achilles' heel. In the early 1920s, Otto Wiedfeldt had urgently demanded its closure. Gustav Krupp had been contemplating a sale of the shipyard since 1925. In January 1933 he started negotiations with the commander in chief of the navy, Admiral Erich Raeder, over the question of subsidies.[13] In March 1933 the talks began again in the new political circumstances. Gustav Krupp opened with the frank observation that he wondered whether he could carry the losses of the Germaniawerft for much longer, and argued that the Germaniawerft was getting much less of the repair business that was crucial to surviving the economic downturn than rival shipyards in the North Sea ports of Bremen and Hamburg. He asked whether he could have a list of the naval orders that might be expected over the next years so that he could be more certain about the prospective level of activity, but succeeded only in extracting an offer of the navy's "serious interest."[14] The problem with the threat of selling the shipyard was: who could possibly be interested in buying the Germaniawerft? Only a rival shipyard with an interest in capacity reduction and rationalization would be able to make a commercially viable purchase, but this would lead to reduced competition and increased prices for naval equipment. The navy consequently emphatically did not want a merger of the Germaniawerft with the partly state-owned Bremen company Deschimag (Deutsche Schiff- und Machinenbau AG), and appealed to Krupp to drop plans for a sale. But the Germaniawerft only began to benefit from submarine and destroyer orders in August 1934. On July 15, 1935, the first submarine was launched at the Kiel shipyard. The yard eventually won the prestige victory of having produced Germany's most famous submarine, the type VII *U-47*, constructed from 1937 to 1938, which under the command of Günther Prien sank thirty Allied merchant ships as well as the British battleship *Royal Oak*.

One of the Krupp directors, Ewald Löser, later asserted that the navy in effect took over the Germaniawerft in 1937/38.[15] But the process of increased navy influence was in reality a rather gradual one, in which the company lost influence in the course of increasingly bitter clashes over procurement policy. In 1937 Krupp appointed Admiral Heusinger von Waldegg, who had just retired from the Supreme Command of the Navy (OKM), to the supervisory board of the Germaniawerft. The hope was that a sympathetic appointment might resolve the clash over the forced pace of production of five destroyers, which were delayed in part because Blohm & Voss

Figure 6.3 A submarine launching at the Germaniawerft in Kiel, c. 1940.
Courtesy of Historical Archives Krupp.

was dilatory in the supply of the boilers and turbines.
Within a few months, the company was taken by surprise
by new state demands. In February 1938, Hitler ordered
an accelerated building of the cruiser "J," which was eventually launched as the *Prinz Eugen* at the high point of the
Sudeten crisis in August 1938. But after these ships were
produced, there were no new naval orders, and the management needed to look for commercial shipping orders
so as to maintain employment levels. Then finally, on
February 7, 1939, the OKM dictated the whole production program of the Germaniawerft. From the perspective of the Essen management, the whole process was
extremely frustrating. The experience of the Germaniawerft seemed no better than it had been in the desolate
days of the Weimar Republic. In 1940 Löser reported

183

that the Germaniawerft had produced no profit, even after 1935.[16]

The problems that crept in with military work lay not just with the Germaniawerft and shipbuilding: the company was suspicious of other military orders as well. Both for naval and army orders, Krupp tried to look for some direct participation of government agencies in the cost of investment. It was reluctant to sink investments into what might be nothing more than a flash-in-the-pan remilitarization. At the supervisory board meeting of January 1936, Gustav Krupp spoke of external pressures that were causing increased difficulties: for instance, the government was pressing for a new crankshaft factory outside Essen for making aero-engine parts. The new factory was eventually constructed near Hamburg at Reinbek, but Krupp put in only 7 percent of the capital, and the investment was financed mostly through the Air Ministry. The E-Programm of 1937 required new production halls for naval artillery and armor, as well as for army tanks. Krupp emphasized in the negotiations that "on commercial grounds we cannot see the lasting need" for the additional capacity. Most of the cost of the program— some RM 88 million—was borne by the government.[17] In the 1937 P-Programm, the second Mechanical Workshop of the Essen Gussstahlfabrik went over directly into the control of the Heereswaffenamt (Army Procurement Agency). The Supreme Command of the Army (OKH) and OKM also directly provided machinery for the Germaniawerft and for the manufacturing of torpedo tubes, shells, and armored cars in the Magdeburg Grusonwerk.

A way of trying to balance the increased significance of military orders and the uncertainty about future development lay in the old company strategy of cultivating global markets. Krupp tried to maintain its share of output going into exports. The proportion fell to 10 percent in 1935/36 but then started to recover. Between 1933 and 1939 the seven most important importers of Krupp products were the Netherlands, Italy, Japan, South Africa, Turkey, Switzerland, and Brazil. In July 1939, of RM 70.9 million earned from Turkish contracts, only 4.1 million were for railway equipment, but 34.6 million were for "war materiel."[18] Nevertheless, the exports were widely diversified: in the late 1930s, for instance, Krupp was supplying steel for the construction of the Bank of China.

Was this looking to export markets a defiance of the orders of the controllers of the German economy? Far from it. In 1938 Göring issued some of his most extravagant threats against the Ruhr industrialists in a meeting in which he was pressing the coal and steel men to export *more* in order to acquire the scarce foreign currency that Germany required in building up its military potential. According to one of the participants at that meeting, Göring argued "that German business has grasped the seriousness of the situation as well as he. If, nonetheless, his goal is not reached, then he will have no alternative to appointing a state commissioner to direct the economy and equipping him with all powers, including to seize specific sectors of business that in his judgment cannot do what the state must demand of them."[19] The company made a point of publicizing the geographic extent and dynamism of its export business.[20]

The problem with trying to follow state, military, or, for that matter, party directions was that they were all wildly inconsistent and changed over time. At times, the government was calling for a concentration on military orders, at other times on exports. Any choice could be politically compliant—or, if the winds changed, politically

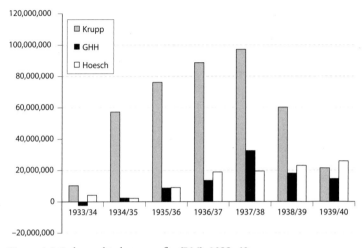

Figure 6.4 Ruhr steel industry profits (RM), 1933–40.

dangerous. The confusion irritated many business leaders. At the outbreak of the war in 1939, Adam Tooze argues, "after three years under the haphazard steel rationing system, these firms had built up a head-steam of frustration that now vented itself on the army procurement office."[21]

The irritation was doubtless born of financial pain. In the first years of rearmament, profits had surged. On a share capital of RM 160 million, the company made profits (according to its tax balance sheet) of RM 97 million in 1937/38, extraordinary levels that seemed to recall the high levels during the Wilhelmine naval expansion. But after 1937/38, profit levels fell off sharply, in the next year by 38 percent, and by 1939/40 they were only 21 million or 22 percent of the 1937/38 peak. The picture was similar at the neighboring GHH, where in the years after 1937/38 profits were 55 percent and then 44 percent of the peak levels, though in Hoesch profitability continued to rise.[22]

The rise and fall of profitability did not correspond directly to the political stance of the company, its owners and its management. In that sense, the simple argument that financial incentives determined the political orientation of this business is clearly inadequate.

POLITICAL GLEICHSCHALTUNG

Gustav Krupp was not a supporter of National Socialism before 1933. He remained a man of the late Wilhelmine era, uncomfortable with modern mass politics. He found Hitler and his movement too radical, too populist, and too socialist. And he was happy to leave political activity to his cultivated and intelligent brother-in-law, Tilo von Wilmowsky, the grandson of one of Wilhelm I's last advisers and the son of the head of the Chancellery Office under Wilhelm II. Indeed, until Gustav Krupp became head of the industrial confederation Reichsverband der Deutschen Industrie (RDI) in October 1931, he tried to maintain a distance from any political activity.

Gustav Krupp had consciously avoided the session of the Düsseldorf Industrieklub on January 26, 1932, when Hitler, dressed stiffly and formally, gave a surprisingly reserved and moderate performance. Fritz Thyssen, a second-generation steel magnate, invited Krupp in October 1932 to a meeting with Hitler, but again Krupp refused to meet the demagogue. Krupp also declined to support Franz von Papen on January 7, 1933, in a meeting in Friedrich Springorum's house in Dortmund, as Papen was preparing plans to share power with the National Socialists. But at this point Papen was talking of a cabinet of "national concentration" and believed that Hitler had abandoned his claims to the chancellorship. Krupp missed the subsequent intrigues, as he was on holiday (and then fell sick) in Campfer in the Swiss Engadin, but he was kept informed by letter and telephone by the general manager of the industrial confederation RDI, Ludwig Kastl. Kastl wrote on January 26 that Papen was planning a "*Bomben-kabinett*" with Hitler and Schacht but that a continuation of the Schleicher government would be preferable from the standpoint of industry. Von Wilmowsky also pleaded for the Schleicher solution. On January 28, after telephoning Krupp, Kastl and Eduard Hamm of the Federation of Chambers of Commerce (*Deutscher Industrie- und Handelstag*) wrote to President von Hindenburg's state secretary, Otto Meissner, that the economy needed political calm and stability.[23] On February 1, after the new government was formed, Gustav Krupp wrote: "I can only with difficulty come to terms with the new turn of events. I fear, that as [Krupp's son] Harald expresses it, the mixture of hydrogen and oxygen will be explosive."[24] Henry Turner rightly speaks of "a widespread myopia on the part of Germany's big businessmen."[25] Gustav Krupp did not appreciate the extent of the vulnerability of the economic and political system of Weimar, or the power and radicalism of the populist impulse. But the terms of the Nazi New Order soon became clear. After Hitler had been appointed chancellor on January 30, the tone of government-industry relations changed dramatically. Papen continued to press for business donations in order to strengthen the nationalist and non-Nazi wing of the government coalition and thus provide a counterweight to Hitler, and he turned directly to Krupp. But Krupp refused, citing his position in the Reichsverband, and instead asked that another Ruhr steel magnate, Fritz Springorum, organize the collection of funds for Papen's "black white red front" in his place.[26]

Kastl in particular was outraged by the Nazi threats and violence, and wrote an extraordinary letter to Krupp in which he conjured up the likelihood of civil war: "What is happening in Prussia in the police and administration will have bad consequences. I find it terrible. The electoral terror and the fighting are unworthy of a civilized people. . . . There are continually the most terrifying rumors. In Munich yesterday I was informed from all different sides that there would be a putsch in the evening. A speech of Hitler, a torchlight procession, shooting, the imposition of a reich commissar, the calling of a monarchy. That is what comes from the threats of the interior minister. . . . The business with the monarchy is not over, because it is hoped in this way to break the power of the Nazis."[27]

On February 20 Gustav Krupp, with over twenty other leading businessmen, was summoned to a meeting at Hermann Göring's official residence, kept waiting for some time, and then subjected to an hour-and-a-half-long harangue by Hitler. Hitler was vague about any policy specifics but emphasized the importance of private property and the "fight against bolshevism," and announced that Germany was about to have its "last election." Krupp, as chairman of the RDI, gave no substantive reply, merely a polite expression of thanks. But his remark that "it is high time to at last reach clarity in domestic political matters in Germany" could be interpreted as support for Hitler (the statement is in fact ambiguous, and might have also been taken as support for the Papen position).[28] After Hitler's departure, Göring spoke again about the forthcoming election, and Schacht then pithily asked the "gentlemen" to pay up.

It was at first because of his position in the RDI, rather than because of the importance of Krupp as a military supplier, that Gustav Krupp was highly vulnerable to political pressure. In the election of March 5, 1933, the Nazis obtained 43 percent of the vote and consequently fell short of an absolute majority. Shortly after, on the day on which Hitler finally announced the government program, which was generally well received by business in that it renounced radical experiments in autarky or with the currency, a meeting of the RDI's presidium took place. Kastl had been highly alarmed: he found his connection with the conservatives in the new government, Finance Minister Lutz Graf Schwerin von Krosigk and Economics Minister Alfred Hugenberg, increasingly strained. Only Hugenberg's state secretary in the Economics Ministry, the Nationalist Paul Bang, seemed a reliable support for the business viewpoint. Kastl was alarmed about the financial recklessness of the government. As he said in a letter to Krupp, "the measures are somewhat unplanned and in any event will cost money. In this way the currency can shake." The idea of a devaluation of the currency, which had allegedly been propagated by Schacht, had been denied by the new government, but Kastl had doubts, and added that "such a measure would be the worst for us." And at the end of the letter he added a political comment as well, to the effect that "when six- and seven-year-old boys and girls go around shouting 'Juda verrecke' [the Jew must die] that is terrible!"[29] At the meeting of the RDI on March 23, Fritz Thyssen, the nationalist and embittered scion of one of the great entrepreneurs of the Wilhelmine era, who felt that the other leading businessmen were out of touch with the new spirit of the age, now launched into an aggressive denunciation of liberalism, the republic, and also the leadership of the RDI. He specifically attacked Gustav

Krupp for conspiring with trade union officials against the new government; and he demanded that the leading figures of the RDI should resign to make way for men who were more in line with the national movement.[30] After the meeting, Thyssen continued aggressively to denounce business leaders with whom he had quarreled, and indeed threatened opponents that he would use his powerful influence in the new state.[31] He then fell out with Hitler because the regime took little notice of his plans for the creation of a corporate state and because he was worried about the regime's militarism; and he allowed a ghost-written book to be produced on how "I paid Hitler." But he continued to denounce: in his view, for instance, Gustav Krupp had turned himself into a "super Nazi."[32]

In fact, some business leaders trusted Krupp sufficiently to try to involve him in a protest against Nazi policy. After the April 1933 anti-Semitic boycott of Jewish-owned stores and businesses, the Hamburg bankers Max Warburg and Carl Melchior, along with the former state secretary in the Finance Ministry, Hans Schäffer, approached Krupp as well as Carl Friedrich von Siemens and the electrical manufacturer Robert Bosch, and asked them to sign a memorandum laying out the deleterious economic and business consequences of the regime's anti-Semitism. But the memorandum was never sent, and does not appear in any government files.[33]

Krupp and Carl Friedrich von Siemens arranged to see Hitler on April 1, but by that time the attack on the RDI and its leadership was already in full swing. Hitler's economic adviser Otto Wagener led a group of strongmen into the RDI building and demanded the immediate dismissal of Ludwig Kastl for having negotiated and supported the Young reparations plan, as well as the dismissal of Jewish employees of the RDI. He also called on Jewish businessmen to step down from the presidium of the RDI. Krupp began to negotiate about the dissolution of the RDI and its replacement by a corporatist and politicized interest organization. He also agreed to the dismissal of Kastl, although the presidium's members voted overwhelmingly in protest against Krupp's acquiescence. But even the protesters recognized that "political opposition would, for an economic association, be utter madness."[34] Kastl was replaced by his deputy, Jacob Herle, but within a year Herle too was forced out by the party after accusations of financial misconduct relating to political payments in 1932.

Krupp stayed on in the Reichsverband, but after the February 27, 1934, "Law on the Organic Construction of the German Economy," which aimed at replacing the business associations by hierarchically structured groups, he became increasingly uncomfortable. He would have stayed as führer of Principal Group I (Industry), but in April 1934 asked Economics Minister Kurt Schmitt to be relieved of his position on health grounds, arguing that a younger and more energetic man could make more of a contribution to the construction of an organic and corporatist state.[35]

THE KRUPP WORKFORCE

The Nazi attack led to changes not just in the RDI but also in the Krupp enterprise. Several members of the Krupp supervisory board were attacked by the Nazis as being Jewish. Anti-Semitism was not the only motive in play: a reorientation away from bankers and bank influence seemed inevitable, as the role of banks in German life was reduced in the aftermath of the economic and financial crisis. Kurt Hirschland stayed in the United States after a business journey in 1933. Jakob Goldschmidt, the discredited head of the failed Darmstädter Bank, was pressed to resign in January 1934. Samuel Ritscher of the state-owned Reichskreditgesellschaft, a highly respected banker, emigrated in 1936. On the other hand, Arthur Klotzbach was reckoned by the Nazis as half Jewish but remained in the Krupp directorate until his death in September 1938. Klotzbach's son also continued to work for Krupp.

The most highly placed Jewish casualty of the Nazi revolution was the director of the research laboratory, Benno Strauss, who had been principally responsible for the development of nonrusting steel and for the very significant hard metal (Widia) production. In the late summer of 1934, he was attacked by the deputy director of the laboratory, Adolf Fry. At the same time, Fry also denounced three younger and dynamic Krupp managers, Paul Goerens, Heinrich Korschan, and Edouard Houdremont, all of whom would later play a prominent part in the Krupp story. Fry used Nazi arguments and language in his attacks, presenting Strauss as Jewish, and Houdremont and Goerens as foreigners who were thus undertaking "high treason." Korschan was merely "suspected of untrustworthiness."[36] The reaction of the firm's owner was to attack the denouncer, not the denounced. Gustav Krupp dismissed Fry without notice: in the letter of dismissal, he stated: "Your accusations have been examined in detail. It became clear that they have no proof or substance. In your actions you have not only damaged the reputations of the gentlemen concerned in the most serious way, but you have also endangered the reputation of the company. We thus dismiss you from our service with immediate effect."[37]

Fry later moved to a state laboratory, the Chemisch-Technische Reichsanstalt, Berlin. Of the men he accused, only the person he denounced as Jewish had to suffer any consequences, but that aftermath was a terrifying one. Strauss was pushed into premature retirement, one year before the end of his contract, with effect at the end of 1934, though he was paid for a further year. He was celebrated at his retirement, which was handled with great dignity, and he was presented with a globe made of nonrusting steel, perhaps a symbol of both Krupp's technology and of its internationalism.[38] But ultimately he was forced out of the business on racial grounds. He was interned in the war and died on September 27, 1944, in a labor camp. Houdremont responded to Fry's attack by taking out German citizenship. Gustav Krupp on the one hand quite bravely resisted the politically inspired denunciations of an ambitious company employee, and he ensured that Strauss suffered no financial disadvantages; but equally he gave in to pressure to remove Strauss from the company.

Within the company, the provisions of the Weimar settlement, in which there had been an organized representation of labor in the Factory Council, were also changed. A new Works Council was elected on March 24, 1933. The communist candidates were banned (in 1931 they had obtained 22.4 percent of the vote), but socialist union representatives won 37.4 percent of the vote and Christian trade unionists 31.7 percent. The NSBO (National Socialist Factory Cell Organization) fared rather poorly, with only 24.7 percent of the vote. Two weeks later, after a law on works councils had been promulgated, the

NSBO simply removed the socialist representatives from the main council. On August 29, finally, the Düsseldorf regional authorities removed all socialist and Christian labor representatives.

The Krupp management tried to reconcile the new Nazi labor activism with the old Kruppianer traditions of a workplace community dedicated to the common good. Nazi politicians also liked to cite Krupp favorably as an exemplar of the German style of business. In 1935 the Reichswirtschaftskammer selected Krupp as one of the factories to show journalists as being most successfully "engaged in mental resistance to industrial undertakings as bearers of capitalist tendencies."[39] In 1937 the Nazi trade union organization German Labor Front (Deutsche Arbeitsfront or DAF) honored Krupp with an award for exemplary training of apprentices.

The Nazi revolution coincided with a general renewal of the high-level management. Klotzbach, the leading figure in the directorate of the late Weimar Republic, stayed on (although he was considered as half Jewish under Nazi racial law), but new managers were added in order to deal with the new politics of labor in the company. Paul Goerens, a metallurgist, was appointed as "führer" of the Essen works, but he did not really behave in the style of a general director, and his tasks were more symbolic in dealing with the NSBO and the "Vertrauensrat" (Council of Confidence) that in 1934 replaced the Works Council.

When the member of the Krupp directorate responsible for finances, Wilhelm Buschfeld, died in October 1936, Gustav Krupp initially tried to replace him with Carl Goerdeler, the mayor of Leipzig who had in 1934 been selected as price commissar but who was increasingly at odds with the regime and seemed a perfect link to the conservative nationalist opposition to Hitler. Krupp had already asked Hitler in person about Goerdeler in June 1936, but in February 1937, after an intervention of the Essen party authorities, Hitler's adjutant informed Krupp that "the Führer would not welcome the appointment of Mayor Goerdeler to the executive board of the Fried. Krupp AG."[40] But Krupp still had a plan for Goerdeler, and with Robert Bosch financed his journey around western capitals in order to widen his range of contacts.

Gustav Krupp then asked von Wilmowsky and Carl Goetz of Dresdner Bank for advice, but most of all listened to Goerdeler himself, and so appointed the man who had been deputy mayor of Leipzig under Goerdeler, Ewald Löser, to the executive board of Krupp, despite some skepticism on the part of Goetz. Like almost all his predecessors as chief executive, Löser came from outside Krupp. He had no experience in heavy industry, and after leaving his position in Leipzig had been the director of the Berlin Hotelbetriebs-AG, a career path that attracted comment and even ridicule, not only from ideological Nazis, but even more from the tight fraternity of Ruhr businessmen. Löser saw himself very much as a figure shaped by his association with Goerdeler. He took particular care to obtain assurances from Krupp that "he would not be obliged to let the firm's policy be influenced by party political considerations."[41]

The most dramatic change was that a member of the family was brought back into management for the first time since the death of Friedrich Alfred Krupp. In 1938 Gustav Krupp appointed his eldest son, Alfried, then aged thirty-one, as a member of the executive board in charge of mining, war materiel sales, and artillery construction. He had already been an alternate director since 1936.

With Alfried Krupp and Ewald Löser as directors, the stage was set for a clash of cultures. Löser came out of the old-style world of German conservatism and nationalism, while Alfried thought of himself as being much more in tune with modern and more radical politics. Conflicts looked inevitable, for exactly the same reasons as Alfred and Friedrich Alfred had in the past struggled with the company's management over how rapidly the company should grow, how expansion should be financed, what sorts of technical initiative were appropriate. But the character of the political regime and the political environment produced by National Socialism ensured that such clashes would be much more violent and disturbing.

FINANCING

In the late 1930s, Gustav Krupp was worried that the costly mistakes—overinvestment and overexpansion—that the company had made during the First World War might be repeated. Instead he preferred to accumulate reserves. By contrast, Löser pressed to use accumulated profits to finance the expansion of the works. Krupp set a ceiling of RM 30 million for borrowing and became increasingly cautious. In 1939 Löser set out a business plan for growth to establish a company that would be competitive at the end of the armaments boom. It required investments of some RM 250 million, but Gustav Krupp subsequently cut back on the management's proposals.[42]

The financing of investment was in general a controversial question in the aftermath of the depression and the collapse of capital markets. Beyond investments that could be financed through the plowing back of profits,

or very specific military projects that were taken directly
into the army or naval budget, the possibilities for raising
money through bond issues was limited. The government
did not want private companies to drive up interest rates
by flooding the market with debt instruments.

In 1936 Krupp put together a 4.5 percent bond issue
of RM 53.8 million, which did not represent new borrowing but simply a conversion of the 1927 bond issue
to take advantage of the fall in interest rates in the 1930s.
Two of the company's traditional bankers, Deutsche Bank
and Mendelssohn, were skeptical about the coupon, since
this was the rate usual for state bonds and most industrial
bonds were paying 5 percent. The Krupp finance director
insisted that the lower coupon was a nonnegotiable matter of prestige.

In 1939 a new 4.5 percent bond issue of RM 40 million
required considerable negotiation with the government
authorities, as the Reichsbank had imposed a stop on new
issues. The Reich Economics Ministry had initially given
priority to bond issues by the Rheinisch-Westfälisches
Elektrizitätswerk and the Gutehoffnungshütte. Löser
argued the Krupp case on military grounds: Krupp was
preparing to build a plant in Upper Silesia that would
be protected against aerial attack. In order to acquire the
necessary permission, Gustav Krupp needed to intervene
personally with the director of the Financial Department
of the Economics Ministry, Kurt Lange.[43]

Most of the major investment projects fitted in with
the autarkic goals and visions of the Nazi regime. One of
Hermann Göring's major worries during the armaments
buildup was Germany's vulnerability because of its dependence on the easily interrupted supply of Swedish iron ore.
The government's response was the development of the

Salzgitter Hermann Göring Werke, which was intended to mine and smelt domestic, low-grade iron ore. The opposition to the Salzgitter project from the Ruhr was intense, but it was led by the Vereinigte Stahlwerke rather than Krupp. Krupp actually worked hard to accommodate the regime's new priorities. The long-term research efforts of Krupp in the 1930s included the pyrotechnical refining (Renn process) plant in Essen Borbeck for the utilization of siliceous ores. In 1936 Krupp agreed with the government on investment in the Fischer-Tropsch process for the production of synthetic fuels.

The new investments were costly, and they lowered Krupp's returns, producing the major profit squeeze of the late 1930s. By 1938 the company, in a brilliantly argued memorandum drawn up by Johannes Schröder, a relatively young man who had come from Dresdner Bank to take a position as an assistant to the finance director, complained bitterly that it was earning a return that was less than the interest paid on Reich bonds.[44] Schröder began with a historical account in which he tried to show Krupp as a victim of its patriotism. In the First World War, the company's investments had been planned by the state. After the collapse of the empire and the institution of the Versailles Treaty, "the owner of the company had decided in the interest of an eventual rearmament of Germany to keep all the workers, the workshops, and the accumulated expertise." Coming to numbers, Schröder argued that the value of the company had been grossly understated: it was RM 219 million according to the tax accounts, RM 67 million in the assessment for the wealth tax, but only RM 17.7 million in the commercial accounts. In addition, Schröder made the improbable claim that the firm's machinery was hardly used between

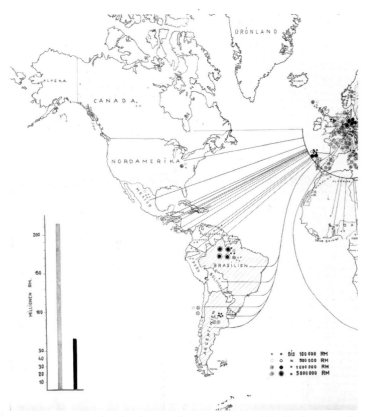

Figure 6.5 Geographic distribution of Krupp exports, 1933–42. Courtesy of Historical Archives Krupp.

1919 and 1933 because of the constant economic crisis. By increasing the calculation of the company's value in this way, Schröder reached a figure of RM 390 million in 1933, and then pointed out that RM 22 million of profits were used to upgrade or replace antiquated or worn equipment. In consequence, he could produce the amazing figure of 1.74 percent as the company's rate of profit between 1934/35 and 1936/37. One final argument

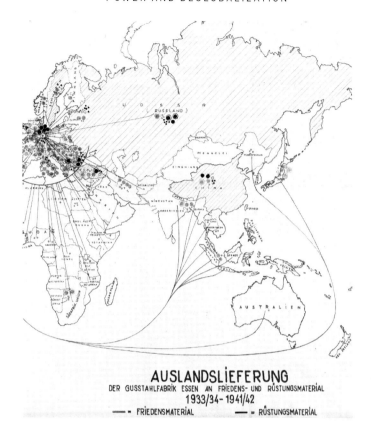

AUSLANDSLIEFERUNG
DER GUSSTAHLFABRIK ESSEN AN FRIEDENS- UND RÜSTUNGSMATERIAL
1933/34- 1941/42
—— ▪ FRIEDENSMATERIAL   ▬▬ ▪ RÜSTUNGSMATERIAL

concerned foreign exchange earnings from exports, which appeared to Göring's planners as increasingly vital so that Germany would be able to import strategically needed raw materials. Between 1933 and 1938, Schröder showed, the company had earned RM 300 million in foreign currency, RM 127 million of which came from exports of coal and coke. This was a sum equivalent to the trade deficit of the whole of Germany in 1938! In

201

short, even if the Göring office was unwilling to swallow the improbable accounting, Germany and its armament program could not do without Krupp.[45]

The negotiations with the military procurement authorities that followed this realization produced a new method of calculation, which allowed a substantially increased depreciation margin. The March 1939 decision of Göring's office was the single most important contribution to the subsequently increased profitability of Krupp, and it was explicitly motivated, according to a notification from the government agency, by "the particular contribution of your enterprise to the development of heavy weapons, your contributions to metallurgy, and your willingness to supply the results of your research to other producers."[46] As a consequence, the profits from 1934 to 1938 were raised by RM 30.7 million, and from 1939 to 1945 the new calculation basis contributed RM 260 million to Krupp's profits.

The statement from the Göring office about its motivation also reflects the view that Krupp was functioning best as a quasi laboratory in which new and innovative products could be developed, rather than as a mass producer of the goods required for German rearmament. Krupp techniques for making nonrusting steel were passed on to two other producers in order to secure high-volume production. Such outsourcing of production led to intense anxiety in Krupp. Widia tools, and also Widia used in shells, proved substandard when made elsewhere, and Krupp at the instigation of the OKH recentralized production. Alfried Krupp in particular urged production in big series, and the adoption of American business practices.

The expansion of weapons production also raised the question, which became much more acute after 1939, of

Figure 6.6 Hitler congratulates Gustav Krupp von Bohlen und Halbach on his seventieth birthday, Villa Hügel, August 1940. Courtesy of Historical Archives Krupp.

the adequacy of energy supplies. Krupp bought in 1937 the Rossenray coalfield on the left bank of the Rhine but never developed the deep pits that would have been needed to realize its potential.

All in all, there was considerable balance in a strategy that continued to place importance on the global market, and which saw opportunities in the industrialization and import-substitution strategies adopted by many non-European as well as European countries in the 1930s. The furnaces for refining low-grade ore constructed in the Gruson works were a major export success: they were sold in Czechoslovakia, Spain, Korea, Japan, and Manchukuo. This was an anticipation of Krupp's corporate course of the 1950s and 1960s, which emphasized the selling of large-scale industrial equipment to countries embarking on industrialization.

WAR AGAIN

On September 1, 1939, Germany invaded Poland, and unleashed a new world war. As the conflict went on, the government's willingness to tolerate hesitance or debate over munitions orders decreased, and disputes over priorities rapidly turned into accusations of incompetence and treason. But the radicalization of the state also in general increased the pains that businesses took in cultivating their political relations. The larger the state becomes, and the less cohesive economic policy-making is, the greater is the attention paid by business leaders to capture political as well as economic rents.

But in the case of Krupp, it is not clear that individual directors and managers were looking out for the overall position of the firm as much as carving out individual empires. They chose different and conflicting strategies. During the war, Löser in particular became the focus of increasing controversy, in part because of his business style, in part because of his politics. In 1941 he tried to appoint his brother-in-law Erich Thiess as the head of the internal audit office. This attempt to build up an internal power base could easily be interpreted by his opponents as cronyism. When put together with Löser's political stance, such maneuvering made for a great vulnerability. In 1942, after "Berlin offices" had commented on Löser's critical remarks about party interference, Krupp reminded Löser that "only support of the Führer is possible; there must be no doubts about this, and no remarks that may be misunderstood."[47]

In 1941 the executive board was unchanged, but six new deputy directors were added: they included Edouard Houdremont, who was in charge of central steel operations; Erich Müller, in charge of artillery; and Fritz Müller in mining. Erich Müller, generally known as "Kanonen-Müller" in order to distinguish him from Fritz, had played a decisive role in the reordering of the war economy in 1940. He achieved fame as the pioneer of the prestigious ultraheavy artillery project that produced "Dora," the 80 cm cannon that was used only once in the course of the war, in the siege of Sevastopol. Müller took a conspicuously different political path from that of Löser. Hitler had become incensed when he saw the low figures for munitions output in the early weeks of 1940, and summoned the architect of the Autobahn network, Fritz Todt, as well as a range of business figures including Erich Müller. On April 8, 1940, in a conversation with Hitler during the course of a train ride, Müller argued passionately against General Karl Becker of the Army Procurement Office,

Figure 6.7 The heavy railcar-mounted cannon "Dora," c. 1941. Courtesy of Historical Archives Krupp.

and added insinuations about the general's personal life. There was also a reprise of an earlier scandal, as one of the complaints of the Krupp company against Becker was that he had been pressing Müller to work closely with the denouncer Adolf Fry from the Chemisch-Technische Anstalt.[48] The business leaders wanted to replace the army munitions regime with a state institution headed by somebody like Todt, who would be closer to businesss. Todt was indeed appointed to head a new Ministry of Munitions. Relations between the new ministry and the house of Krupp immediately showed a substantial improvement over those that had prevailed in the last years of peace. In November 1940 Müller was appointed by Todt to chair a new committee (Sonderausschuss "X") to oversee guns and artillery production.[49]

While the Krupp managers took different paths, the owners started to worry as much about the family position as about the financial position of the company. Gustav Krupp feared the tax implications of the death of the company's owner, Bertha Krupp, and consequently thought of altering the legal status of the enterprise. He had become an increasingly isolated and remote figure, more and more distanced from the actual conduct of business. His own health was faltering; he had a series of strokes and largely withdrew to Schloss Blühnbach, his mountain estate near Salzburg. Klöckner and Friedrich Flick advised against creating a family foundation. At the instigation of Gustav Krupp, Alfried Krupp began negotiations on the Obersalzberg with the Führer's secretary Martin Bormann; and Krupp wrote to Hitler on November 11, 1942, that his personal experience confirmed "that the concentration of responsibility in a single head, especially in critical times, of which I have experienced several, cannot be valued highly enough."[50] Hitler was highly sympathetic to the request, and ordered the head of the Reich Chancellery, Hans Heinrich Lammers, to draw up a draft decree. On November 12, 1943, a Führer decree (which became known as "Lex Krupp") specified that "the owner of the Krupp family wealth is empowered to create a family enterprise with a particular regulation of succession." A final clause of the decree allowed interventions by the justice and economics ministers. On December 15, 1943, a family statute was worked out, and on December 29 the Fried. Krupp AG was converted into a simple company, whose principal owner, Bertha Krupp, immediately nominated her eldest son, Alfried, as her successor and transferred her shares in the company. In addition, a family council was put in place, as well as regulations for compensation and a family fund for Alfried Krupp's brothers and sisters.

The new ownership structure had an immediate impact on the company's management. Alfried had found relations with Löser increasingly strained. He thought Löser to be vain, ambitious, arrogant, and deceptive, and presented him as "unsocial" and "capitalist in the bad sense," as he had rejected the idea of building workers' accommodation for the new wartime employees. Löser in turn believed that Alfried was too influenced by Nazi ideology and had too many "dubious friends" in the party and in the office of the head of the German Labor Front (Deutsche Arbeitsfront), Robert Ley.[51] Löser left the firm once it ceased being an AG, and Alfried took the position of chairman of the executive board.

Alfried Krupp indeed cultivated his political links, but without much energy or enthusiasm. As a student, he had already joined the SS in 1931 as a "patron." On the other hand, it was only when he was already a member of the Krupp board that he joined the party, in 1938. When Albert Speer met Alfried for the first time, on May 28, 1942, he was immediately impressed and concluded that the young Krupp should join the central industrial munitions council and also that he should become deputy chairman of the Iron Association. Göring however preferred another candidate, Hermann Röchling from the Saar, who was playing a major role in the integration of the French economy into the German war effort. And Speer rapidly found that Alfried Krupp was in reality not a very effective presence in meetings and discussions. In 1945, after the German defeat, the British military authorities noted that "in spite of the many important posts which he now holds, on the boards of the firm's sub-sidiaries as well as on those of external companies, very little has been heard of him. This appears to be due to lack of colour and initiative in his personality rather than to his youth."[52] This was Golo Mann's verdict also: the last Krupp was not "evil, but was pretty much a nothing."[53]

Speer in the end found it easier to deal with other Krupp managers, in particular with Edouard Houdremont, the specialist for steel alloys who since 1940 had headed a group concerned with scarce metals and had worked on nickel and on using chrome and molybdenum as substi-tutes for the tungsten and nickel that Germany found it difficult and expensive to import. In November 1944, Speer noted: "The visit to Krupp produced the pleasant discovery that under the new director of Krupp, Herr Houdremont, a large part of the outmoded Krupp spirit has already vanished. Everywhere new young employees can be seen, who grasp the problems with more energy than up to now was the case."[54]

Did Alfried's new position and his half-hearted search for political influence really make any difference to the firm's strategy? With the outbreak of war in September 1939, the historian Werner Abelshauser considers that there was no more room for "entrepreneurial autonomy."[55] The Gussstahlfabrik was subject to the directions of the Supreme Command of the Armed Forces (Oberkom-mando der Wehrmacht or OKW). But the problem was that the demands were continually changing. Hence the enhanced efforts of business to tip developments in a particular direction. The situation could be regarded as a classic problem of monopsony, but it was monopsony with a curious twist, what might be termed polycratically (dis)organized monopsony.

Procurement priorities were constantly clashing, and frequently altered. At the outbreak of war, 24 percent of armaments orders were canceled, because they had become obsolete in the wake of planning changes. In August 1939, the army tried to stop the continued Krupp production of civilian trucks. Krupp at first resisted, but at the beginning of 1940 a complete stop on civilian construction was imposed.[56] Nevertheless, agricultural machinery was produced until 1942, although the number of types was reduced. The death of Fritz Todt on February 8, 1942, and the appointment of Albert Speer changed the conditions under which German business operated. In May 1942, directors of Rings and Committees (the new organizational structures of the Speer ministry) were instructed to carry out their duties "not by persuasion but by clear and sharp instructions and orders to industry."[57] After heavy bombing attacks in June 1943, the Gussstahlfabrik was inspected by the Technical Commission of the Armaments Commission to ascertain the effectiveness of reconstruction. What the inspectors saw was chaos. At this point Speer and the plenipotentiary for labor Gauleiter Fritz Sauckel considered imposing a commissar to run the factory. From spring 1944, after heavy Allied bombing, the Gussstahlfabrik was placed under the direction of a special emissary of the Speer Ministry, but less and less could be produced there. In October 1944, after a new bombing attack, further production became impossible, and in any case Essen was by now effectively cut off from the rest of Germany.

Naval orders were especially problematic, just as they had been during the peacetime phase of rearmament. Löser had for a long time wanted to sell the Germaniawerft. Instead, in December 1941, the Krupp corporation bought 54 percent of the share capital of the rival ship-yard Deschimag, which was partly owned by the state of Bremen and partly by the German government. But in 1943 Admiral Doenitz imposed a stop on the production of large ships in order to concentrate on the expansion of the submarine fleet. Deschimag took a substantial number of orders but increasingly lagged behind in fulfillment. The plant supplied only forty-three of the eighty-eight type XXI 1,600-ton submarines. Franz Stapelfeldt, the general manager of Deschimag, was arrested by the Gestapo in October 1944 after a visitation by Speer's chief of staff Karl Otto Saur, and remained in prison until March 1945. As an outcome of the Stapelfeldt scandal, the Krupp management simply refused to take responsibility for operating Deschimag as a privately run naval shipyard: it was safer, it seemed, to leave the responsibility to the state.

Other Krupp acquisitions under the Nazi regime included the Austrian Berndorf silverware plant (the mid-nineteenth century creation of a much older Krupp concept of global markets) after the death of the chief representative of the Austrian branch of the family, Arthur Krupp, in 1938 and the *Anschluss* of Austria. In October 1939, Löser also made clear his interest in taking over a blast furnace and cokery in Upper Silesia. Hermann Göring wanted to push Krupp into taking over a Silesian steel works, in large part as a consequence of an attempt to shift some production farther east and away from the range of British bombers, but was reluctant to give Krupp any coalfields in the East. There were intensive negotiations with the Göring office over the Bismarckhütte, the most modern Silesian steel plant, as well as less enthusiastic discussions over the Laurahütte and the Falvahütte. But the state-owned Reichswerke Hermann Göring took the only suitable source of coking coal, the Dubensko mine; and in the end, in September 1941, Krupp abandoned the idea of a Silesian expansion. In the meantime, Friedrich Flick had ensured that opinion in the Göring office shifted against Krupp when he told State Secretary Paul Körner that Krupp directors had let it be known in the Ruhr that they were being "forced" to take over the Bismarckhütte.[58]

There were also Krupp acquisitions and engagements farther east, as the German offensive expanded into Soviet territory. Speer allocated the Azov work in Mariupol in Ukraine to Krupp, as well as an engineering firm in Kramatorsk and an agricultural equipment plant in Berdjansk to a Krupp trusteeship; but these plants were abandoned shortly afterward, in 1943, because of military developments. In 1942 Krupp also participated in the "Ivan Programm," producing munitions and shells under license in the Donets basin.

The major theme of the midwar years was the attempt to shift production eastward, primarily for strategic reasons, in that the Ruhr was exposed to Allied bombing attacks, but also because the government was pressing Krupp to shift its character and make a transition to mass production as part of the mobilization for war. Such a transformation could occur much more easily on a green-field site than in the more chaotic conditions of the Gussstahlfabrik, which looked more like (and indeed was) a chance aggregation of historically accumulated craft workshops.

In the late 1930s, the naval command suggested the construction of a new plant for heavy naval artillery, away from the vulnerable Ruhr district. The site eventually chosen was a two-thousand-hectare area at Markstädt, near Breslau. On September 24, 1941, the Fried. Krupp Schlesische Industriebau GmbH was established as a joint subsidiary of the Fried. Krupp AG and the Afes (the Krupp holding company established in the 1920s). Originally, the plans specified 8.8 cm and 10.5 cm anti-aircraft weapons; in March 1942, in a discussion in the Führerhauptquartier in Rastenburg, Hitler personally changed the priorities to light and heavy howitzers, and Speer told the group (which included Erich Müller, the Krupp artillery expert) that the new Krupp works near Breslau would be a perfect production location. Then the Heereswaffenamt reduced the resources allocated to construction, and reduced the number of machine halls. In June 1942, Krupp was instructed to undertake the additional construction with its own resources. By July Saur was demanding that the whole project be stopped. Alfried Krupp then intervened personally with Albert Speer, and construction resumed in October 1942. The advantages of the project listed by Krupp included not only location but also a saving in skilled labor, and the possible employment of prisoners and Jews for the construction of the machine halls.[59]

The construction became more urgent after a major British bombing raid on March 5, 1943, on the Essen works. The Krupp site had become a major target for the bombing offensive of the RAF in western Germany, which in the course of the war dropped one and a half million tons of explosive on Essen.[60] In fact, the Allies dropped more explosives tonnage on Essen than the steel output of the Krupp works (520,000 tons in 1942/43 and 475,000 tons in 1943/44).[61] Consequently German planners wanted to shift the bulk of munitions production to more protected eastern areas. Hitler now ordered the construction of two additional halls at the Markstädt site, for tank equipment and aircraft shafts. The production of some components for the light howitzers started as early as February 1943, even though only a tenth of the machinery needed was in place.

Skilled workers were sent from western Germany, but the proportion of skilled labor remained relatively low (6 percent). The Speer authority suggested that the slave labor that had been engaged for the construction should also continue to be employed in production. The objections of the Krupp management largely concerned the absence of sanitary facilities and the threat of infection of the skilled German workers.[62]

In January 1943 the Markstädt factory was renamed as the Berthawerk, and the Heeres-Rüstungskredit-AG took over a "war risk clause" guaranteeing compensation for government orders in the case of a stopping of military procurement. As the highest priority was now given to the production of tanks in Essen and Magdeburg, the Berthawerk was unable to supply the first hundred light howitzers due in May 1943. The initial hopes of establishing a green-field factory operating along the principles of fordist production proved illusory.

There were also more and more problems with the supply of coal in the eastern works, which proved to be an increasing constraint on steel production. Alfried Krupp tried to negotiate with Göring for the acquisition of a stake in the Karwin-Trzynietz AG mining operation and ironworks, to supply pig iron and coal. But the concerns were sold instead to Deutsche Bank and Dresdner Bank. After the March 1943 air raid, Alfried Krupp tried in addition to get a source of coal, and intervened through Martin Bormann. But again the request was unsuccessful.

Because of both the fuel situation and the slowness with which new plant capacity was constructed, production was sporadic. Two tilting electric furnaces were shipped to Markstädt from the dismantled Ilva works in Piombino, Italy, but never used. When Saur visited the Berthawerk on October 15, 1943, he complained violently about the "slackness" of the management and inserted a special commissar into the Berthawerk to supervise the howitzer program. Alfried Krupp complained that this constituted a "moral discrimination." But he was also forced to recognize that the performance of the plant was inadequate, and that the future of the Berthawerk as part of the Krupp empire was in question.[63] He put the Berthawerk under a new manager, Hans Girod, who had a reputation for brutality. But Saur continued to complain about the insufficient work. In December 1944 he was still referring to the "hair-raising conditions." Only one month later, the plant was evacuated because of the approach of the Red Army.

A large part of the conflicts with the government revolved around labor shortages, which severely affected the Krupp tradition of highly skilled production. This issue went back as far as the peacetime years. There were increasing labor shortages after 1936, and in 1938 Krupp recruited three hundred workers from the "Ostmark." In April 1939 an initial group of ninety Czech miners arrived in Essen. In 1940 small numbers of Dutch and Belgians began to work in Gussstahlfabrik, and by September 1941 there were also over a thousand Italians. But many of these foreign workers quickly moved away from Krupp to look for more attractive conditions of work.[64]

Prisoners of war did not have this kind of freedom, but their employment immediately raised severe feeding and housing difficulties. In 1940, some 1,275 French

POWs were engaged in Essen. But the company needed much larger numbers for wartime production, and Russian POWs as well as recruited workers began to arrive at the Gussstahlfabrik in early 1942. The Krupp foremen and managers rapidly complained about their poor physical condition and consequent inability to work, but remarkably little was done to improve the conditions of work. Most were never given adequate clothing or shoes, and many preferred to go barefoot rather than deal with the injuries inflicted by heavy wooden clogs. Adam Tooze records that "Krupp (and this is certainly true for most other German businesses) employed foreign workers because there was no alternative. . . . After 1942, employing foreign labor was simply the entry ticket for the war economy."[65]

At a high level of management, a discussion of the working conditions in the Krupp factories developed, but it produced no effective—not to speak of just or moral—solutions. Gustav Krupp's brother-in-law, Tilo von Wilmowsky, a Christian conservative who was increasingly alienated from the regime, had been informed about the conditions of Russian workers by the director of the Konsumanstalt, and tried at first unsuccessfully to contact Löser before addressing Alfried Krupp. He protested about the economic folly of not using the "productive powers" of the workers, and the scandal that workers had been recruited with written promises and then were held in Essen behind barbed wire and with inadequate food. But Alfried offered little in the way of a response.[66] What paltry improvement occurred took place more as a result of state than of company initiatives. It was not just the Krupp managers who were concerned about the consequences of poor nutrition and housing, above all

Figure 6.8 Forced labor at Krupp Essen works, c. 1943. Courtesy of Historical Archives Krupp.

because of the impact on labor productivity. Albert Speer also complained about the unproductive use of the Russian workers. The barbed wire was taken away and rations increased to the levels of German "normal consumers." In the autumn of 1943 new incentives, additional pay and leave, as well as a meaningless promise to limit the time of labor service to two years, were added.

In June 1942 another large group of Russian workers arrived, this time as a result of compulsory recruitment. By November 1942, 2,522 Soviet POWs and 5,469 Russian civilian workers were working in the Gussstahlfabrik. The peak of foreign employment (almost 25,000) was reached at the beginning of 1943, with the largest contingent coming from France (8,423). Overall, during the war some 100,000 forced-labor workers were employed by the Krupp company.

As in Silesia, coal shortages originating in labor shortages began to be a bottleneck for production in the Ruhr. Overwhelming numbers of Italian miners simply left the coalfields. In the summer of 1942, large numbers of Russians were sent to the Ruhr mines to replace them. How should they be treated? The regime sent quite inconsistent messages. Some government figures seemed to advocate harsh treatment for the most cynical reasons, emphasizing that the brutality would necessarily create a solidarity based on shared complicity between the regime and German employers, managers, and workers. Others worried about the implications of cruelty on labor productivity and industrial output. On October 4, 1942, the leader of the German Labor Front, Robert Ley, told Ruhr managers, including representatives of Krupp, that "the coal must be mined, so or so. . . . if not with you, then against you, gentlemen. . . . We have burnt all the bridges behind us, intentionally. We have practically solved the Jewish question in Germany. Even that alone is a colossal achievement." If a "Russian pig" was beaten, the responsibility would fall on individual workers, "because you and I won't do that."[67] Labor Commissar Sauckel by contrast was worried about reducing the Russians' capacity for work and ordered that "every mistreatment should be avoided; on the contrary, it is necessary to avoid anything that might diminish their will to work."[68] Three days after the brutally frank meeting with Ley, the director of the Krupp Personnel Department, Max Ihn, instructed managers to ensure a correct (more humane) treatment of Russian workers.

In September 1942, the company authorized a RM 2 million investment in order to build parts for automatic weapons and detonators in Auschwitz, with the aim of using slave labor from the concentration camp. In this case too, labor considerations seem to have driven the company's production strategy. But the plant was in the end constructed not by Krupp but by another and unrelated company (Union Gesellschaft für Metallindustrie Sils, van de Loo & Co.). One year later, another Krupp memorandum tried to explain delays in manufacturing these parts to the impatient military authorities. In the end, the production of detonators was moved from Essen to Wüstegiersdorf in Silesia instead of to Auschwitz, and 250 female inmates of Auschwitz were selected for work in the detonator plant by the Krupp work manager Weinhold. But the workers were relatively well cared for; they received medical attention, and there is only one recorded case of a death, a woman from Novi Sad who died of tuberculosis. The conditions at Wüstegiersdorf were indeed substantially better than in Essen.[69]

In late 1942, Löser asked for a precise calculation of the comparative costs of domestic and foreign labor. The additional transport, security, and administrative costs paid to the state and the SS for using foreign workers amounted to much more than their low pay levels saved, and meant that the foreign workers (at least in the case of males) became more expensive than their German counterparts. Similar calculations were made in other enterprises, and can be used to show the increasingly irrational as well as murderously immoral character of the German war economy. But these were hypothetical calculations, in that there were no alternative German workers available; and in the light of labor shortages, compulsion became the key to the organization of the labor force.

From February 1942, West European workers reaching the end of their contract terms were more and more often forcibly retained (*Dienstverpflichtung*). For Russians, this compulsory retention was applied from March 1943. In September 1942, the Munition Committee in the Speer authority asked Krupp where Jewish prisoners might be sent as part of the labor contingent. Krupp announced that the firm was willing to take around 1,000 specialized Jewish workers and made specific requests for 258 turners, 242 fitters, 150 milling operatives, and so on; but this formulation was (perhaps deliberately) unrealistic, and no Jewish workers were actually sent in response to the Speer initiative. With increasing shortfalls in production, Krupp managers became more desperate to find workers. In the bombing raid of March 5, 1943, a large number of barrack huts were destroyed and forty-six workers killed. After this, workers were dispersed in the region around Essen, and spent long hours in weary and sometimes deadly guarded treks through an increasingly dysfunctional and cruel city. In June 1944, however, after the Essen prison too had been destroyed by bombs, Alfried Krupp asked the local authorities whether he might employ the prisoners in locomotive construction. The Rolling Mill II and the Electrode Workshop also requested concentration camp prisoners.

But the bombing and the destruction of accommodations also meant that the employment of any kind of labor became an increasingly futile and inhuman process. In some instances in Essen and in Magdeburg, forced workers were prevented from taking shelter against the bombing raids even in public air raid shelters, although the company's own shelters were used by foreign workers.[70] In August 1944, 520 Hungarian female prisoners from Buchenwald worked in Rolling Mill II, but their effective employment was thwarted by increasing disruption because of bombing. The women were forcibly marched back to Buchenwald on March 17, 1945.[71]

By the time of the German collapse in May 1945, the Krupp company had become indelibly associated with the Nazi regime: as an iconic German firm; as a consequence of the deliberate Nazi strategy of drawing companies into its program of economic and military mobilization; and as a consequence also of the inevitable tensions produced by the transition from one generation to another within a family firm. As early as March 1945, Edouard Houdremont noted that relations between the Krupp managers in the Rheinhausen steel works, on the left bank of the Rhine, and Allied occupation authorities would be of crucial importance for the future of the whole company.[72]

Since October 1944, the Essen works had produced almost nothing, as the military front moved closer. But the U.S. Army reached Rheinhausen only on March 5,

1945, and the Villa Hügel only on April 11. Essen had been largely evacuated on the orders of Deputy Gauleiter (party district leader) Fritz Schlessmann. Alfried Krupp was arrested by American soldiers but quickly allowed to return to the villa under house arrest before he was taken away again on June 19. On April 27 the Krupp directorate was already presenting a plan for the reconstruction of the Essen works, and on June 25 asked for permission to restart fourteen branches of iron- and steelmaking. But by this time the military authority had passed from the U.S. to the British army, and although some production of specialty hard metal (Widia) and railway material was permitted, on September 8 the British definitively ordered all steelmaking activity to be closed down, and two days later all but one of the directors were arrested. The only exception, Fritz Müller, was in charge of the Krupp mines. On November 16, the British army formally took over the Gussstahlfabrik and the Friedrich-Alfred-Hütte, and E. L. Douglas Fowles began to function as "controller." On November 22, the Krupp coal mines were also sequestrated.

On November 30, the Friedrich-Alfred-Hütte in Rheinhausen and the locomotive works were given a "permit" to start up production. By December 1945 Fowles was arguing that the Krupp capacity in repairing equipment was desperately needed, and he also argued in favor of a resumption of activity at the Borbeck steel mill. But the Gussstahlfabrik was split into individual activities: the Widia hard metal products, the locomotive workshop, the trucks department, and so on. The Borbeck works were allocated to the Soviet Union, however, as war reparation. Dismantling started in February 1946, and some 75,000 tons of steelmaking equipment were shipped for reassembly as a Soviet factory. In June 1947 the Disarmament Department of the Allied Control Commission ordered the dismantling of twenty-three production halls in the Gussstahlfabrik. That order led to a substantial protest from the Essen population, but the final form of the order produced an even more radical form of dismantling. So as well as the estimated 45 percent of the factory that had been destroyed by bombing, another additional 30 percent was dismantled, and the empty buildings were destroyed.

By contrast with Essen, the Soviet occupation led to a quick resumption of production in Magdeburg, and until the spring of 1948 there were regular contacts between the Gruson works and the Essen directorate.

The trial of Gustav Krupp as one of the twenty-four defendants accused as major war criminals before the International Military Tribunal in Nuremberg turned into a fiasco. Gustav Krupp had clearly deteriorated mentally, but the British Foreign Office was hostile to the idea of substituting his son for him. That seemed too arbitrary, too close to the idea of inherited guilt and the totalitarian practice of arresting relatives in *Sippenhaft*. Justice Robert Jackson read out a powerful indictment: "Four generations of the Krupp family have owned and operated the great armament and munitions plants which have been the chief source of Germany's war supplies. For over 130 years this family has been the focus, the symbol, and the beneficiary of the most sinister forces engaged in menacing the peace of Europe. . . . It was at all times however a Krupp family enterprise." But the senile Krupp was not tried.

Instead, the company was the subject of one of the U.S. successor trials to the major war criminals trial. Case

10, which was heard from November 1947 to July 1948, involved Alfried Krupp and all the Krupp directors with the exception of Fritz Müller. There appears to have been many and in some instances multiple violations of standard judicial practice. Alfried Krupp and his lawyer complained repeatedly that he was deprived of the assistance of his American lawyer, Earl J. Carroll, and indeed of any legal advice until the beginning of the trial. Two-thirds of the witnesses were not heard by the whole court but by commissioners. The case appears to have been argued more on the level of the importance of Krupp as a symbol than on concrete actions. A great deal of the prosecution case focused on the assertion, implausible even at that time, that corporations such as Krupp had put Hitler in power. The peroration of the prosecutor, General Telford Taylor, was based on Gustav Krupp's words when he received a party "Golden Banner" award for the factory from Rudolf Hess in 1940: "These words accurately epitomize the defendants. Nothing need be added. The tradition of the Krupp firm, and the 'social-political' attitude for which it stood, was exactly suited to the moral climate of the Third Reich. There was no crime such a state could commit—whether it was war, plunder, or slavery—in which these men would not participate. Long before the Nazis came to power, Krupp was a 'National Socialist model plant.'"[73]

In the end, the Krupp directors were cleared of the charge of aggressive war but convicted for slave labor and for the plunder of occupied Europe. Alfried Krupp, whose involvement in business decisions was never clearly delineated at the trial, was sentenced to twelve years imprisonment and his entire fortune confiscated. He was sent to the military prison in Landsberg am Lech. Ewald Löser, who had left the Krupp directorate in 1943 and was the most obviously anti-Nazi of the Krupp directors, was sentenced to seven years. The Krupp company had undoubtedly been a large beneficiary of the armaments economy, and its treatment of slave workers was vile. But the idea that Krupp had been a driving force behind the high-level making of Nazi policy, rather than a participant in a massive web of ideologically driven immorality, was an absurd fantasy, derived from a preexisting view of the iconic and national character of the enterprise. Now that company was fragmented, its management convicted, and its owner expropriated.

SEVEN

REGLOBALIZATION

Alfried Krupp von Bohlen und Halbach and Berthold Beitz

The chronicler of Germany's postwar years in popular fiction and film was Will Tremper, a film script writer who achieved fame with a movie on the postwar German youth phenomenon (*Die Halbstarken*, 1956). In the early 1970s, Tremper wanted to make a thinly disguised film about the Krupps—one of many fictional or semifictional versions that periodically passed across German cinema and television screens. But the television channel Westdeutscher Rundfunk was not very enthusiastic about the prospect, and the actor Carl Raddatz, whom Tremper thought would have been ideal for his central figure, was not available. So Tremper wrote a roman à clef instead, which was published in 1973 under the title *Das Tall-Komplott*.

The book is an attempt to unmask the sinister influence of banks in the German economy. It deals with the fall of a highly charismatic top manager, Benjamin Bach, known as "BB," as a result of an intrigue carried out by bankers. In particular, a cynical and duplicitous old financier named Josef Maria Diergard swears to "destroy" Bach. Bach is the incarnation of the new and pushy dynamism of the Federal Republic, while Diergard is the representative of the corrupt practices of the old world that 1960s Germany was rapidly leaving behind. Bach thinks that he could

Figure 7.1 Berthold Beitz (*left*) and Alfried Krupp von Bohlen und Halbach (*right*), 1967. Courtesy of Historical Archives Krupp.

make his own foreign policy and concludes a big deal to supply four complete steel works to China, but is unable to agree with the banks to finance the deal. In order to get the financing package, he is obliged to negotiate with a bank that he has not dealt with previously, and which is a rival of his own house bank, and that bank has Diergard as the chairman of its supervisory board. The main hinge of the novel is the demand of the banks for a complete financial statement on the affairs of the private company: or what Tremper regularly calls "letting down the trousers."[1]

Josef Maria Diergard in fact bears a striking resemblance to Hermann Josef Abs, the chairman at the time of the Krupp crisis of 1967 of the Deutsche Bank supervisory board; while "BB" is unmistakably modeled after the Krupp manager Berthold Beitz, whom Tremper claimed to have met two dozen times, and who was best known to the public as the foremost exponent of an economic *Ostpolitik*.[2] The book is a sensationalized reflection on the struggle for control in German business between ambitious company managers and the powerful universal banks that in the immediate postwar era were turning themselves into the core of an interconnected and interdependent economy of relationships that was often characterized as "Deutschland AG."

A PROMISE AND AN IMAGE

Why were banks so uniquely powerful in the postwar German industrial recovery? And how was their influence eventually reduced? German business began the new era with very limited financial resources. Krupp was a particularly dramatic example. But the problems went well beyond the merely financial.

The Ruhr business elite was scandalized by the severity of the sentences the U.S. military tribunal imposed on Alfried Krupp and the Krupp directors in July 1948, and by the expropriation of Krupp. The decision had come just as Germany looked as if it was starting in a new and prosperous direction in the wake of the June 1948 currency reform. Some of Krupp's friends and associates started a campaign against the verdict. In particular, Krupp's lawyers Otto Kranzbühler and Klaus Hennig drew up a memorandum with the title "Drei Amerikaner richten Krupp" (Three Americans Condemn Krupp). Gustav Krupp von Bohlen und Halbach's brother-in-law, Tilo von Wilmowsky, persuaded Kranzbühler to expand it into a book. At the suggestion of the publisher, the memorandum was rewritten by the prominent former National Socialist constitutional lawyer Ernst Rudolf Huber. The title was changed first to "Krupp, Victim of a Myth" and then to "Why Was Krupp Condemned?" and the result was published under Wilmowsky's name. Wilmowsky, together with his wife, had been imprisoned by the Nazis after the July 1944 bomb plot against Hitler, and a work appearing under his name could not easily be accused of being National Socialist in sympathy. Indeed the book was, as intended, influential in Germany. Chancellor Konrad Adenauer, for instance, read it and came to the conclusion that Alfried Krupp had been wrongly convicted. Although it was never translated into English, it may have had some influence on Allied High Commissioner John McCloy.[3]

In January 1951 McCloy amnestied Alfried Krupp and the Krupp directors. Alfried Krupp, he explained, "was not the real Krupp . . . and exerted very little if any influence in the management of the company."[4] Also the confiscation of his property was revoked.

Figure 7.2 Release of Alfried Krupp von Bohlen und Halbach (*center*) from Landsberg prison, February 1951. Courtesy of Historical Archives Krupp.

Released from the Landsberg prison, Alfried Krupp returned to Essen and eventually in March 1953 returned to the company offices and the direction of the firm, though not to the Villa Hügel, which was transferred to the Krupp company in 1955. From a business perspective, he faced an almost insuperable challenge. Building the firm up again looked to be a question of taking the fish

230

soup of individual businesses created by the Allies in the course of economic deconcentration (*Entflechtung*) and turning it back into a German aquarium: a fundamentally impossible task, in which no one could ever really succeed.

Above all, the reconstruction of Krupp was not simply or primarily a problem of finding the appropriate business strategy. It involved the whole question of the appropriate political order of Germany and of Europe. In negotiating about deconcentration with the Combined Steel Group in Düsseldorf, it was not enough for Krupp to rely on the leading Krupp managers, in particular Friedrich Janssen and Finance Director Johannes Schröder, or on his Nuremberg attorneys, the German Otto Kranzbühler and the Americans Earl J. Carroll and Joseph S. Robinson. Krupp, and the Ruhr industrial sector in general, needed high-level political support. Relations with the German government were as essential for the survival of the firm as they had been in the mid-nineteenth century or during the interwar years.

The question of the future shape of the German steel and coal industry was at the heart of political debate in Germany, but also in other countries, and especially, in France. The Ruhr Statute of December 1948 was designed to ensure that the natural resources of the Ruhr would not used for aggression but in the interests of a new and peaceful order. Law 27 of the Allied High Commission, titled "Reorganization of the German Coal and Iron and Steel Industries" (May 16, 1950), which provided for deconcentration, started with a declaration that the commission's policy was to "decentralize the German economy for the purpose of eliminating excessive concentrations of economic power and preventing the development of a war potential." But the preamble also stated that "the question of the eventual ownership of the coal and iron and steel industries should be left to the determination of a representative, freely elected German government." France and its high commissioner, André François-Poncet, however, viewed Law 27 as a precondition of realizing the Schuman Plan, in which German and French heavy industry would be brought together. The French plans in turn led the SPD opposition in Germany to suggest that Adenauer and the German government were making too many concessions to the deconcentration proposals, and that their only aim was to weaken the German economy.[5] On October 19, 1951, the Allies had agreed to the abolition of foreign controls on the steel industry but required Law 27 to remain in effect, and on May 25, 1952, provided contractual agreements in which Germany acceded to the deconcentration and decartelization programs and in which a dispute resolution mechanism was created.

Particular conditions were applied to the businesses that had once constituted the Krupp enterprise. At the beginning of 1952, the Allied authorities began to demand that as a precondition for the return of the Krupp finishing works, Alfried Krupp should issue a statement renouncing any participation in steel production. Krupp was prepared to agree only because he worried that in the absence of a "statement" the Krupp enterprise would be completely broken up. According to the head of the Krupp Law Department, Hermann Maschke, the French representative said that the statement had "practically no meaning and no legal effect, but it should be formulated in a way so that the political elements in France are satisfied." The German government also formulated the view that such an agreement could not be legally binding.[6] Partially secured in this way, Alfried Krupp on July 22, 1952, signed the statement, a promise that "He will not through the use of the proceeds of the aforementioned sale of securities, acquire securities of any enterprise engaged directly or indirectly in the steel or iron producing industries in Germany or in the coal mining industry in Germany or otherwise acquire a controlling interest in any such enterprise of attain a dominant position therein." Was there a time limit to this commitment to sell the Krupp steel and coal holdings? And which authority would be in a position to enforce it? There inevitably followed a protracted struggle about the meaning of the "statement" and whether it might be modified.

This personal guarantee of Alfried Krupp's was highly controversial in Germany. Friedrich Flick liked to boast of the fact that unlike Krupp he had not given any kind of assurance.[7] The German government struggled desperately to avoid any commitment at all to guarantee the implementation of the program. Krupp secured a letter of Walter Hallstein, the influential state secretary in the Bonn Auswärtiges Amt, that the "binding limit of the statement ends with the end of Allied Law 27" on deconcentration. But when was that? There was repeated Allied discussion of the particulars of the Krupp case. On October 15, 1952, it formed the subject of a debate in the British parliament, and the leader of the British Liberal Party attacked the idea of compensation to "this family, whose activities were of such assistance to Hitler and all his evil associates." In 1953 the fiery young Labour Party politician Barbara Castle asked the foreign secretary, "Is the right hon. Gentleman aware that a new attempt is being made to infiltrate, by Nazi influence, into the free democratic party in Germany and that the former Nazi

233

officials who are trying to capture this party are backed by money from the Ruhr industries? In view of this great danger of a revival of Nazism in Germany, does the Foreign Secretary not agree that it is urgent to find a means of breaking down the concentration of economic power in the hands of former Ruhr industrialists?"[8] In these impropitious external circumstances, German authorities started to defend Krupp, and Ludger Westrick, the state secretary in the Economics Ministry, negotiated skillfully on Krupp's behalf. Westrick had been the head of Vereinigte Stahlwerke's Balkan Division until 1933, and the French negotiators rightly regarded him as actively promoting the cause of the German steel industrialists.[9] Westrick's major effort initially involved attempting to set a term limit for the applicability of Law 27, for instance five years, but the Allies rejected that proposal. In fact the deconcentration plan for Krupp was only officially abandoned in 1968, after Alfried Krupp's death. Even then, when the executor of Krupp's will, Berthold Beitz, argued that with the death of Alfried Krupp the sales obligation was irrelevant, he faced an immediate protest from the British embassy in Bonn, which explained that the Allied deconcentration plan "was not dependent on the owner of Fried. Krupp."[10]

The decisions on the Krupp case were of such far-ranging significance that Chancellor Adenauer was inevitably involved in the debate about Krupp's statement. François-Poncet was concerned that the influence of heavy industry on Adenauer was "growing every day."[11] Adenauer personally was in fact quite irritated by pushiness on the side of Krupp—and especially from the Krupp manager Berthold Beitz, who in his first meeting with the veteran chancellor in late 1956 had rather directly asked whether the Krupps were "second-class citizens" who did not deserve the freedom to practice their chosen occupation that was guaranteed by the German Basic Law.[12]

In the end, the Allied High Commission sent an assurance that the duration of the law would not be extended by prohibitive measures included in any individual deconcentration plan. Alfried Krupp was then prepared to sign a new declaration on February 22, 1953.[13] On March 4, 1953, he reached an agreement with Allied representatives (known as the Mehlem Agreement) on a deconcentration plan. At the same time, the property relations of the Krupp family were regulated by the transfer of cash or securities to his brothers Berthold and Harald and sisters Irmgard and Waldtraut, as well as to the son of Claus von Bohlen und Halbach (who had been killed in the war) and to his own son Arndt von Bohlen und Halbach.

Deconcentration could be viewed in a number of ways. Some American lawyers viewed it as essentially the application of the competition policy that had been applied very successfully in the so-called second New Deal in the later 1930s: trusts and oligopolies should be dismantled in order to create greater competition. Applied to Germany, such a doctrine meant the end of a specifically German way of doing business, in which cartel arrangements had been common. But who would buy the split-up businesses, at a moment when their business prospects were very uncertain? There was a major problem in that the capital market in Germany in the early 1950s was not developed or dynamic enough to provide easy financing for such sales. A second option, which had major implications for European security, was that some of the strategic German companies could be sold to France. Such an approach would be much more in accordance with the

235

European and transnational vision of the Schuman Plan. In 1947 and 1948, before the foundation of the Federal Republic, the banker Robert Pferdmenges, Adenauer's friend and business adviser, had actively promoted the idea that Ruhr coal holdings could be sold to French steel interests. In that way, the seventy-five-year conflict over the control of Europe's strategic coal and iron resources would come to an end, and this economic integration would bring political peace.

In the early 1950s, the balance between these contrasting views of deconcentration was changed by the introduction in 1951 of special codetermination rules for the coal and steel industry (*Montanmitbestimmung*). The solution offered by the 1951 law was intended to deal with another aspect of the historical problem of the power of the Ruhr barons: it was argued that if workers were represented on the supervisory boards to such an extent that they controlled half the seats, the political intrigues of the interwar years would be ruled out. But codetermination also influenced the course of the European-level negotiations. Tying workers' representatives, and the powerful trade unions, into the coal and steel industry meant that these interests would be more likely to support a national solution to deconcentration, and would not be sympathetic to increased French engagement. Codetermination appeared to be an essential feature of what would become known as "Deutschland AG." But in the light of the prevailing capital shortage, a sale to German interests really amounted to nothing more than a reshuffling of cards already in play in the German business deck. There were no German outsiders with the money to finance any expensive participation in heavy industry. A further argument put forward by the representatives of labor, and then taken up by the business negotiators, consisted in the way in which the German companies had heavy responsibilities to workers and former workers in the form of pension commitments; worker representatives worried about the threat to company pensions in the event of a sale of the business. Berthold von Bohlen und Halbach noted in 1951 that Krupp had a total workforce of 14,000, of which 2,200 were working in the administration of social programs, and 16,000 pensioners (by contrast, in January 1939, there had been 60,000 employees and 9,850 pensioners and widows).[14] The pension incomes of a large number of elderly people thus depended on the continued existence of an enterprise that was heavily burdened by social commitments. In a curious way, in consequence, trade unions and the major opposition party in parliament, the SPD, thus were tied into supporting German business interests.

The parts of the Krupp enterprise not subject to deconcentration, including the plant making locomotives, the truck-making plant, and the AG Weser shipyard, were quite quickly freed from Allied control. The collieries that had been at the center of the iron and steel complex were spun off into five separate companies. The Friedrich-Alfred-Hütte was transferred to a company established in 1947, the Hüttenwerk Rheinhausen AG. The share capital of Rheinhausen (DM 65 million) was to be held by administrative trustees until the company was sold through a banking consortium.

Some of the separated enterprises were sold off, in accordance with the commitment Krupp had undertaken: the Emscher-Lippe Bergbau AG to the state-owned Hibernia, the Krupp share of Harz-Lahn-Erzbergbau AG to Klöckner, Mannesmann, and the Westfalenhütte; but there was no compulsion on Krupp to sell immediately at what would have been fire-sale prices. And some of the pieces were sold to other Krupp companies, so that for instance the coal mine Constantin der Grosse was sold via the Bochumer Verein to the Hütten- und Bergwerke Rheinhausen AG. The Constantin negotiations are a neat example of the Krupp negotiating strategy, and the anxieties it provoked in Germany's neighbors. The French group SIDECHAR, which had been built around the historical Lorraine steel family de Wendel, started to negotiate for a controlling stake, which would have given the Lorraine steel industry access to one of the most productive Ruhr coal pits. But in May 1953, an Italian group appeared that outbid the French, and the negotiations with SIDECHAR collapsed, allowing Germans to step in and buy the mine.[15]

The saga of the Krupp sale of the Constantin mine indirectly to another Krupp company runs in an opposite direction to that of Friedrich Flick's long negotiations in which he eventually sold a majority stake of the Harpener Bergbau to SIDECHAR. Transport Minister Hans-Christoph Seebohm was worried about the alienation of German mines, and contemplated a purchase by the state-owned railway system Deutsche Bundesbahn; and Adenauer also spoke in this case about national political interests. The chairman of the general German trade union association, Walter Freitag, called the sale of German mines to French companies "national treason."[16] The extent of the hostility of the official German response to the Flick transaction, and the considerable public sympathy that flowed in response to Krupp's way of handling the business, indicate in a remarkable way the extent to which political sentiment had shifted in the direction of a national response rather than of the internationalized solution of the Ruhr problem.

Just after the Allied decartelization plan came into existence, on March 12, 1953, Alfried Krupp formally returned to the head of an enterprise that consisted of the machine-building workshops, the hard metal production of Widia, locomotive and truck plants, the "Konsumanstalt" as well as Stahlbau Rheinhausen, and a majority stake in the Schiffswerft AG Weser (the former Deschimag complex acquired in 1941). The company became a centrally directed enterprise with twenty-one main operations and ninety-five departments: but this was clearly a reduced and scaled-down version of the old firm.

REMAKING KRUPP

How could an enterprise be rebuilt? Friedrich Janssen, one of the wartime Krupp directors who had been tried at Nuremberg, was appointed as a general plenipotentiary. But it is clear that Alfried Krupp did not entirely trust the existing Krupp directors, and wanted a fresh approach to management. The old traditions had reached a dead end. Houdremont was kept entirely out of the new business. Alfried Krupp decided on a relatively young man, a complete outsider to the Ruhr, whom he had met in the house of the sculptor Jean Sprenger: this was Berthold Beitz, the general director of the Iduna-Germania Insurance Company in Hamburg, who in November 1953 was appointed alongside Janssen as a further general plenipotentiary. Beitz had been born in 1913, in relatively humble circumstances in Pomerania, and had been through an apprenticeship at a bank. In the Second World War, he had a spectacular and genuinely heroic career.

As the young and enterprising commercial director of the Karpathen-Öl AG in Boryslaw, Beitz had saved substantial numbers of Jewish workers, as well as dependent women and children, from being deported to annihilation. His energy and organizational talent in managing the food supply of a large enterprise (which employed and fed some 80 percent of the population of Boryslaw) had meant a stable supply of petroleum for Germany; and with that, Beitz gained sufficient influence with the SS and the military to be able to protect his workforce for a substantial period of time, though many of the Boryslaw workers were eventually deported as the German armies retreated. The historians Thomas Sandkühler and Joachim Käpper calculate that Beitz saved several hundred Jews.[17] After the war, Beitz moved to Hamburg and worked briefly in the supervision office for insurance in the British zone. From 1953, he dedicated his life to the Krupp business. And after Janssen's death in 1956, he remained as the sole plenipotentiary.

Beitz later explained the nature of Alfried Krupp's attraction: he "wanted to have a man who was not related and married into the Ruhr industry, but was one hundred percent his man."[18] Krupp was highly possessive and suspicious of Beitz's relations with anyone else; he viewed in particular Beitz's close personal friendship with the entrepreneur Max Grundig as a potential difficulty, although Grundig never took any interest in Krupp business. Beitz also seemed iconoclastic, and to be bringing a wave of fresh northern air to the stuffy Ruhr. He liked to say how before the war, in the old Ruhr, it would have been impossible for someone with his modest background to become the leading manager. People referred to him as "der Amerikaner," and he in turn thought that the weight of tradition had been a "sleeping pill" for the company. What was needed was emancipation. Beitz later complained about Alfried's pronounced proclivity to accept authority, and Golo Mann duly reproduced this view in his failed attempt at a biography. The journalist Rudolf Augstein, an acquaintance of Beitz's from Hamburg times and a neighbor on the summer resort island of Sylt, later recalled that he had visited Alfried Krupp in Kampen on the island of Sylt and found him on a side street with a piece of paper in his hand. When asked what he was doing, Krupp replied that he was counting the different types of cars that passed. Augstein then asked whether he had time for such an activity, and Krupp replied: "I have the time, but that isn't so important. What is important is that there is someone who sees that the really important things are done."[19]

At the same time as Krupp and Beitz tried to break with tradition, they also set about reconstructing the old Krupp enterprise, justifying it by reference to the preservation of jobs as well as "the old Krupp tradition of technical and economic progress" that they hoped would come back "after the lifting of controls."[20] This view reflected the strong compact with labor in which the unions helped to fight off the threats of foreign control and foreign ownership. It rested on an image of a shared tradition that created common commitments and loyalties. Alfried Krupp apparently once told Beitz, when Beitz was suggesting stopping the building of locomotives: "My great grandfather built locomotive parts; we will continue to build locomotives. Profit is important, but one cannot separate it from other social obligations." Beitz later commented that "Kruppianer could not simply be sold."[21] Old-style patriarchalism came back as a business strategy.

That was not enough. The firm reinvented itself as an image before it really became a firm again. The company needed public relations, and for that it turned to the director of the Krupp Widia plant. Carl Hundhausen had worked briefly for Krupp in the 1920s before going to the United States and writing about his experience of U.S. commercial culture (which in the Nazi period he had attacked using Nazi racial terminology). In the new postwar environment, he wrote an influential book that set out new strategies for postwar German business: *Werben um öffentliches Vertrauen* (*Winning the Public Trust*—the book was also issued in English). He was soon rehired by Krupp to produce a positive image. Hundhausen's major argument was that German society had been atomized by modernity, and then by the shock of the Nazi dictatorship and the war. Corporations could offer a new pole of loyalty and focus. Hundhausen explained that the company had a "permanent life." "Through the continual assumption of new forces, which are assimilated in the spirit of the enterprise, the company can acquire those powers, capabilities and talents that it needs to develop independently and productively in particular areas such as production, research, accounting, human resources, and the top leadership." He liked to use a phrase of the U.S. philosopher of management Edward L. Bernays on the "engineering of consent." The leadership of a firm would have to balance all the continual conflicts produced by individuals seeking power and seeking to subordinate others.[22]

More generally, a new image of business was required. Together with other Ruhr businesses, the Krupp management was very active in hiring a prominent American journalist, Louis Lochner from Associated Press, whose Berlin office he had headed in the 1930s. Lochner would write a book published in both the United States and Germany in 1954 as *Tycoons and Tyrant: German Industry from Hitler to Adenauer*. Hundhausen wrote to Beitz to explain that "there is no better advocate for Krupp than Lochner."[23]

Krupp publicists also tried to recast the image of Krupp in a modern way. There were spectacular PR actions, such as the provision of a diving sphere for the charismatic marine explorer Auguste Piccard in 1960, which Beitz saw enthusiastically as "sensational, merciless salesmanship."[24] The Villa Hügel was opened up for exhibitions and concerts, as well as for formal and commemorative company events. There were 400,000 visitors to the first exhibition, on church art, in 1953. A fashion show of Christian Dior introduced a new concept of modernity and elegance in dress. An industrial film of 1961, *Technik: Drei Studien in Jazz*, used modern music to establish "a new relationship between images and music" in three movements taken from the story of steel production: casting, forging, and mechanics.[25]

A new image by itself would not accomplish the task of remaking the enterprise. The firm needed to be recast. Beitz in 1955 declared to the news magazine *Der Spiegel*: "If Alfried Krupp does not say it, because he has signed a document, I can according to my conscience say it: the obligation to sell has to go, because the Krupp enterprises belong together, just as on a farm there are good and bad fields."[26] It was a somewhat peculiar metaphor, which underlined the oddity of the Krupp association with a large variety of engineering products. Krupp directors were placed on the supervisory boards of the enterprises that were supposed to be sold, on the grounds, as a Federal Economics Ministry official put it in a letter to Beitz, that "it can only ease negotiations if the management of the companies that are to be sold are supervised by persons who have the confidence of the owner."[27] In 1957 the headquarters of the Rheinhausen steel company were moved to Essen.

Shadows of the past could tarnish the optimistic new vision of the corporation. In the Wollheim settlement of 1957, IG Farben paid DM 30 million as compensation for forced labor, and the German industrial federation BDI started a general discussion of the corporate responsibility of companies to the victims of National Socialism. Krupp was opposed to such an initiative, but needed to respond to a letter of June 1958 in which the former high commissioner John McCloy asked Krupp to consider compensation out of a "concern to help Germany and to ensure that German industry could keep its good name in the world." McCloy asked whether the Krupp company might act in order to what was "right and just in making good the depredations of the Nazi regime."[28] In response the Krupp Legal Department started to work on a plan, and in 1959, after negotiations with Nahum Goldman and Jacob Blaustein of the Jewish Claims conference, Berthold Beitz reached an agreement to pay DM 10 million, or DM 5,000 for each worker. The 1959 agreement, which was the first such agreement by a German industrial company, was specifically oriented to Jewish slave labor. It was only after the end of communism in the early 1990s that the question of compensation for other slave and forced laborers, the group described by Stuart Eizenstat as the "double victims" of Nazism and communism, was raised. In 1998/99 the Fried. Krupp AG Hoesch-Krupp was one of twelve founding firms that established a Foundation Initiative of German Business (Stiftungsinitiative der deutschen Wirtschaft) to provide a total of DM 10,000 million for the compensation of slave and forced workers.

In January 1958, Krupp submitted an application to the Economics Ministry asking for an extension of the sale requirement, and in April the German government submitted the request to the Allies. That request was dealt with according to the mechanism established under Article 5 of the Convention of May 25, 1952. In October 1959 a Mixed Committee under the chairmanship of a Swiss banker and with three German and three Allied members granted that permission; the committee then proceeded to grant annual renewals in a rather automatic way every year. The last such renewal was granted in July 1967, shortly before the death of Alfried Krupp. In the meantime, Krupp had become a very large company again: in 1958, it was indeed briefly the largest German firm as measured by turnover. Such a development raised anxieties in other European countries. Especially in Britain, in consequence, the extensions of the sale requirement were hugely controversial. The Labour Party politician Denis Healey asked in 1960 about the "extraordinary and unconscionable delay" in selling off the steel and coal holdings of Krupp. Only in 1968, following the transformation of ownership after the death of Alfried Krupp and an economic crisis that made Krupp seem much less of a threat, was the Labour foreign secretary Michael Stewart prepared to say: "I think that this is the right and proper outcome."[29]

From the point of view of the company's self-image as a business that still had steelmaking at its core, it was crucial to expand steel production again. Beitz liked to put the point rather crudely, saying that a company without a steel basis was like a woman without the lower part of her body. In 1959 the Hütten- und Bergwerke Rheinhausen AG secured permission from the European

245

Coal and Steel Community to buy Krupp's old competitor from the nineteenth century, the Bochumer Verein.[30] In 1964 Rheinhausen bought a 50 percent stake in the Westfälische Drahtindustrie, and in 1965 Rheinhausen took back the historic name when it was renamed the Fried. Krupp Hüttenwerke AG. Krupp had reverted to tradition.

The problem was that steelmaking technology was changing very rapidly in the 1950s and 1960s, with the first major technological shifts since the mid-nineteenth-century innovations of the Bessemer, Siemens-Martin, and Gilchrist-Thomas processes. Oxygen steelmaking was developed in Austria, then taken up on a big scale in the United States and elsewhere. By 1971, only 7 percent of German steel was produced by the Thomas process and 21 percent by Siemens-Martin; all the rest, 72 percent, was oxygen steel. Much more capital was required for this process than could easily be raised by a family firm. The German company that reacted most effectively to the challenges of the new environment was Thyssen, under the dynamic leadership of Hans-Günther Sohl. Sohl proposed European mergers, arguing for instance that a combination of Thyssen and the French group de Wendel would be able to compete effectively with the American giant U.S. Steel. In Germany, Sohl also openly discussed the idea of a merger between Thyssen and Krupp. But Krupp and Thyssen had quite different emphases, which corresponded to their moments of birth: Krupp remained true to the philosophy of a craft producer of the early nineteenth century, making a wide range of products, though on an ever larger scale; Thyssen had developed at the end of the nineteenth century and surged as a mass-producer of steel goods. In the 1960s, the vision of a business focused on flat-rolled steel production, conducted on a European scale, was the driving one for Thyssen.

Krupp had never simply been a mass-production steelmaker but had specialized in particular uses of steel. In line with the back-to-tradition philosophy, the Krupp company also looked for substitutes for the businesses that had been stripped away. If a satisfactory aquarium could not be made by putting all the old fish back together again, it would simply be necessary to buy some new fish. The Maschinenbau Kiel (MaK) company in Kiel made ship engines, just as the Germaniawerft had done, as well as other transportation equipment; and Ardelt in Wilhelmshaven was bought as a substitute for the crane manufacturing plant in the Magdeburg Gruson Werk.[31]

The Krupp company was, in short, consistently held together by an idea of what it had been in the past. Berthold Beitz, at the celebrations in 1961 of the 150th anniversary of the founding, stated: "The performance of yesterday has its place in history. The performance of yesterday is also the basis for the performance of tomorrow. If we achieve it collectively, then we will best keep the tradition of the Firma Krupp."[32]

The historian Lothar Gall describes the remnants of the Gussstahlfabrik as an "odds-and-ends store with centrifugal tendencies."[33] It was more of a conglomerate than a *Konzern*, but it remained centrally organized and controlled: in this respect too it represented a major contrast with Thyssen, which kept the commitment already developed before the First World War to a multidivision structure. In this way, different and conflicting corporate cultures in Germany's major steel companies survived the political and economic turmoils of wars, revolutions, dictatorships, inflations, and depressions.

GLOBAL ORIENTATION

The Krupp tradition of looking to export markets was equally durable. Krupp saw at an early stage that a German engineering firm could be a powerful supplier to countries embarking on their own industrialization. In March 1952, the French high commissioner André François-Poncet complained that the Krupp company was planning in the long term to conquer the Latin American market.[34] In 1954 Alfried Krupp announced: "We must export, in order to create employment at our plants, in order to be able to import raw materials and foodstuffs."[35] In 1961 Beitz stated that "the whole globe is the market of tomorrow."[36]

When Krupp participated for the first time in a trade fair after the Second World War, in 1954, it was in Mexico. Emperor Haile Selassie of Ethiopia visited Essen in 1954. Alfried Krupp undertook an exceptionally energetic travel program; so too did Berthold Beitz. Krupp's travels as well as his hospitality at the Villa Hügel looked like an iron devotion to duty, and a return to his great-grandfather's tradition of cultivating foreign clients. For Beitz, there always seemed to be a political element in the search for new business areas. Long before the chief economist of Goldman Sachs, Jim O'Neill, invented the sobriquet BRICs in 2002 to describe large and dynamic emerging-market economies (Brazil, Russia, India, China), Beitz had decided to concentrate on the very large countries that were underdeveloped and had markets that were difficult to sell in as a consequence of the tariffs and import regime that followed from the adoption of a strategy of industrialization through import substitution. In part, the powerful impetus to build plants in what were then called underdeveloped countries lay in the policies of trade protection.

The first Latin American country to adopt such an explicit import-substitution strategy had been Brazil in the 1930s, under the leadership of President Getulio Vargas. Along with the Soviet industrialization of the same era, Brazil provided a powerful inspiration to many developing countries. The Krupp Grusonwerk in 1938 had supplied a complete oil factory. In 1952, as a demonstration of what it could do, Krupp sent a large locomotive to Brazil, the largest built in postwar Germany, and then set about building up a Brazilian producer. In 1954 Krupp founded the Industria Nacional de Locomotivas (or JNL) Ltd. After disputes about locomotive and truck production, it shifted its emphasis to the provision of automobile parts from a new factory built on the site of a former coffee warehouse in Campo Limpo. The drop-forge plant Krupp Metalúrgica Campo Limpo S.A. started production in 1961 and established itself as one of Krupp's most successful international ventures. Krupp also sent other products required for industrialization to Brazil: docking equipment, a cement factory, a paper and cellulose factory.

India's industrialization strategy under Prime Minister Nehru in the 1950s was more firmly oriented toward the Soviet model: India embarked on a series of Seven Year Plans. As in the Soviet experience, steel was at the center, and India became something of a Cold War test case with rival teams of Soviet and Western experts engaged in building up their type of steel plant. Already in 1953 India concluded an agreement with Krupp and the Duisburg firm DEMAG to advise the Hindustan Steel Limited company in building a mixed steelworks, and in 1955 the German companies won a contract to build a

Figure 7.3 Inauguration of the Rourkela steelworks, India, January 1960. Courtesy of Historical Archives Krupp.

vast modern steelworks that used the advanced oxygen-steel process in Rourkela. The new steel works began production in 1959 but suffered from multiple problems. In 1961, it was only producing at less than one-third of capacity. By the middle 1960s its performance was being judged more positively.

In 1954 the Krupp directorate discussed the possibility of building up industrial relations with Eastern Europe and the Soviet Union, and sent a small delegation to visit Moscow, Minsk, and Riga. Initially the German government was skeptical, and Adenauer worried that Moscow would use commercial interests to undermine his anti-communist Cold War policy. In 1957 Beitz agreed to a contract for the construction of a synthetic fibers plant in the Soviet Union.

Beitz took up the Krupp tradition of diplomacy and *Ostpolitik* that had already been practiced in the Weimar Republic by Otto Wiedfeldt. He had a special advantage in dealing with Poland because of his heroic wartime record, and when he visited Warsaw in 1958, he was received with great enthusiasm. Prime Minister Józef Cyrankiewicz explained that Beitz was "an excellent ambassador of Germany, a friend of Poland who has proved himself for twenty years."[37] For some Germans, however, his enthusiastic welcome in the Eastern bloc raised suspicions. Immediately after Beitz came back from Warsaw and Moscow, Chancellor Adenauer went so far as to say that "one may doubt the national reliability of Herr Beitz."[38] But within two years, Adenauer was prepared to use Beitz as an informal contact with Warsaw, and in January 1961 he asked Beitz to make soundings about whether Poland might resume diplomatic relations with the Federal Republic.[39] It was not just a question of dealing with Poland and the

Soviet Union. Beitz undertook commercial and political visits that were disguised as hunting trips with Hungary's Janos Kádár; he also started to take up contacts with Yugoslavia. But Krupp's relationship with the German government was never free of strains as a result of Beitz appearing to be a parallel ambassador carrying out a rather different type of foreign policy than officially articulated in Bonn. Adenauer in particular was greatly irritated when the Krupp consultant and former director Carl Hundhausen met the East German party boss Walter Ulbricht at the Leipzig spring trade fair in 1960.

When Beitz visited the Soviet Union again in May 1963 and was received by Khrushchev, he spoke explicitly of how more members of the German government were in favor of increased commercial contacts with Eastern European countries. Khrushchev expressed an interest in improved relations, and suggested specifically an ending of the German embargo on pipeline components. *Der Spiegel* started its report with a Lenin quote: "The steppe must become a bread factory and Krupp must help us."[40] Khrushchev saw the Krupp initiative as the beginning of a long-term new orientation of Soviet development strategy, in which the Soviet Union would leverage its raw materials in order to obtain access to high technology. But he was also extraordinarily explicit about his vision of a long-term future based on German-Soviet collaboration, which he presented as a continuation of the strategy of the Rapallo meeting of 1920, when it looked as if Germany and the Soviet Union were forming an economic alliance against the Western powers. The Rapallo Treaty, Khrushchev explained, had been made on "the basis of the strong economic interests of the two countries, and it was a full success." Even more extraordinarily, he said that he would like to see the dissolution of both the NATO alliance and the Warsaw Pact.[41] Such an ambitious program seemed beyond the bounds of the politically possible, and Beitz was hesitant in his responses. But the strategy of using business contacts to build a new politics was at the core of the subsequent decades of German foreign policy. At a political level, this trade opening provided a substantial underpinning to the *Ostpolitik* pursued by Willy Brandt after 1966.

There was a brief but short-lived increase in Krupp exports to China in 1961; the rapid opening up of the Chinese market only occurred later. Beitz headed a delegation of German economic experts, which included Alfred Herrhausen of Deutsche Bank, sent to China in 1973, and met Chou En Lai. As in the case of Russia, there is little doubt that the resonance of the Krupp name was an attraction, and the Chinese asked whether it was still possible to buy the famous nineteenth-century 8.8 cm Krupp cannon. Beitz came back promising a new era in economic relations with China, and explained: "The Chinese expect good technology, prompt deliveries and also support in technical-economic cooperation. We hope for good business from the Chinese. That's what we live from." He also said that he was impressed by the "relaxed attitude, the peace and the security with which the Chinese consider their problems."[42] In 1976 the company secured an order to supply a chemical plant in Tientsin, which was complete in 1981. The immediate aftermath of the 1973 trip produced little, but it placed Krupp in an advantageous position when the reform process of the Chinese economy began under Deng Xiaoping after 1979. In 1984 Krupp agreed to a contract to build a rolling mill for copper wire; in 1985 there was a contract

Figure 7.4 Berthold Beitz meets Prime Minister Chou En Lai in Beijing, May 1973 (Sven Simon photo). Courtesy of Historical Archives Krupp.

to build a magnesite sintering plant; in 1987 a plant for specialty steels was ordered. In 1988 Widia constructed a hard metal plant for the Tianjin Carbide Tool Company; and there was a joint-venture agreement between Krupp Koppers (Koppers was a major producer of cookery equipment that had been established in 1901 and taken over by Krupp in 1974) and the China Anshan Coking and Refractory Engineering Consulting Corporation to build a plant for producing coking coal.

Such foreign engagements could not have occurred without a substantial relationship with German politics and policy making, and Beitz sought contacts with both of the major political parties: with Willy Brandt and Johannes Rau in the SPD, but also with the new generation of Christian Democrat politicians. In 1965 a new political leverage arose when Beitz appointed a promising and dynamic thirty-six-year old CDU Bundestag deputy, Gerhard Stoltenberg, as director, even though Stoltenberg had not studied law or economics but rather history and philosophy. But Stoltenberg soon went back to politics as minister-president of Schleswig-Holstein.

FINANCIAL CRISIS

Beitz's energetic foreign diplomacy and the search for foreign markets were reflected in the character of the company's financing in the 1960s. The capital basis on which the postwar recovery was built was very thin. Krupp depended for a great part of its activities on financing from the Ausfuhr-Kredit-Gesellschaft mbH (AKA), a Frankfurt firm that was owned by German banks in order to provide trade credit.

Internally, Krupp finance director Johannes Schröder had warned with increasing insistence about the dangers of the company's high level of debt, although there were conflicts about other issues: Schröder had worried after the construction of the Berlin Wall in August 1961 about the vulnerability of the Federal Republic, and at his own initiative and without consulting Beitz or Alfried Krupp had placed substantial sums of Krupp money as an emergency reserve in Switzerland. Beitz was quick to suspect personal corruption, the more so as Schröder demanded that special payments be made to his secretary. Such conflicts eventually led to Schröder's dismissal, and he seemed to be taking his revenge when he published an explosive article in the business newspaper *Handelsblatt* on July 27/28, 1962. The title was "The Financial Heart Attack," and the message was very explicit: "The danger of such a heart attack is particularly evident in companies that do not publish their accounts. They are not controlled by a doctor (in this case by the public). Thus they cannot be warned in time." At the end of the article, he concluded that "since the economic development of Germany had already passed its high point, many firms will surely have to ask whether they are living within their financial means or whether they also run the danger of a financial heart attack."[43]

In 1963 Beitz asked his auditors for the first time to prepare a consolidated balance sheet of the whole *Konzern*. But in November 1963 British newspapers sparked a new round of jitters about Krupp's financial status when they reported on the company's liquidity problems. The Krupp managers immediately suspected that the old hostility to the name of Krupp and its connotations of arms and aggression was flaring up again. But the financial nervousness was by no means confined to Krupp: many of the best-known names in German industry were vulnerable. The family business model that had been at the heart of much of German postwar reconstruction was at risk because it was undercapitalized. Stinnes declared near bankruptcy in 1963. Alfred Haniel wrote to the board of the Franz Haniel holding company to say that "these events are just a further link in a long chain of failures of precisely such first-class and well-known firms which bear the label of family firm. Some examples are Borsig, Henschel, Heyl von Herrnsheim, Maffei, Borgward, Schlieker. . . . It is certain only that economic downturns will do great damage, now as earlier."[44] After 1965 Krupp was hit by Germany's real postwar recession. In 1966 Alfried Krupp began to speak of the necessity of "a new style of business planning."[45] In particular, the coal mine holdings were rationalized, and Krupp's coal output fell by 40 percent from 1964 to 1966.

Some 270 creditor banks were increasingly worried about the position of Krupp. In December 1966, the AKA refused a Krupp demand for new credit for a contract to supply Poland, since Krupp already had DM 360 million in credit and did not have a 30 percent collateral in capital assets to cover its debt.

Beitz then embarked on frantic negotiations with the new federal economics minister of the Great Coalition government, Karl Schiller, and the bankers, in particular the commanding figure of Hermann Josef Abs of Deutsche Bank, with whom Beitz had what he would later describe as a love-hate relationship. Beitz liked to repeat the warnings about the pernicious and antientrepreneurial bank influence that had been a traditional part of the business culture of the Ruhr. On March 7, 1967, a rescue package was announced, with a federal government guarantee of DM 300 million and an additional DM 150 million guarantee from the state of Nordrhein-Westfalen. The federal and state governments' financial backstop allowed the banks to provide a new export credit of DM 100 million, and to promise to maintain their existing credit lines until the end of 1968. But the outcome initially looked like a defeat for Beitz's philosophy. He felt acutely humiliated by the way in which the package was announced by Abs, Economics Minister Schiller, and Finance Minister Franz Josef Strauss while he had to stand off to one side.[46]

But was it a real crisis? The state guarantees were never used. Hermann Josef Abs later suggested that the problems lay with the nervousness of the banks, which "had lost control of the situation," and that in reality "there

Figure 7.5 Berthold Beitz (*farthest right*) versus the banker and the politicians (*left to right*): Hermann Josef Abs, Karl Schiller, and Franz Josef Strauss, 1967. Courtesy of Historical Archives Krupp.

was no Krupp crisis."[47] Beitz always reminded critics that the East European business ventures had been profitable and that the credit of East European governments was impeccable: communist countries became the world's most reliable debtors (until they were hit by the massive debt crisis of the early 1980s). But in a letter to Beitz in 1968, Abs referred much more to problems that were specific to Krupp: "The particular structure of a single firm [Krupp], which you have represented for so long, also carried the disadvantage of the management's limited responsibility. In the difficult years that lie behind us, that surely did not lead to the recruiting into top positions of the strongest personalities, who would have been needed in tackling the problems. That resulted in the owner, who did not participate in the daily management of the company, bearing responsibilities that he really could not carry."[48]

The government and bank assistance came at a price: Krupp needed to have the more effective corporate governance that would follow from the institution of a proper board of directors (*Verwaltungsrat*) and the transformation into a more regular form of German company, either a joint-stock company (*Aktiengesellschaft*) or a limited liability company (*GmbH*). The influence of the owners would be reduced. Beitz feared that the bankers would take control and turn Krupp into simply a run-of-the-mill joint-stock corporation. The American newsmagazine *Time* commented that the bankers "in effect ordained the end of the house of Krupp."[49] A new chief executive, Günter Vogelsang, was appointed, and a new era of managerial capitalism began. Some assets were sold off: the Munich graphite works Kropfmühl (Graphitwerk Kropfmühl AG) as well as a hotel and a department store; and in January 1968 Vogelsang stopped the loss-making production of trucks and sold the distribution network to Daimler-Benz. The company became a limited liability company, GmbH, instead of a private company.

Vogelsang was a veteran of Krupp, who had worked as the head of the Audit and Organization Department (1954–58) and then as a member of the executive board of the Bochumer Verein für Gussstahlfabrikation from 1958 to 1960 before going as finance director to Mannesmann. His second stay in Krupp did not last very long. There were conflicts over whether to build a high-temperature thorium reactor for a nuclear power plant (Vogelsang was skeptical); over Beitz's demands for an increased payout to the new Alfried Krupp von Bohlen und Halbach Foundation; and in general over the degree to which the management could take decisions autonomously of the owners. In 1972 Vogelsang declined a renewal of his contract. Beitz initially tried to engage the charismatic young star of the Deutsche Bank Alfred Herrhausen, who had grown up in Essen and felt powerfully attracted to the Krupp tradition; but Deutsche Bank refused to let him go. Instead an "internal" candidate, Jürgen Krackow, who came from the AG Weser, was appointed, but only lasted six weeks; and his successor, Ernst Wolf Mommsen, was only an interim solution because of his age (sixty-two).

The traditions of Krupp were coming to an end. In 1974 the Konsumanstalt, which had been one of the pioneering monuments of nineteenth-century corporate paternalism, was sold to the supermarket chain Coop. With that move, there was no longer a company shop. In 1976 the rather gloomy headquarters erected in 1911 on the Altendorferstrasse in Essen were demolished.

THE FOUNDATION

Beitz, who had looked so marginalized in the bank crisis of 1967, came back into the business—via the Alfried Krupp von Bohlen und Halbach Foundation. The financial crunch came at the same time as plans matured to transform the family firm, subject to the vagaries of human mortality and the chance of succession, into a foundation. As far back as 1952, Tilo von Wilmowsky had proposed a family foundation as a way of managing the industrial holding. The plan of transforming the company into a foundation had already been actively discussed in the early 1960s. Meanwhile, Alfried Krupp became an increasingly isolated and remote figure in his new house not far from the Hügel, in the Berenberger Mark. His two marriages had ended in failure and loneliness. The first, in 1937, to the divorced Annelise Bahr, had been bitterly opposed by his parents Gustav and Bertha Krupp von Bohlen und Halbach, and collapsed in 1941, three years after the birth of Arndt, and the mother was left to bring up the child in unpropitious circumstances. The second marriage, in 1952, to thrice-divorced Vera Hossenfeldt, also ended after five years. To his brothers and sisters and their children, he exuded glaciality. Diana Maria Friz, the granddaughter of Gustav and Bertha Krupp and the daughter of Waldtraut von Bohlen und Halbach, complained of "a lack of heartiness, of attention or of interest," while she thought that the house emanated "a feeling of coldness, distance and rebuffal."[50]

Krupp had also been distant from his only son, Arndt, who had been largely brought up by his mother and in boarding schools in Bavaria and Switzerland. Like Alfred Krupp in the nineteenth century, Alfried Krupp had doubts about the capacity of his son as the future heir of the company. Arndt at first seemed shy and remote. But then he began to cultivate an ostentatious and hedonistic life as a homosexual playboy, and made it clear that he did not like or want the restraints imposed by the Krupp tradition. He explained: "I am not a man like my father, who sacrifices his whole life for something, not knowing whether it is really worth it in our time." Krupp traditions, he said, had "brought my forebears a lot of unhappiness."[51] Alternative solutions such as transferring the company to one of Alfried's brothers would have raised tax problems in that legacies between brothers were treated very differently in Germany than legacies to children. Such reflections had indeed even begun during the war, when Gustav Krupp had written to Hans Lammers, the head of Hitler's Reich Chancellery, to ask permission to establish a mechanism under which a single inheritor of the company could be designated in the eventuality of Alfried's premature death. Arndt at this time was six years old, but the family was already looking for a means to avoid any strict interpretation of primogeniture.[52]

Only in the 1960s was the issue resolved. Alfried Krupp was determined to convert the company into a public company controlled through a foundation. In the course of an emotional evening of September 16/17, 1966, Beitz negotiated an agreement by which Arndt would receive an annual income of DM 2 million, with some participation also in revenues flowing from Krupp coal mines, in return for the renunciation of his inheritance. He could devote himself to leisure in Marrakech and in the estate that he had bought with his mother in Brazil at Campina do Monte Alegre.[53] Later Arndt regarded his renunciation of the inheritance as an act whereby he paid off his debts to Germany and the family past.[54] He seemed to have broken with every Krupp tradition. He died in 1986, a convert to Roman Catholicism who had been received into the church by the Cardinal Archbishop of Manila.

The renunciation by Arndt von Bohlen und Halbach made possible a corporate transformation. Alfried Krupp then drew up a will in which he left his property to a foundation, the Alfried Krupp von Bohlen und Halbach-Stiftung. The foundation was intended to secure the "unity" of the company: in accordance with the principles that had prevailed ever since the 1840s, it should not be broken up to meet the possible financial requirements of family members. It would devote its income to the general good, in the form of charitable support. With its funds it supports projects in Germany but also internationally in five areas: science in research and teaching;

Figure 7.6 Arndt von Bohlen und Halbach, pen in hand, and Berthold Beitz at the signing for the transformation of the firm, December 31, 1967. Courtesy of Historical Archives Krupp.

education and training; health services; sports and literature; music and art.

The *Stiftung* continued such traditional Krupp social engagements as the provision of a state-of-the-art hospital for the city of Essen (Alfried Krupp Krankenhaus) but also worked in education, giving prizes for talented university teachers and endowing professorships in a wide range of subjects. The first was a chair for European Studies at Harvard, whose incumbents have included the distinguished historian Charles Maier. But the main emphasis was in the revival and renewal of the local region, as Essen and the Ruhr suffered from the changes in Germany's industrial structure. In particular, the foundation saw cultural life as a way of combating urban decline. In 2009/10 the Folkwang Museum in Essen was expensively remodeled and enlarged. That vision was also applied to the problematic legacy of East Germany. The foundation played a special role in developing educational institutions in former East Germany, including the launching of an Institute of Advanced Studies (Alfried Krupp Kolleg) in Greifswald, which began activities in 2002. The engagement in East German education had even predated 1989: Beitz had been given an honorary doctorate at the University of Greifswald as an acknowledgment of his involvement in restoration projects in Greifswald and Stralsund. The Stiftung also provided substantial resources for the reconstruction of cultural monuments in eastern Germany, including the Dresden Opera House (Semperoper), which had been badly damaged in flooding in 2002. Around 15 percent of the Stiftung's funding went outside Germany. In general, its work reflects the belief that what might be termed "public-interest capitalism" can help in the revival of particular communities.

Foundations are an essential part of the postwar Americanization of German business culture. Some major U.S. foundations had a very prominent role in rebuilding politics and culture in Germany in the wake of the collapse of the Nazi dictatorship, and it is not surprising that many large German firms saw a new potential for corporate existence by means of a foundation. Models for German business emulation were provided by the Carnegie Endowment and the Ford Foundation. Andrew Carnegie, the American equivalent of Krupp and the builder of the major corporations that eventually went into U.S. Steel, created the endowment on his seventy-fifth birthday in 1910 as a demonstration of his horror of war, and with the explicit goal "to hasten the abolition of international war, the foulest blot upon our civilization." The Ford Foundation was probably the best-known American foundation in Europe, created in 1936 and focused on "scientific, educational and charitable purposes, all for the public welfare." By the 1950s, it was playing a major role in higher education and the arts, as well as in economic development and environmental protection. The Rockefeller Foundation had played a key role in helping European intellectuals in exile from fascism and National Socialism. German business figures had already established some charitable institutions, notably hospitals, but the 1950s brought some direct imitations of the U.S. model. In 1958 the Carl Friedrich von Siemens Stiftung and in 1959 the Fritz Thyssen Stiftung were established, both with fundamentally scientific and academic visions. In 1964 the Bosch family transferred its shares to the Vermögensverwaltung Bosch GmbH, which in 1969 changed its name to the Robert Bosch Stiftung GmbH. Alfried Krupp and his advisers also looked at the U.S. models, and their German imitations, as a specific way of furthering a clearly defined public good, rather than as a tax-sheltered way of planning family wealth, which was how most German family firms treated the legal provisions for establishing a Stiftung. It was in fact John McCloy, the chairman of the Ford Foundation and former American high commissioner in Germany, who not only intervened in the dispute over the compensation of wartime forced workers but also recommended to Krupp and Beitz the

Ford Foundation as a model for Krupp corporate governance. In particular, McCloy recommended that it would be helpful "if the Krupp foundation gave money to Harvard, Oxford, Delhi etc. and other non-German institutions." At a lunch meeting with McCloy on February 19, 1962, Beitz mentioned that there was a plan to establish a Krupp foundation.[55]

The American patterns differed considerably from their German emulators, however, in that the foundations soon developed an independence from the originating company. Between 1955 and 1974, for instance, the large Ford Foundation divested itself completely of its holdings of nonvoting stock in the Ford Motor Company, on the grounds that the move would optimize and smooth investment returns but also that it would demonstrate the foundation's independence from the corporation. The German model by contrast included two potentially diverging goals: the foundation would act as a charitable institution, but it would also control the corporation. As a result, the stakeholders of the corporation were protected by a secure ownership structure: unlike a joint-stock company, but even unlike a company held by a multiplicity of family members who might be tempted to sell their investments at some moment as a result of unfavorable business developments or simply because of a split in the family, it was impossible for the corporation to be sold or taken over. The *Frankfurter Allgemeine Zeitung* commented in 1967 that "the existence of the [Krupp] Foundation will take this great industrial wealth for all time and irrevocably away from any personal interest and claim and thus ensure that it is held together."[56] But it also helped later to consolidate a defense of the company against corporate raiders. The foundation became a classic case of what corporate analysts call a "poison pill" defense. A highly innovative company such as Bosch, which functioned primarily as a supplier of automobile components, would in the United States have undoubtedly been taken over by a big automobile producer; but in Germany, Daimler was unable to swallow Bosch because of the protection offered by ownership through a foundation. The intention of both Alfried Krupp and Berthold Beitz was to protect Krupp in the same way. In that sense the Stiftung represented a provision not just for the general good but also for the specific good of the Krupp employees.

Alfried Krupp died on July 30, 1967, less than a year after the arrangements were in place, and only three months after the plans had been publicly announced. On November 29, 1967, the foundation received its authorization from the state of Nordrhein-Westfalen, and the corporate restructuring could begin. The enterprises of Fried. Krupp were now transferred to the Fried. Krupp GmbH, which was completely owned by the foundation.

The surviving members of the Krupp family felt excluded from the foundation. Beitz had initially been rather coldly treated by the family, with the exception of Alfried's mother Bertha and her sister Barbara von Wilmowsky and her husband Tilo von Wilmowsky. After the death of Alfried, the situation became more and more conflictual.

In part this was a consequence of Kaiser Wilhelm II's patent of 1906, which restricted the use of the name Krupp to Gustav von Bohlen and Halbach and the heir to the firm, in the event his eldest son. Beitz could consequently announce that "there is no Krupp family anymore," and "I am the last person to hold up the name of Krupp."[57] What remained of the family unsurprisingly found this stance provocative. But Beitz constantly referred to Alfried Krupp's last will excluding family members from the foundation.

Beitz was equally resolute in warding off the challenge of the bankers. Initially, the new Krupp holding company had a supervisory board chaired by Hermann Josef Abs. Beitz joined the supervisory board in 1968 as first deputy chairman; at the beginning of 1970, he asked Abs to arrive earlier for a routine board meeting in Essen, and then confronted him with Otto Brenner, the head of the metalworkers' trade union IG Metall and the second deputy chairman of the board, a man who was on excellent terms with Beitz. Brenner announced that the workers' representatives were going to vote Abs off the chairmanship. Abs responded that the agenda did not include such a discussion, but at the next meeting in June 1970 he resigned and was replaced by Beitz. In this way, by an act of managerial liberation, both family and bank interests were removed from the strategical operation of the corporation.

THE QUEST FOR AN OPTIMAL SIZE

From the 1970s, the words "steel" and "crisis" regularly appeared together. There were severe setbacks to the German steel industry as a whole in 1975, in 1981, in 1992/23, and in 2008/9, as well as a milder version in 1971. On each occasion, analyses emphasized the same multiple reasons: a decline in the need for "old" industrial production as opposed to newer sectors of the economy, a shifting geography of economic development toward developing or emerging markets, labor rigidities, too much dispersion of business among too many firms well below their optimal size, and companies with excessive debt levels, outdated equipment, antiquated management structures, and high energy costs.[58] It seemed as if crisis had become a perpetual state of the norm for the industry.

Beitz's most important long-term strategical move in the 1970s was to secure an adequate capital basis for the Krupp enterprise. In July 1974, Iran took a 25.04 percent stake in the Fried. Krupp Hüttenwerke AG via the National Iranian Steel Industries Co., and from 1976 to 1978 also in the Fried. Krupp GmbH. The new owners brought a total injection of some DM 1,400 million, and secured representation on the supervisory board. The Iranian state and Krupp also set up a joint company based in Zurich. The Iranian holding followed intense and personal negotiations between Beitz and Shah Reza Pahlavi. In particular Beitz did not inform the banks about his diplomacy, which was intended to free the company from financial tutelage. He was especially delighted that he succeeded in obtaining a price that was more than double the figure suggested by the banks as the value of a stake in Krupp. Beitz explained that the engagement represented a long-term commitment of the German company not only to the economic and technical development of Iran but also to projects in other rapidly developing countries. The chair of Krupp's board of management, Ernst Wolf Mommsen, argued that this was a much more stable mechanism for recycling petrodollars than short-term deposits in Western banks.[59]

The Iranian participation became a source of great concern in Germany, but also in other industrial countries, after the Iranian Revolution and the overthrow of the shah, who had negotiated the Iranian stake. The Islamic government nominated new figures to represent Iran on

269

the Krupp board, and there was considerable uncertainty about how the new owners would see their role—followed by great relief when the Iranian representatives actually appeared at their first supervisory board meeting in September 1979. The new arrivals were technically well-prepared men and not fanatical ideologues: Mahmoud Ahmadzadeh-Hervari, the new Mining and Industry minister, had been a professor at the Technical University of Teheran and had studied for four years at the German mining academy of Clausthal. Krupp's financial director, Alfred Lukac, reported that he and the new state secretary Reza Salimi were "more pleasant than all the Harvard people" who had been sent by the shah.[60] From 1991, as a consequence of mergers, the Iranian holding in the company shrank, and after 2003 it fell below 5 percent.

The Iranian participation drew attention to the increasing importance of developing countries, as well as the OPEC countries, for Krupp exports. In the 1970s, export growth seemed to shift away from the traditional industrial countries. The Polysius Division specialized in the supply of cement-making equipment: it had been founded in 1870 by Gottfried Polysius and bought by Krupp in 1971. In 1974 Krupp fulfilled the biggest-ever contract in its history so far, a DM 200 million cement plant in Saudi Arabia. There was also a large increase in the demand for the specialized desalinization equipment that Krupp built, which mostly was sold in Gulf countries. Krupp developed a steelmaking process based on the sponge-iron process for countries that lacked cokable coal. South Africa was one of the first major customers. In 1975, while steel and metallurgy sales fell off quite severely, by 15 percent, there was a 40 percent increase in sales of complete factories. As the industrial world was hit by stagflation, 43 percent of foreign sales went to developing countries, and 11 percent to OPEC. The diversification even included a modest return to armaments production, which had been a taboo in the 1950s and 1960s. From 1977 MaK, the vehicle products division, was involved in the construction of the Leopard 2 tank, produced mostly for the German army and for NATO partners; and Krupp-Atlas Elektronik developed its range and targeting system in the early 1980s.

Iran brought a considerable injection of cash, but there was no strategic reorientation of the company: in that sense, a powerful opportunity to remake Krupp was squandered. There was a general steel crisis in Europe, with too many producers, dominated by powerful managers trying to preserve their independence. In Germany, the major steel companies initially responded to the crisis by attempting to rationalize. Between 1974 and 1980, the major Ruhr firms reduced their workforces: Hoesch by 20 percent, Thyssen by 14.5 percent, and Krupp by only 6.6 percent.[61] The historical pattern of the 1870s was replicated, when Krupp had also been the steelmaker that succeeded in keeping more of its workforce than its competitors. But the experience led to major losses in 1975 (DM 61 million) and 1978 (DM 19 million).[62] The same crisis-adjustment mechanism was evident in the early 1980s, when the combination of a second oil price shock and a new monetary policy in the United States produced a new, major worldwide recession (which affected above all the industrial countries). In Europe, Krupp and other large steel manufacturers also suffered from the competition of the cheaper Italian minimills. A logical response was to move more into steelmaking equipment rather than steel. In 1981 there was a surge in the number of contracts for complete factories (an increase of around 120 percent), which were sold mostly to developing countries, while basic steel production fell in response to a fall of demand in the industrialized world. A heating plant was built for the GDR, a steelworks for Libya.

A better response to the crisis might have been a more general industrial rationalization and a reconfiguring of the steel industry. In 1979 Economics Minister Otto Graf Lambsdorff had agreed to a French proposal that the provisions of the European Coal and Steel Community that limited state subsidies should be suspended in the face of the new crisis, and that the German government should now use the leverage of government subsidies to push for steel rationalization. Greater industrial concentration looked like an obvious answer to the difficulties of overcapacity. But there were many difficulties in the way, and the 1980s became the decade of failed mergers. The problems of that decade were treated as specific to the steel industry; by contrast, in the 1990s, mergers were more easy to push through because the whole social model of the Federal Republic had come under enormous pressure. In the early 1980s, on the other hand, the push to rationalize seemed to be coming primarily from the outside, and from the government. The state was, however, relatively ineffective in dealing with the powerfully entrenched managers of the steel business.

Hoesch had already merged in 1972 with the Dutch company Hoogovens to form Estel, and needed to be removed before it could again be merged into a larger Ruhr company. The German government proposed a rationalization program that would be backed by public investment and guarantees, as well as help in dealing with the unemployment that might result from rationalization.

In February 1982, the supervisory boards of Krupp and Hoesch drew up a plan to form a new Ruhrstahl AG, which might provide a framework for lowering overall capacity (from a total capacity in 1979 of 15.5 million tons of crude steel to 11 million tons by 1987), as well as for new investment for a new oxygen-steel plant on the Westfalen-Hütte site in Dortmund. But the negotiations were undermined by later discussions in 1982 on cooperation between Krupp and Thyssen on specialty steels, and the rationalization plan collapsed. The head of Thyssen, Dieter Spethmann, bitterly criticized the subvention policy of the European Community as a revival of eighteenth-century-style interventionism as practiced by Emperor Joseph II.[63]

The government then gave three "steel moderators" (*Moderatoren*), outsiders who had a substantial connection with the steel business, the task of producing a plan for rescuing the industry as a whole. With an election looming, Chancellor Helmut Kohl impressed on the moderators the urgency of a steel solution.[64] One of the "moderators," Günter Vogelsang, had been a former chief executive of Krupp but was then on the supervisory boards of Veba, Deutsche Bank, and Daimler-Benz as well as Thyssen; the banker Alfred Herrhausen of Deutsche Bank was on the supervisory board of what was by far the weakest German steel company, Klöckner; and Marcus Bierich of the Allianz insurance company had been the financial director of Mannesmann. The suggestion of these business experts to reorganize German steel in a "Ruhr group" of Hoesch, Klöckner, and Salzgitter and a "Rhine" group of Thyssen and Krupp also came to nothing.[65] The "moderators" were a powerful exemplification of the notion of a "Deutschland AG" controlled by banks and insurance companies:[66] financial institutions drove many mergers, though on some spectacular occasions, as in the case of a proposed Daimler merger with BMW in the late 1920s and then again in the late 1950s, they also failed. The steel initiative of the early 1980s belongs to the failures, not the successes of "Deutschland AG."

Some other mergers in the sprawling Krupp empire also failed. The story of the AG Weser seemed to repeat the rather dismal loss-making story of the Germania-werft. A proposal to merge the AG Weser with the Hapag Lloyd Werft GmbH and the Bremer Vulkanwerft AG collapsed in 1983. In 1984 the Bremen shipyard AG Weser was closed, two thousand workers were laid off, and the AG Weser's production moved to Bremerhaven.

Steel production in Germany only began to recover in the mid-1980s, starting in 1984. By the mid-1980s, the largest developing countries were hit by the aftermath of the international debt crisis that broke out in Latin America in 1982; the most dynamic Eastern bloc economies, Poland and Hungary, had run into a similar kind of debt crisis and also into a broader political crisis. These problems made the Krupp business model seem vulnerable. In 1985, 22 percent of Krupp's exports went to developing countries, 20 percent to OPEC producers, and 8 percent to communist countries. There was clearly a need to refocus again on products for advanced countries, and Krupp indeed sold very successfully a new process (PRENFLO or Pressurized Entrained Flow) for the gasification of coal for power generation. In 1986 Polysius also supplied the most advanced European cement plant for Ketton in England.

The turning point in the modernization of Krupp came as a consequence of increasing tension between Beitz and the chief executive, Wilhelm Scheider, in the late 1980s. The losses of the company increased, amounting to DM 202 million in 1988 and DM 452 million in 1989. Losses were especially heavy in the division that produced industrial equipment. Beitz lost confidence in Scheider's ability to find an appropriate strategy to return the company to profitability. He promptly persuaded Scheider to leave Krupp before his contract expired. But there was also increasing criticism of Beitz, and one member of the supervisory board, Rudolf von Bennigsen-Foerder, resigned. Beitz now trawled widely among the heads of big German companies to find not one but two senior managers, one to be chief executive and the other to chair the supervisory board. The head of Hoesch, Detlev Rohwedder, declined an offer to become chief executive. As mentioned earlier, Beitz even tried to persuade the highly charismatic head of Deutsche Bank, Alfred Herrhausen, to move to Essen in order to save Krupp as chair of the supervisory board. Herrhausen was inclined to accept but was dissuaded in a three-hour-long meeting of Deutsche Bank's executive board.[67] In the end Manfred Lennings, a former head of the steel and engineering concern GHH (the old Krupp rival, the Gutehoffnungshütte) who had been forced out and had then run the industrial holdings of the Westdeutsche Landesbank, became chair of the supervisory board; and Gerhard Cromme, who had had a stellar career in the French company Saint-Gobain before joining Krupp as the head of Krupp Stahl, in 1989 succeeded Scheider as chief executive.

An often-remarked feature of the German-style capitalism of the "Deutschland AG" is that it is better at the pursuit of incremental change than at fundamental technological shifts and structural breaks in production.[68]

Like Japanese business, with which there are strong parallels, it is essentially about the management of perfection through an emphasis on continuity. But the problems of the steel business in Germany were now so severe that they demanded a radical break with the past. Cromme had a very clear modernization strategy involving diversification and also the shifting of production sites, and he dressed the new course with a quite radical rhetoric. He sometimes complained that Krupp was selling "products of the second industrial revolution."[69] He was also very clearly aware of the dangers of failure: "If we do not want to go under, we have to strive for a European dimension."[70]

The most dramatic sign that the era had changed was that the Rheinhausen steelworks, the venerable Friedrich-Alfred-Hütte, was finally closed in 1993. Rheinhausen had been since the end of the nineteenth century one of the most striking symbols of Krupp tradition. The closure thus took on a symbolic role in remaking a business culture, analogous to Ronald Reagan's dismissal of striking air-traffic controllers or Margaret Thatcher's struggle with British coal miners. The closure had initially been announced by Krupp Stahl AG more than ten years earlier, in December 1982. A new announcement was made in 1987, and it provoked bitter protests. Krupp workers from Rheinhausen demonstrated in the Villa Hügel, interrupted a supervisory board meeting, ate the canapés, and smoked the cigars; they also occupied the bridge across the Rhine between Rheinhausen and Duisburg. They complained that they could not find anyone in the Krupp corporation to speak with.[71] Cromme made it clear that he was determined to succeed where his predecessors had failed, but he also convinced the labor representatives that the move was a necessary part of an adjustment strategy. In the end, and after a considerable personal engagement of Beitz on the side of Cromme, all the worker representatives on the Krupp supervisory board voted for Cromme's appointment as chief executive with the exception of the Rheinhausen representative, who abstained. The Rheinhausen works were closed without dismissals, and employees were offered jobs in other factories, including the Krupp-Mannesmann works in Duisburg-Huckingen. Cromme turned himself into a virtuoso of the peculiar system of German labor relations, with one British observer remarking that he played on *Mitbestimmung* (workers' participation in management) as on a Stradivarius.

The most obvious way forward was to consolidate the steel industry in Germany. The big names in German steel, accustomed to see each other as competitors or rivals, started to engage in some forms of cooperation. In 1990 the Hüttenwerke Krupp-Mannesmann AG was established to create semifinished steel products.

In 1991 Krupp secretly bought up just under a quarter of the shares of Hoesch and then launched a hostile takeover, one of the very first in Germany. Takeovers had previously been thought of as a peculiarity of a radically aggressive form of Anglo-Saxon capitalism, not as an appropriate method for restructuring German industry to meet global challenges. In preparation for the takeover, Krupp transformed itself from a limited liability company (GmbH) into a joint-stock company (Aktiengesellschaft) in March 1992. In December 1992 the two enterprises merged as the Fried. Krupp AG Hoesch-Krupp, which was 51.61 percent owned by the Alfried Krupp von Bohlen und Halbach-Stiftung and 23.55 percent by the Islamic Republic of Iran. The Stiftung was thus still the holder of the majority of the stock. It was still a steel-based company, though the steel share of its business gradually fell. Steel accounted for about 35 percent of external sales in 1993. The takeover occurred at the moment of a severe recession, and the new enterprise incurred high losses in 1992 (DM 250 million) and 1993 (DM 589 million). The number of workers was reduced by sixteen thousand in the course of two years. But the stock market was enthusiastic about the new company. Its shares, which were traded from January 1993, for some time outperformed the German market. In 1996 the company established a Department for Investor Relations. By 1995 there was a return to profitability, although there was a pronounced difference in culture between the two companies and managers continued to refer to themselves as "Kruppianer" or "Hoeschianer." Cromme attempted to bridge the divide with a program for "reengineering" the company emphasizing four "Ks" (Cs in English): Customers, Costs, Creativity, Communication.

Between 1992 and 1998, Cromme reduced the number of companies in the group from 160 to 75, and production abroad increased from 10 percent to 40 percent.[72] The vehicle products division (MaK) had been spun off as a separate entity in 1992, and in 1996 was sold to the U.S. company Caterpillar; the traffic engineering sector was sold to Siemens. Krupp took over Acciai Speciali Terni in the course of the breaking up and privatization of the Italian state-owned steel company ILVA between 1994 and 1998. Terni was a steelworks established in 1884 that was in many ways the historical Italian equivalent of Krupp, which it had used as a model for its own development. It had been created in an old ironworking town; in the 1880s it started to work with a giant 108-ton hammer, and to specialize in military equipment. It hit a series of crises in the interwar period, but unlike Krupp, it was taken over by the government. At the same time, in 1997 Krupp acquired the only substantial Mexican producer of flat steel products, Mexinox S.A. de C. V. Krupp was moving out of steel mass production and into the manufacture of specialty steels.

One sign of the new ethos of globalization was that in 1994 separate companies were created for steel flat products, special heavy items, and long products, in part because the new specialized companies would no longer be subject to the workers' representation provisions of the *Montanmitbestimmung* laws. In the mid-1970s, when Beitz was selling a share of Krupp to Iran, he had explained that he had no objection to *Montanmitbestimmung*. Consensual labor relations were for a long time a crucial element in the German way of doing business. Twenty years later, the business climate had changed, and the postwar German tradition looked like an obstacle to the modernization of business strategies.

After absorbing Hoesch, Krupp turned to a bigger company. Thyssen had been even more badly hit by the collapse of the early 1990s than Krupp. Much more of a mass producer, it did not even consider buying into the decrepit East German steel industry but instead bought about twenty-seven smaller enterprises in engineering and services. The head of Thyssen, Heinz Kriwet, at this time even contemplated a complete exit from steel. Back in 1987, Thyssen had tried to buy out Krupp but had been turned down by Beitz, who referred to the will of Alfried Krupp. In 1995 there was a limited form of cooperation in that Krupp and Thyssen merged their stainless steel operations in a venture that was 60 percent owned by Krupp: Krupp-Thyssen Nirosta.

In September 1995, the heirs of the Thyssen family sold their stakes, so that that enterprise too was no longer a family firm. Only a very small stake was held by the Fritz Thyssen Foundation. The company was hit by scandal in 1996 when the chief executive, together with nine other senior managers, was charged with fraud in a case that involved an investigation of government funds used for the privatization of an East German metal-trading company. In 1996 Thyssen tried but failed to establish a collaboration on telecommunications with Deutsche Bahn. In 1997 it sold its stake in a cellular phone company. At the same time, it moved to further internationalization, by buying the largest U.S. machine toolmaker, Giddings & Lewis Inc., as well as the North American elevator operations of the Dover Corporation. Despite its problems, Thyssen was substantially bigger and also more profitable than Krupp.

In March 1997, Krupp launched a hostile takeover bid for Thyssen, backed by Deutsche Morgan Grenfell and Goldman Sachs, who offered Krupp an apparently immense credit line (an estimated DM 18 billion, or three times the capitalization of Krupp). As in the 1980s, the idea of rationalization in the steel industry was again backed by the government, though on this occasion more on the *Land* level, where the prime minister of Nordrhein-Westfalen, Johannes Rau, was a firm advocate of rationalization, although he was opposed to the idea of a hostile takeover. The Krupp bid attracted widespread opprobrium. It seemed to many Germans to be the introduction of "Anglo-Saxon capitalism" or the beginning of a "Wild West." Many commentators stressed the oddity of Krupp being the smaller and less profitable company of the two (DM 28 billion sales in 1996 with a market capitalization of DM 5.9 billion, while Thyssen had DM 38.7 billion in sales and a market capitalization of DM 10.8billion). There was an additional peculiarity in that the Deutsche Bank was advising Krupp on the deal but was also represented on the board of Thyssen. The *Financial Times* quoted one of the bankers involved to the effect that "this move is being made in accordance with the rules of the capital market rather than in the old clubby way such deals have often taken place in Germany."[73] But initially the parent banks, Deutsche and Dresdner, hesitated in the face of public criticism, and the deal collapsed.[74] There was for the moment only a more modest cooperation agreement.

The merger talks resumed in a more cooperative spirit. In late 1997 Krupp and Thyssen agreed on a cooperation in Thyssen Krupp Stahl to manufacture flat products; and there followed an agreement on a complete merger, on the basis of a valuation of two thirds (Thyssen) to one third (Krupp). Five main product areas would constitute the new company: steel, automotive, industrial, engineering, materials and services. There would be "no losers" in the merger, and Gerhard Cromme from Krupp and Ekkehard Schulz from Thyssen would be joint chief executives. But the facts that Krupp would have four seats on the nine-man executive board (*Vorstand*) and that Dieter Vogel, the chair of Thyssen, had been sidelined were widely interpreted as a success for Krupp. The merger was approved by an extraordinary shareholders' meeting of Krupp on November 30, 1998, and by Thyssen on December 4. The cost-saving synergies were estimated at DM 66 million for 1998/99 and would rise to DM 440 million in 2000/2001.[75] In March 1999 the new company announced that it aimed to reduce employment in steel from 22,600 to 19,300 by 2001.

The merger mania of German industry continued. Germans spoke of "fusionitis" and of "the endgame of the giants." Soon there were rumors that Mannesmann too would be sucked into the merger.[76] But unlike what had happened in the chemical industry, where Hoechst and Rhône-Poulenc merged into Aventis, or in automobiles, where the unwieldy German-American giant Daimler-Chrysler was the outcome of "fusionitis," German steel remained mostly German. By the 2000s, "avoiding Mittal" (the family firm, of Indian origin, that was acquiring a dominant position in the European steel business) was indeed often given as a rationale of the ownership structure anchored around the foundation when this position was criticized by other ThyssenKrupp shareholders.

International pressures also changed the structure of the ownership. After the terrorist attacks of September 11, 2001, the United States pressed ThyssenKrupp to reduce the holding by the Iranian state to under 5 percent and to exclude Iranians from the supervisory board. The operation of buying out Iran was an expensive one, as Thyssen-Krupp in 2003 paid €406 million or €24 a share, three times the current market value.[77]

The management of ThyssenKrupp suggested the sale of the Hamburg shipyard Blohm & Voss and the Nordsee-werke Emden, on the grounds that they were "no longer core businesses."[78] In December 2006, the supply of tank parts was sold to Krauss Maffei Wegmann. In May 2004, the shipyards were merged with Howaldtswerke-Deutsche Werft, with the hope that this might form the basis for a European-level cooperation with the French shipbuilder and defense contractor Thales. There were also plans to let the steel branch go public, but these were not realized because of the unfavorable economic environment. The new core was that export business which Krupp had for a long time identified as central to its business model: exports of systems to emerging markets. In particular, the deal that seemed to establish the reputation of the new company was the creation of a high-speed rail system, the Transrapid, for China. ThyssenKrupp Stahl, the original core business, was to be floated separately in an IPO, but the outbreak of the world financial crisis frustrated this operation.

The company looked to external sources of renewal. In 1999 all nine members of the executive board of the new company came from either Krupp or Thyssen; ten years later only two, Ekkehard Schulz and Ulrich Middelmann, were veterans of the original board, and the other four board members came with an outside background. In 2010 a new chief executive of ThyssenKrupp was appointed from outside the company: Heinrich Hiesinger from Siemens.

A move that reasserted some of the Krupp tradition provoked controversy. In January 2007, the Alfried Krupp von Bohlen und Halbach-Stiftung, whose postmerger share of the capital of ThyssenKrupp had originally been a mere 17.36 percent and was gradually increased to 25.33 percent, was given the permanent right to nominate three members of the supervisory board. This looked like exactly the kind of "poison pill" used for instance by Arcelor to prevent ThyssenKrupp taking over the Canadian steelmaker Dofasco. The German fund manager Christian Strenger was quoted as saying that the move "stunts the rightful influence of other shareholders."[79] Another reassertion of tradition came with the decision to move the headquarters of ThyssenKrupp away from the architecturally ambitious, modernistic Düsseldorf "Dreischeibenhaus" (Three Wedges) house built in the

Figure 7.7 A reconstructed version of the Krupp Stammhaus and the new ThyssenKrupp central office, Essen, 2010 (Peter Wieler photo). Courtesy of Historical Archives Krupp.

late 1950s to a dramatic postmodern cubic building (by Chaix & Morel and JSWD Architekten) as part of a company campus situated on the Altendorfer Strasse on the outskirts of Essen, right next to a reconstructed version of the original Krupp Stammhaus. In this way, the company returned as it were to the womb, to the site where everything had started some two hundred years before.

In the economic and financial crisis after 2007, sales fell off very sharply: for the fiscal year 2008/9 sales of €40.6 billion were three-quarters of the level in the year before. There was a renewed threat of labor unrest, with announcements of protest meetings and a demonstration outside the Villa Hügel, but union representatives and management agreed in June 2009 on the "Essen Declaration," which resumed a Krupp tradition in promising a restructuring without dismissals and protection of the principle of codetermination (*Mitbestimmung*). German workers had been worried in particular about the company's strategy of international diversification, with big steel-plant investments in Brazil and the United States, which also continued in spite of the economic and financial crisis. The $5 billion steel mill constructed in Calvert, Alabama, is the largest single German plant investment ever made in the United States. The new Brazilian works was inaugurated in June 2010, at a moment when Brazil's economy was widely seen as the most successful and crisis-resistant of the big emerging markets.

OUTLOOK

For much of the twentieth century, large enterprises seemed to be very stable and enduring institutions. Japan's lifelong employment traditions were only an extreme variant of a worldwide theme that was also very well developed in Germany. In particular in Krupp, third-generation workers were not uncommon, and the enterprise apparently offered a cradle-to-grave enclave of social protection. But in the last decades of the century a dramatic change occurred, and corporate existence across the world became much more unstable and uncertain. This has certainly been evident among the great nineteenth-century steelmaking rivals of Krupp. Among those in other European countries, Vickers was bought in 1999 by Rolls-Royce after substantial financial difficulties; Skoda was sold to a Dutch-registered holding company, Appian Group, in 2003, with a substantial lack of clarity about the ultimate ownership; and only the French firm Schneider remains as an independent company, but now it is specializing mainly in electrical products and retains little connection to the old enterprise. The giant French steel company Wendel became a financial holding company. Of the great old German steel and engineering groups, the rump of the Gutehoffnungshütte merged in 2008 with the French company Valdunes, which had emerged out of the Belgian Cockerill works; and Mannesmann has completely transformed itself from a tube company to mobile telephone enterprise after a controversial hostile takeover by Vodaphone in 2000. Hoesch and Thyssen had merged with Krupp.

The German business model changed with the global transformation of corporate cultures, as many critics complained about slow growth and rigidity in Germany. Some people presented this globalization as an Americanization, forgetting that there had been previous eras in which the transformation of German enterprise was also described as Americanization: in the early twentieth

century, when the process was also called fordism or tay-
lorism; and in the immediate postwar period, when figures
such as Hundhausen had held out American methods as
the key to successful German reconstruction. In reality,
at the beginning of the twenty-first century, as in earlier epochs, the supposed influence of foreign models or
best practice is part of a continuing process of corporate
reinvention, rebuilding, and rebranding. After 2007, the
global financial crisis produced a return to rather upbeat
assessments of German prospects in manufacturing and
especially in engineering (though not in the undercapitalized and underperforming banking sector). Germany,
until 2010 the world's largest exporter, benefited greatly
from its traditions of workmanship, reliability, and technical innovation, and from the demand for engineering
products and machine tools in the rapidly growing emerging markets. The foundations of this business model were
old and traditional: the values of craftsmanship, devotion
to technical innovation, and suspicion of financial capitalism all go back to the world of the nineteenth century
and to the visions of Alfred Krupp. It was an old German
model that began to shine again, though the jewels in the
crown were brand new.

Why has Krupp survived in the turbulent corporate
environment of a globalizing German economy? The
name has a powerful brand recognition, but especially in
the early postwar period the connotations in most foreign
countries (communist China was an exception) were
highly negative, associated with war, not peace. The company was put together again very effectively in the 1950s
by Berthold Beitz; and the transformation of ownership
to the foundation in 1967/68 provided a new and more
stable ownership structure that preserved the positive

elements of being a family firm without the drawbacks. But by themselves, even these measures would not have been enough; and a process of transformation was required in the 1990s and 2000s to create a coherent company vision for what had now become an integrated technology group rather than a rather diverse conglomerate that was a chance outcome of badly needed mergers between small enterprises that had lost their globally competitive edge. How did that new vision and new focus emerge?

The 1990s were the decade in which globalization began to erode the complex institutions that had come to be known as "Deutschland AG," in which banks held controlling stakes in some major companies while other large corporations were controlled by family holdings. Instead, institutional shareholders and private-equity firms became more important, and shareholding became more diversified. The transition to a new corporate governance was furthered by legislative and tax measures. Laws of 1998 and 2002 abolished multiple voting shares and increased the controlling functions of supervisory boards. In addition, the socialist-environmentalist coalition government of Gerhard Schröder overhauled benefits in order to make for greater labor flexibility. Some family groups emerged strengthened from this era of corporate upheaval and tried themselves to play the private-equity game, using capital markets and bond issues to create high degrees of leverage. Such a strategy also involved playing according to the rules of a global game, which had changed in the direction of greater openness and transparency. Some of Germany's best-known public companies—Volkswagen and Siemens—became enmeshed in corruption and bribery scandals. And some large family enterprises miscalculated badly and overstretched themselves: Schaeffler

Group, for example, which launched an ill-considered bid for the much larger Continental; and the complex business empires of Adolf Merckle centered on generic pharmaceuticals. These developments of the turn of the millennium posed a challenge to traditional German notions of how business should be conducted. What was the response of corporate Germany?

1. Ownership became more important, and market pressure on stock markets meant that managers had to become sensitive to share valuations. This doctrine, popularly termed "shareholder value," was highly controversial because it looked as if the new focus in its current was transferring wealth from stakeholders (such as the workforce, or the local community generally) to shareholders. In consequence, it was inevitable that Germans began to ask about the identity of the owners of large companies, and worried about the exclusion of a wider group of stakeholders.

2. Profitability mattered much more. In the past, owners had had a vision that focused on technology rather than an orientation to cash flow. In addition, managerial incentives were not closely aligned with profitability. The nineteenth-century Krupps had frequently been dismissive of the significance of profits, as had Alfried Krupp von Bohlen und Halbach in the years of the postwar boom. Late-twentieth-century managers in many large German companies had largely ignored owners and their interests. Cromme reemphasized profitability and the interests of owners, and justified his course by arguing that cost saving was the only way that Germany could remain internationally competitive. The "Modell Deutschland" as it had developed in the years of the postwar "economic miracle," when profitability mattered

289

less than the maintenance of social cohesion and a gamble on growth, required significant modification.

3. International competition became a major criterion for judging a company's stature—as in the days of the early nineteenth century, when Alfred Krupp was worried above all about his firm's ability to compete with English products. There was a return to the globalized vision that had already characterized the company in its early history, before the first half of the twentieth century brought a reorientation in national terms.

4. Patriarchal philosophies appeared obsolete. Already before the First World War, paternalism had been under fire, and Friedrich Alfred Krupp had tried to reduce the rigidities of his father's model of labor relations; and a more inclusive management philosophy began to emerge. In the immediate postwar era, there had been a strategic bargain in which industry had worked closely with labor in order to fight off the threat of foreign ownership. By the new millennium, that very simple bargain appeared to be obsolete. There was a new premium on labor flexibility that was actively promoted by governments and which seemed to mark a new type of social compact.

5. Company inheritances became problematic as the corporate landscape began to change rapidly. The megamergers of the past two decades have thrown together some unlikely bedfellows. In every case, there was an inevitable shock to well-established corporate cultures, symbols, and routines. Some mergers, especially those crossing national boundaries, were spectacularly conflictual and eventually unsuccessful (the Daimler-Chrysler fusion, and BMW's takeover of Rover, were the most conspicuous failures). The German steel industry was historically built on different cultures, associated with specific

and rather unique urban settings: Hoesch in Dortmund, Thyssen in Duisburg, and Krupp in Essen. The whole concept of "Kruppianer" involved a particular Essen patriotism, in which other Ruhr cities were thought of as less sophisticated. Though the Ruhr cities are quite close, no further apart than the constituents of the Los Angeles conurbation, and are often indeed considered by geographers to be simply part of a Ruhr megalopolis, they had unique profiles, which could be fused and synthesized only with great difficulty. But remaking the company after the merger involved reinvigorating the whole region, and thinking about the connections of local and regional identities in a globally integrated economy.

6. The central role of banks in the German economy eroded, as bank lending was replaced by the capital market. In the postwar years, when companies had found it hard to raise capital for new investments, banks had played a major part in reconstruction; and in the last decades of the twentieth century, large mergers and acquisitions needed to be financed. But such financing could be handled more cheaply and effectively through the capital market. The new banks that mattered were investment banks, often American banks such as Goldman Sachs, as well as the German banks, such as Deutsche Bank, that had turned into Anglo-Saxon-style investment banks. The new relationships were quite different from the traditional German concept of a business run in a very close relationship with a particular "house" bank (a concept that Krupp had always been uneasy about). A sign of the new liberation from banks was their decreased importance on supervisory boards. In January 2010 the last banker, Martin Kohlhaussen of Commerzbank, departed from the board of ThyssenKrupp.

7. There was no complete retreat of the state from involvement in business. Large industrial undertakings still obviously have a major impact on the development of whole societies, and in that sense they are inevitably political. Indeed it is striking that the last banker on the supervisory board of ThyssenKrupp was replaced by a very recent German finance minister who was as well a former minister-president of Nordrhein-Westfalen, Peer Steinbrück.[80] The question of who occupies such a position in a major industry is still—as it was in the 1950s—a matter of politics.

ThyssenKrupp is an incarnation of this transition of corporate culture. The two component companies had been central to Germany's steel and engineering traditions and had evolved deeply different and contrasting managerial philosophies, with Krupp widely seen as highly centralized and Thyssen celebrated as a pioneer of the multidivision form. But both looked as if they had reached the end of a particular track, and had been severely hit by crisis in the 1990s. They then remade themselves in the new style. At the same time the characteristically German form of the foundation as a holder of property rights created an institutional peculiarity, looking back to an age in which there was an *affectio societatis*, or a company held together by an idea and a vision. It was a way of preserving the virtues—or the familiarity—of family capitalism, without the well-known drawbacks of fratricidal struggles and destructive succession disputes that so often tear a well-established business unit apart.

Modern management theory, especially as preached in U.S. business schools and practiced by their graduates, treats managers in particular, but also company employees in general, as individuals driven by isolated

gain-maximizing strategies. It is diametrically opposed
to the traditional German and perhaps European vision
of a company as an embodiment of some overarching
value system, in which a corporation is a microcosm of
a general social equilibrium. In that European tradition,
profitability is not everything, but rather flows from the
success of the business venture and the business philosophy. Without the sense of community, a search for
profitability would subvert itself, in that it encourages
individual managers and employees to internalize the
goals of profit maximization and turn them against the
firm as a broader unit. Over much of the past two centuries, companies were often believed to be alternatives to
other, more conflictual models of society: a society based
on intense antagonism of classes, a century ago; and in
recent years the radical individualism and market funda-
mentalism that seemed to German observers to emanate
from the Anglo-Saxon world. There were of course class
conflicts and tensions in the factory, just as there were
problematic managers (as had become especially appar-
ent in the general dissolution of values in the Nazi period,
when managers started denouncing each other). But the
community of the factory nevertheless could serve as a
sort of ideal or dream that might inspire a better (and
ultimately also more profitable) corporate life.

The answers to economic challenges of the last twenty
years have taken up some of the themes that had emerged
in Germany's striking postwar recovery. As German
society and politics disintegrated in the mid-twentieth
century in the wake of dictatorship and war, corporate
existence and loyalty, in which a company represented
"permanent life," looked like a way of rebuilding society around an idea of community. Over sixty years later,

293

there is still a debate about how business can be appropriately anchored in a broader framework of obligations and responsibilities. But now it involves much more reflection on how local communities can survive in a global economy. A foundation that guides a corporation is an institutional way of realizing a vision of a society not just held together by the clashes and competitions of individual agents, but bound by cooperation for a higher purpose or general good. That vision might be termed "public interest capitalism." Its realization or implementation makes quite obsolete the kind of fierce dispute between bankers and business leaders that characterized the 1960s and 1970s and that even recalled Alfred Krupp's struggle against finance in the 1870s. A Stiftung or foundation preserves the virtues of a family business structure—which the bankers had fought against—and offers a way of emphasizing the long-term vision rather than a short-term speculative position. That was exactly the philosophy that Alfred Krupp had evolved, of a company that was—whether large or small—a microcosm of the general society in which it existed, and a source of dynamism and development. In that sense, the modern reinvention of the company goes back to the roots of German industrial culture.

APPENDIX 1: FAMILY TREE

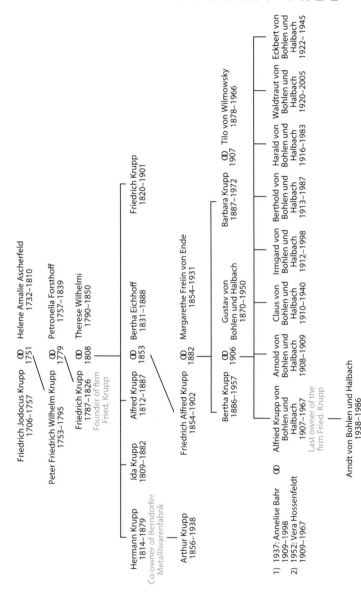

APPENDIX 2: BUSINESS RESULTS, 1811-2010

Revenues and Profits / Losses, 1811–2010

Year	Revenues Marks	After-tax profit / loss Marks
1811/12		–6,728
1813	317	–17,867
1814	2,996	–13,796
1815/16	4,495	–13,665
1817	6,069	–6,332
1818	9,317	–11,084
1819	6,972	–9,231
1820	7,929	–4,416
1821	8,828	–5,704
1822	8,281	–10,341
1823	10,024	–4,409
1824	3,592	–10,441
1825	3,969	–7,864
1826	3,795	–8,039
1827	4,692	Loss
1828	5,931	Loss
1829	10,197	Loss
1830	6,540	Loss
1831	11,256	Loss?
1832	11,028	Loss?
1833	10,677	Loss?
1834	18,732	Loss?
1835	33,147	Loss?
1836	69,960	(–11,426)
1837	96,744	(22,012)
1838	92,607	(25,052)
1839	100,590	(25,052)
1840	84,219	(15,442)
1841	165,042	(14,569)
1842	98,871	(14,569)

(*continues*)

Revenues and Profits / Losses, 1811–2010 (*continued*)

Year	Revenues Marks	After-tax profit / loss Marks
1843	78,252	(21,957)
1844	144,480	(27,200)
1845	132,903	(13,747)
1846	238,803	(–26,509)
1847	128,028	(–26,590)
1848	156,534	(49,601)
1849	204,900	(49,601)
1850	470,726	(49,601)
1851	387,518	149,887
1852	566,032	90,180
1853	597,144	59,388
1854	935,695	220,077
1855	1,513,468	228,103
1856	2,002,766	282,994
1857	2,779,196	704,088
1858	2,669,799	658,081
1859	2,711,499	660,701
1860	3,045,711	630,091
1861	4,145,771	774,609
1862	5,280,080	1,247,386
1863	7,090,762	2,049,018
1864	11,641,274	4,135,222
1865	15,722,360	6,066,673
1866	20,430,788	6,769,535
1867	20,166,149	5,528,246
1868	16,376,339	3,199,955
1869	24,232,515	6,278,704
1870-I	9,737,464	2,707,111
1870/71	29,074,126	6,551,257
1871/72	35,114,268	8,341,249
1872/73	35,089,918	10,675,827
1873/74	40,810,768	363,160
1874/75	46,513,565	–440,609
1875/76	41,578,333	2,473,341
1876/77	41,279,004	3,172,952
1877/78	48,050,381	3,163,106
1878/79	38,431,179	1,378,437
1879/80	30,037,345	–1,778,551
1880/81	40,595,681	2,601,601
1881/82	46,402,878	3,770,149
1882/83	46,026,993	4,570,595

Year	Revenues Marks	After-tax profit / loss Marks
1883/84	36,512,250	2,165,845
1884/85	42,559,537	4,642,041
1885/86	47,318,145	4,208,543
1886/87	42,201,110	3,937,258
1887/88	47,470,883	7,786,916
1888/89	47,890,466	6,542,457
1889/90	51,406,004	6,220,815
1890/91	55,854,718	5,691,661
1891/92	57,574,506	6,713,177
1892/93	47,629,410	3,919,491
1893/94	75,336,785	6,081,894
1894/95	58,660,831	4,821,651
1895/96	74,136,498	5,595,029
1896/97	74,650,182	4,790,106
1897/98	82,525,183	9,034,988
1898/99	103,082,991	7,561,300
1899/1900	119,752,495	13,529,067
1900/1901	119,178,537	6,796,875
1901/2	101,373,295	7,710,467
1902/3	125,803,983	8,087,215
1903/4	126,254,823	11,562,762
1904/5	179,006,770	16,413,053
1905/6	228,456,644	20,738,095
1906/7	283,895,394	24,844,266
1907/8	271,471,797	18,488,170
1908/9	243,679,045	15,607,625
1909/10	280,335,531	21,265,307
1910/11	313,991,412	28,712,265
1911/12	363,146,018	29,528,881
1912/13	430,738,792	36,635,070
1913/14	409,767,619	33,904,224
1914/15	494,611,712	86,465,611
1915/16	745,491,179	49,657,309
1916/17	1,098,212,130	40,976,456
1917/18	1,620,337,208	4,927,944
1918/19	1,545,500,413	−36,140,101
1919/20	2,390,143,899	79,658,027
1920/21	4,457,113,894	93,690,316
1921/22	9,332,062,186	147,783,214
1922/23	868,178,110,814	48,948,551,576
1923/24	240,555,091	2,141,963

(*continues*)

Revenues and Profits / Losses, 1811–2010 (*continued*)

	Reichsmarks	Reichsmarks
1924/25	393,119,423	–15,293,773
1925/26	352,017,246	–2,106,227
1926/27	457,726,240	13,036,674
1927/28	516,606,105	5,977,210
1928/29	515,080,230	6,905,228
1929/30	464,114,019	–4,450,656
1930/31	328,527,575	–10,884,188
1931/32	199,256,447	–15,231,642
1932/33	223,031,532	–3,069,449
1933/34	335,866,679	6,651,601
1934/35	488,191,705	9,689,548
1935/36	604,367,482	14,354,206
1936/37	674,003,823	16,226,877
1937/38	772,539,608	21,111,743
1938/39	920,255,/18	22,705,615
1939/40	1,007,988,751	10,719,666
1940/41	1,079,853,673	10,894,132
1941/42	1,208,906,753	10,115,320
1942/43	1,068,751,071	780,191
1943/44	1,013,092,000	
1944/45	1,082,987,834	–109,710,267
1945	151,805,941	–32,604,683
1945/46	160,948,308	
1946/47	143,672,955	
1947/48	126,839,881	
	Deutsche Marks	Deutsche Marks
1948/49	1,088,000,000	–83,328,879
1949/50	994,000,000	–64,640,954
1950/51	1,385,000,000	–1,324,831
1951/52	1,931,000,000	30,374,467
1952/53	2,139,000,000	–4,173,000
1953/54	2,305,000,000	4,790,561
1954/55	3,657,000,000	3,102,788
1955	376,000,000	–11,546,830
1956	3,026,000,000	–44,488,724
1957	3,431,000,000	–10,837,183
1958	4,082,000,000	7,873,037
1959	4,434,000,000	–24,100,000
1960	5,082,000,000	48,900,000

	Deutsche Marks	Deutsche Marks
1961	5,215,000,000	11,570,000
1962	5,217,000,000	888,000
1963	5,175,000,000	52,254,000
1964	6,018,000,000	38,300,000
1965	6,271,000,000	−170,900,000
1966	6,153,000,000	−43,000,000
1967	5,954,000,000	58,432,627
1968	5,766,000,000	−10,000,000
1969	6,426,000,000	63,000,000
1970	7,190,000,000	110,000,000
1971	7,437,000,000	16,000,000
1972	7,678,000,000	13,000,000
1973	8,866,000,000	83,000,000
1974	10,707,000,000	87,000,000
1975	10,683,000,000	−61,000,000
1976	11,138,000,000	1,000,000
1977	12,648,000,000	3,000,000
1978	13,320,000,000	−19,000,000
1979	14,266,000,000	119,000,000
1980	15,550,000,000	98,000,000
1981	16,811,000,000	−37,000,000
1982	18,758,000,000	439,000,000
1983	19,104,000,000	−301,000,000
1984	20,179,000,000	108,000,000
1985	19,953,000,000	124,000,000
1986	17,165,000,000	126,000,000
1987	15,504,000,000	42,000,000
1988	16,692,000,000	−202,000,000
1989	19,663,000,000	−452,000,000
1990	16,670,000,000	217,000,000
1991	16,207,000,000	305,000,000
1992	27,866,000,000	−250,000,000
1993	24,181,000,000	−589,000,000
1994	24,214,000,000	40,000,000
1995	27,679,000,000	505,000,000
1996	27,931,000,000	208,000,000
1997	27,625,000,000	437,000,000
1998	19,043,000,000	433,000,000

(continues)

Revenues and Profits / Losses, 1811–2010 (*continued*)

	Euros	*Euros*
1999/2000	40,687,000,000	527,000,000
2000/2001	40,765,000,000	665,000,000
2001/2	39,118,000,000	215,000,000
2002/3	38,705,000,000	552,000,000
2003/4	42,759,000,000	904,000,000
2004/5	45,977,000,000	1,079,000,000
2005/6	49,861,000,000	1,704,000,000
2006/7	55,191,000,000	2,190,000,000
2007/8	56,580,000,000	2,276,000,000
2008/9	42,953,000,000	−1,873,000,000
2009/10	45,687,000,000	927,000,000

Employees, Krupp Group, 1812–2010

1812	2	1864	6,900	1/1/1916	133,168	12/31/1966	102,806
1813	8	1865	9,100	1/1/1917	163,609	12/31/1967	90,628
1814	6	1866	7,200	1/1/1918	201,697	12/31/1968	87,404
1815	4	1867	7,800	1/1/1919	89,264	12/31/1969	79,500
1816	5	1868	7,200	1/1/1920	85,870	12/31/1970	80,340
1817	6	1869	7,400	1/1/1921	96,238	12/31/1971	79,663
1818	10	1870	8,400	1/1/1922	98,732	12/31/1972	74,931
1819	8	1871	10,400	1/1/1923	102,997	12/31/1973	76,100
1820	8	1872	14,800	1/1/1924	80,035	12/31/1974	80,892
1821	8	1873	16,000	1/1/1925	74,966	12/31/1975	78,912
1822	8	1874	15,200	1/1/1926	60,606	12/31/1976	76,161
1823	8	1875	13,900	1/1/1927	51,714	12/31/1977	86,574
1824	6	1876	13,100	1/1/1928	68,617	12/31/1978	84,713
1825	6	1877	12,800	9/30/1928	92,347	12/31/1979	86,172
1826	4	1878	14,000	9/30/1929	89,737	12/31/1980	85,706
1827	6	1879	13,400	9/30/1930	75,242	12/31/1981	82,194
1828	6	1880	15,500	9/30/1931	56,856	12/31/1982	78,201
1829	8	1881	17,600	9/30/1932	46,107	12/31/1983	69,291
1830	8	1882	18,300	9/30/1933	55,722	12/31/1984	66,320
1831	9	1883	17,800	9/30/1934	75,240	12/31/1985	67,402
1832	9	1884	17,000	9/30/1935	91,507	12/31/1986	68,043
1833	11	1885	17,100	9/30/1936	98,341	12/31/1987	65,205
1834	30	1886	18,300	9/30/1937	108,765	12/31/1988	63,391
1835	67	1887	20,200	9/30/1938	123,408	12/31/1989	63,557
1836	80	1888	21,000	9/30/1939	139,259	12/31/1990	59,044
1837	55	1889	22,300	9/30/1940	149,290	12/31/1991	53,115
1838	65	1890	24,000	9/30/1941	159,308	12/31/1992	91,411
1839	60	1891	24,600	9/30/1942	178,071	12/31/1993	78,376
1840	60	1892	25,000	9/30/1943	235,304	12/31/1994	66,138
1841	95	1/1/1893	25,517	9/30/1944	277,382	12/31/1995	66,352
1842	95	1/1/1894	28,662	10/1/1945	57,412	12/31/1996	69,608
1843	99	1/1/1895	27,692	10/1/1946	59,102	12/31/1997	57,938
1844	109	1/1/1896	29,420	10/1/1947	65,210	9/30/1998	58,392
1845	124	1/1/1897	32,332	10/1/1948	70,039	9/30/1999	184,770
1846	122	1/1/1898	36,706	10/1/1949	68,747	9/30/2000	193,316
1847	95	1/1/1899	41,750	10/1/1950	70,349	9/30/2001	193,516
1848	74	1/1/1900	46,088	10/1/1951	74,689	9/30/2002	191,254
1849	109	1/1/1901	47,129	10/1/1952	76,993	9/30/2003	190,102
1850	241	1/1/1902	43,555	10/1/1953	77,457	9/30/2004	187,036
1851	195	1/1/1903	40,951	9/30/1954	80,600	9/30/2005	185,932
1852	345	1/1/1904	43,826	9/30/1955	81,520	9/30/2006	187,586
1853	357	1/1/1905	52,392	12/31/1955	82,169	9/30/2007	191,350
1854	365	1/1/1906	61,754	12/31/1956	89,826	9/30/2008	199,374
1855	704	1/1/1907	64,354	12/31/1957	85,296	9/30/2009	187,495
1856	985	1/1/1908	63,084	12/31/1958	98,405	9/30/2010	177,346
1857	1,007	1/1/1909	63,191	12/31/1959	106,826		
1858	1,063	1/1/1910	67,166	12/31/1960	110,738		
1859	1,410	1/1/1911	67,533	12/31/1961	112,443		
1860	1,785	1/1/1912	70,999	12/31/1962	109,030		
1861	2,108	1/1/1913	75,429	12/31/1963	105,934		
1862	2,543	1/1/1914	81,001	12/31/1964	114,118		
1863	4,229	1/1/1915	99,336	12/31/1965	112,406		

NOTES

The names of the Krupp family after 1906 are simplified in the text to improve readability. On October 15, 1906, Gustav von Bohlen und Halbach married Bertha Krupp; both were allowed by an Imperial decree to bear the name "Krupp von Bohlen und Halbach." Their children reverted to "von Bohlen und Halbach," with the exception of the oldest son who was named "Krupp von Bohlen und Halbach" when he took over the firm. His son Arndt reverted to the "von Bohlen und Halbach" name.

INTRODUCTION: A NATION AND A NAME

1. Adolf Hitler, *Mein Kampf*, vol. 1, Munich: Eher, 1927, p. 392; Donald C. Watt (ed.), *Hitler's Mein Kampf*, London: Hutchinson, 1969, p. 324; Max Domarus (ed.), *Hitler Reden und Proklamationen 1932–1945*, Wiesbaden: Löwit, 1973, 1/2 (second half-volume of volume 1), pp. 532–33.

2. www.g7.utoronto.ca/finance/fm070209.htm, accessed November 1, 2010.

3. From appendix of Alfred Chandler, *Scale and scope: The dynamics of industrial capitalism*, Cambridge, Mass.: Belknap Press of Harvard University, 1990; also Rudolf Martin, *Jahrbuch des Vermögens und Einkommens der Millionäre der Rheinprovinz*, Berlin: Martin, 1913, p. v. Christopher J. Schmitz, *The growth*

of big business in the United States and Western Europe, 1850–1939, Houndmills, Basingstoke, Hampshire: Macmillan, 1993, pp. 32–33.

4. Michel Albert (trans. Paul Haviland), *Capitalism against capitalism*, London: Whurr, 1993.

CHAPTER 1: RISK

1. Theo Barker and Maurice Lévy-Leboyer, "An inquiry into the Buddenbrooks effect in Europe," paper presented at the Eighth International Economic History Congress, Budapest: From Family Business to Professional Management, 1982; Shigeaka Yasuoka, "Capital ownership in family companies: Japanese firms compared with those in other countries," in Aki Okochi and Shigeaki Yasuoka (eds.), *Family business in the era of industrial growth: Its ownership and management*, Proceedings of the Fuji International Conference on Business History, 10, Tokyo, 1984, pp. 1–32; Michael Mendel and Nikolaus Piper, *Stabwechsel: Die schwierige Suche nach dem richtigen Nachfolger*, Munich, 2005.

2. Anke Probst, *Helene Amalie Krupp, Zeitschrift für Unternehmensgeschichte, Beiheft 33*, Wiesbaden: Franz Steiner, 1985, p. 32.

3. Helene Amalie Krupp to Königliche Pr. Kriegs-und Domainen-Kammer, Cleve, December 10, 1799: Historisches Archiv Krupp, Essen, Germany (hereinafter HAK), FAH 1 B 3.

4. Probst, *Krupp*, p. 43.

5. Burkhard Beyer, *Vom Tiegelstahl zum Kruppstahl: Technik- und Unternehmensgeschichte der Gussstahlfabrik von Friedrich Krupp in der ersten Hälfte des 19. Jahrhunderts*, Essen: Klartext, 2007, p. 162.

6. See Jürgen Lindenlaub and Renate Köhne-Lindenlaub, "Unternehmensfinanzierung bei Krupp 1811–1848: Ein

Beitrag zur Kapital- und Vermögensentwicklung," *Beiträge zur Geschichte von Stadt und Stift Essen* 102, 1988, p. 100.

7. *Krupp 1812–1912: Zum 100 Jährigen Bestehen der Firma Krupp und der Gussstahlfabirk zu Essen Herausgegeben auf den hundertsten Geburtstag Alfred Krupps*, Jena: Gustav Fischer, 1912, p. 25.

8. Beyer, *Tiegelstahl*, p. 200, fn. 143.

9. See Thomas J. Sargent and François R. Velde, *The big problem of small change*, Princeton, N.J.: Princeton University Press, 2001.

10. Beyer, *Tiegelstahl*, p. 202.

11. *Krupp 1812–1912*, p. 31.

12. Beyer, *Tiegelstahl*, p. 122.

13. Announcement of Therese Krupp (Beilage zum Rheinisch-Westfälischen Anzeiger No. 86), October 28, 1826: HAK, FAH 1 B 129.

CHAPTER 2: STEEL

1. Alfred Krupp memorandum of December 15, 1873: HAK, WA 4/269, S. 30; also cited in Burkhard Beyer, *Vom Tiegelstahl zum Kruppstahl: Technik- und Unternehmensgeschichte der Gussstahlfabrik von Friedrich Krupp in der ersten Hälfte des 19. Jahrhunderts*, Essen: Klartext, 2007, p. 529.

2. Alfred Krupp to his brother Hermann, July 27, 1838; as edited in Wilhelm Berdrow (ed.), *Friedrich Krupp, der Gründer der Gussstahlfabrik: in Briefen und Urkunden*, Essen, 1915, p. 46.

3. Alfred Krupp to F. A. Krupp, n.d. [c. 1876/77]: HAK, FAH 2 B 218.

4. Krupp to Firma, October 11, 1871; as edited in Berdrow, *Briefe*, pp. 263–64.

5. Krupp to Prokura, December 26, 1871: HAK, FAH 2 B 180, S. 93; also edited in Berdrow, *Briefe*, p. 269.

6. Program for audience at Kaiser Wilhelm I, April 21, 1871; HAK, WA 7 f/1688.

7. Jürgen Lindenlaub and Renate Köhne-Lindenlaub, "Unternehmensfinanzierung bei Krupp 1811–1848: Ein Beitrag zur Kapital- und Vermögensentwicklung," *Beiträge zur Geschichte von Stadt und Stift Essen* 102, 1988, p. 114.

8. Beyer, *Tiegelstahl*, pp. 321, 319; Hermann Krupp to Alfred Krupp, Paris, 1843: HAK, FAH 2 B 91; and Alfred Krupp to Favre Baudit, 22.9.1836: HAK, FAH 2 B 87.

9. Beyer, *Tiegelstahl*, p. 425.

10. Barbara Wolbring, *Krupp und die Öffentlichkeit im 19. Jahrhundert*, Munich: C. H. Beck, 2000, p. 144.

11. *Krupp 1812–1912: Zum 100 Jährigen Bestehen der Firma Krupp und der Gussstahlfabrik zu Essen Herausgegeben auf den hundertsten Geburtstag Alfred Krupps*, Jena: Gustav Fischer, p. 166.

12. *Krupp 1812–1912*, p. 173.

13. Alfred Krupp to Fried. Krupp, Paris (Heinrich Haass), 19.1.1859: HAK, WA 3/23e; also edited in Berdrow, *Briefe*, p. 166.

14. *Krupp 1812–1912*, p. 188.

15. Harald Regner, "Schumpeterian German firms before and after World War I: The innovative few and the non-innovative many," *Zeitschrift für Unternehmensgeschichte* 54/1, 2009, pp. 50–72.

16. Klaus Tenfelde, *Bilder von Krupp: Fotografie und Geschichte im Industriezeitalter*, Munich: Beck, 1994, pp. 42, 53; Wolbring, *Krupp*, pp. 33, 138.

17. Tenfelde, *Bilder*, p. 42.

18. Alfred Krupp to Hanns Jencke, July 28, 1880; as edited in Berdrow, *Briefe*, p. 376.

19. Krupp to Friedrich Sölling, February 18, 1846: HAK, FAH 2 B 104; also edited in Berdrow, *Briefe*, p. 87.

20. Berdrow, *Briefe*, p. 35.

21. Krupp to Friedrich Alfred Krupp, August 24, 1875; as edited in Berdrow, *Briefe*, p. 321.

22. Berdrow, *Briefe*, p. 50.

23. Wilhelm Berdrow, *Alfred Krupp*, Band I, Berlin: Reimar Hobbing, 1928, pp. 128–29.

24. HAK, WA 4/76, October 1867 reports.

25. Jeffrey A. Auerbach, *The Great Exhibition of 1851: A nation on display*, New Haven: Yale University Press, 1999, pp. 161, 163.

26. Krupp to Collegium, April 13, 1851: HAK, FAH 2 B 20; also edited in Berdrow, *Briefe*, p. 119.

27. Wolbring, *Krupp*, p. 97.

28. Berdrow, *Briefe*, p. 122.

29. Louis Konstanz Berger, *Der alte Harkort. Ein westfälisches Lebens- und Zeitbild*, Leipzig: Baedeker, 1890, S. 474.

30. Krupp to von Todtleben, May 21, 1864; as edited in Berdrow, *Briefe*, pp. 205–6.

31. *Krupp 1812–1912*, p. 151.

32. Krupp to Firma, November 1871; as edited in Berdrow, *Briefe*, pp. 265, 266.

33. See Ralf Stremmel, "Globalisierung im 19. und 20 Jahrhundert: Ausgewählte Daten zum Export der Firma Krupp," *Essener Beiträge: Beiträge zur Geschichte von Stadt und Stift Essen* 133, 2009.

34. Krupp to Friedrich Alfred Krupp, January 1, 1875; as edited in Berdrow, *Briefe*, p. 309.

35. Wen-tang Yü, *Die deutsch-chinesische Beziehungen 1860–1880*, Bochum: Brockmeyer, 1981, pp. 129–33.

36. Krupp to Prokura, February 13, 1875; as edited in Berdrow, *Briefe*, p. 314; Jane E. Elliott, *Some did it for civilization, some did it for their country: A revised view of the Boxer War*, Hong Kong: Chinese University of Hong Kong Press, 2002,

p. 482; Shellen Wu, "Underground Empires," Princeton University PhD diss., 2010, p. 144.

37. Berdrow, *Briefe*, p. 12.

38. Krupp to Freiherrn von Bodelschwingh-Velmede, November 11, 1835: HAK, FAH 2 B 1; also edited in Berdrow, *Briefe*, pp. 28, 30.

39. Krupp to Leutnant von Donat, July 16, 1843: HAK, FAH 2 B 97; also edited in Berdrow, *Briefe*, p. 68.

40. Berdrow, *Briefe*, p. 74. Also *Krupp 1812–1912*, p. 141; Beyer, *Tiegelstahl*, p. 370.

41. Krupp to Richter and Hagdorn, June 10, 1848: HAK, FAH 2 P 125; also edited in Berdrow, *Briefe*, p. 106.

42. Berdrow, *Briefe*, p. 131.

43. Berdrow, *Briefe*, p. 133.

44. Berdrow, *Briefe*, p. 135.

45. *Krupp 1812–1912*, p. 133.

46. Berdrow, *Briefe*, p. 173.

47. Krupp to Prince Regent William, March 8, 1860; as edited in Berdrow, *Briefe*, p. 176.

48. *Krupp 1812–1912*, p. 143.

49. Friedrich Sölling to Krupp, July 17, 1852: HAK, WA 9 v 103.

50. Berdrow, *Briefe*, p. 172.

51. Berdrow, *Briefe*, p. 144.

52. Krupp to Carl Meyer, April 13, 1857: HAK, FAH 2 B 199; also edited in Berdrow, *Briefe*, p. 154.

53. Beyer, *Tiegelstahl*, pp. 549–50.

54. Berdrow, *Briefe*, p. 169.

55. Krupp to von Roon, June 1, 1860; as edited in Berdrow, *Briefe*, p. 180.

56. Krupp to Alexander von Humboldt, January 4, 1858: HAK, FAH 2 C 21; also edited in Berdrow, *Briefe*, p. 160.

57. Konstantin Bernhard von Voigts-Rhetz to Krupp, July 9, 1866: HAK, FAH 2 C 1; also edited in Berdrow, *Briefe*, p. 223.

58. Berdrow, *Briefe*, p. 195.

59. Berdrow, *Briefe*, p. 218.

60. Krupp to Albrecht von Roon, April 13, 1866: HAK, FAH 2 B 51; Wolbring, *Krupp*, p. 46.

61. Berdrow, *Briefe*, p. 229.

62. Krupp to Kaiser Wilhelm I, April 23, 1871: HAK, WA 4/3502; also edited in Berdrow, *Briefe*, pp. 257, 259.

63. Alfred Krupp, "Ansprache an die Angehörigen meiner Gussstahlfabrik und der meiner Firma Fried. Krupp gehörenden Berg- und Hüttenwerke," February 1887: HAK, FAH 2 F 8; also edited in Berdrow, *Briefe*, p. 422.

64. *Krupp 1812–1912*, p. 274.

65. Wolbring, *Krupp*, pp. 43–44.

66. Berdrow, *Briefe*, p. 271.

67. Krupp to Crown Prince, January 16, 1880; Berdrow, *Briefe*, p. 372.

68. Wolbring, *Krupp*, pp. 138–41.

69. Memorandum of Alfred Krupp, July 1879: HAK, WA 7 c/22 (typewritten copy of 1905 as annex to letter of November 11, 1905, to Landrat Rötge and Director Eccius).

70. Hansard, House of Commons, *Parliamentary debates* (hereinafter HC *Deb*), vol. 243, p. 1861, February 27, 1879 (John Nolan); HC *Deb*, vol. 177, p. 963, March 2, 1865 (Henry Baillie); HC *Deb*, vol. 259, p. 1398, March 18, 1881 (W. H. Smith).

71. *Essener Zeitung*, no. 182, August 7, 1879, p. 2.

72. Berdrow, *Briefe*, p. 32.

73. Krupp to Konstantin Bernhard von Voigts-Rhetz, October 13, 1859: HAK, FAH 2 B 199.

74. See Lindenlaub and Köhne-Lindenlaub, "Unternehmensfinanzierung," p. 121.

75. Krupp to Freiherrn Kübeck von Kübau, July 16, 1842: HAK, FAH 2 B 14; also edited in Berdrow, *Briefe*, p. 65.

76. Berdrow, *Briefe*, p. 92.

77. Lindenlaub and Köhne-Lindenlaub, "Unternehmensfinanzierung," p. 143.

78. Friedrich Sölling to Krupp, July 10, 1855: HAK, WA 9 v 96.

79. Krupp to Ernst Waldthausen, March 28, 1857: HAK, WA 4/111; also edited in Berdrow, *Briefe*, p. 153.

80. Berdrow, *Briefe*, p. 170.

81. W. S. Deichmann to Krupp, October 16, 1864: HAK, FAH 2 B 56; also edited in Berdrow, *Briefe*, p. 208.

82. *Krupp 1812–1912*, p. 200.

83. Weise of Disconto-Gesellschaft to Ernst Waldthausen, 1856: HAK, WA 9 d 354.

84. Krupp to Prokura, July 26, 1873; as edited in Berdrow, *Briefe*, p. 290.

85. Lother Gall, *Krupp: der Aufstieg eines Industrieimperiums*, Berlin: Siedler, 2000, p. 184; Ulrich Wengenroth, "Krisen in der deutschen Stahlindustrie im Kaiserreich und in der Zwischenkriegszeit," in Friedrich-Wilhelm Henning (ed.), *Krisen und Krisenbewältigung vom 19. Jahrhundert bis heute*, Frankfurt: Peter Land, 1998, p. 55; Gert von Klass, *Die drei Ringe: Lebensgeschichte eines Industrieunternehmens*, Tübingen und Stuttgart 1953, p. 121; Richard Tilly, "Die Industrialisierung des Ruhrgebietes und das Problem der Kapitalmobilisierung," in Richard Tilly (ed.), *Kapital, Staat und sozialer Protest in der deutschen Industrialisierung*, Göttingen: Vandenhoeck & Ruprecht, 1980, p. 66; Volker Wellhöner, *Grossbanken und Grossindustrie im Kaiserreich*, Göttingen: Vandenhoeck & Ruprecht, 1989, p. 158; Jürgen Lindenlaub, *Die Finanzierung des Aufstiegs von Krupp. Die Personengesellschaft Krupp im Vergleich zu den Kapitalgesellschaften Bochumer Verein, Hoerder Verein und Phoenix 1850 bis 1880*, Essen: Klartext, 2006.

86. "Memoire" of Krupp: HAK, FAH 2 B 229.

87. Gall, *Krupp*, p. 173.

88. Cited in Wolbring, *Krupp*, pp. 51–52.

89. Ernst Eichhoff to Krupp, April 24, 1873: HAK, FAH 2 B 229.

90. Cited in Wellhöner, *Grossbanken*, p. 157.

91. Berdrow, *Briefe*, p. 316.

92. Berdrow, *Briefe*, p. 84.

93. Krupp to Wilhelm Loerbroks and Firma, October 6, 1871: HAK, FAH 2 B 180; also edited in Berdrow, *Briefe*, p. 262.

94. Krupp to Ludwig Wiegand (Prokura), January 15, 1865: HAK, FAH 2 B 185; also edited in Berdrow, *Briefe*, p. 209.

95. Berdrow, *Briefe*, p. 311.

96. Berdrow, *Briefe*, p. 324.

97. Berdrow, *Briefe*, p. 81.

98. See Heinz Reif, "'Ein seltener Kreis von Freunden': Arbeitsprozesse und Arbeitserfahrungen bei Krupp 1840–1914," in (ed.) Klaus Tenfelde, *Arbeit und Arbeitserfahrung in der Geschichte*, Göttingen: Vandenhoeck & Ruprecht, 1986.

99. Krupp to Firma, March 2, 1867: HAK, FAH 2 P 106; also edited in Berdrow, *Briefe*, p. 228.

100. Krupp, 1873: HAK, FAH 2 F 2.

101. Krupp to Firma, February 24, 1870: HAK, WA 4/269; also edited in Berdrow, *Briefe*, p. 243.

102. Krupp to Ernst Eichhoff, September 1, 1872: HAK, FAH 2 B 181; also edited in Berdrow, *Briefe*, p. 275.

103. See Ernst Schröder, "Alfred Krupps Generalregulativ," *Tradition* 1, 1956, pp. 35–77.

104. Schröder, "Alfred Krupps Generalregulativ," p. 41; *Krupp 1812–1912*, p. 289.

105. Schröder, "Alfred Krupps Generalregulativ," p. 46.

106. Berdrow, *Briefe*, p. 301.

107. Krupp to Prokura, December 31, 1874; as edited in Berdrow, *Briefe*, p. 307.

108. Gall, *Krupp*, p. 186.

109. *Krupp 1812–1912*, p. 290.

110. Krupp to Ernst Eichhoff, December 6, 1871: HAK, FAH 2 B 180; also edited in Berdrow, *Briefe*, p. 267.

111. Beyer, *Tiegelstahl*, p. 104.

112. *Krupp 1812–1912*, p. 103.

113. Beyer, *Tiegelstahl*, p. 111.

114. Gall, *Krupp*, p. 79.

115. Beyer, *Tiegelstahl*, p. 379.

116. Bertha Krupp to Alfred Krupp, July 25, 1857; as edited in Berdrow, *Briefe*, p. 157.

117. Krupp to Firma, October 10, 1871: HAK, FAH 2 B 180; also edited in Berdrow, *Briefe*, p. 263.

118. See Renate Köhne-Lindenlaub, *The Villa Hügel: An entrepreneur's residence in the course of time*, Berlin: Deutscher Kunstverlag, 2003; Tilman Buddensieg (ed.), *Villa Hügel: Das Wohnhaus Krupp in Essen*, Berlin: Siedler, 1984.

119. Cited in Knut Borchardt, "Der Unternehmerhaushalt als Wirtschaftsbetrieb," in Buddensieg (ed.), *Villa Hügel*, p. 12.

120. Fahri Türk, *Die deutsche Rüstungsindustrie in ihren Türkengeschäften zwischen 1871 und 1914*, Frankfurt: Peter Lang, 2007, p. 177.

121. Borchardt, "Der Unternehmerhaushalt als Wirtschaftsbetrieb," p. 27.

122. Krupp to Prokura, July 18, 1884; as edited in Berdrow, *Briefe*, p. 403.

123. Krupp to Friedrich Alfred Krupp, December 22, 1874; as edited in Berdrow, *Briefe*, p. 306.

124. Krupp to Friedrich Alfred Krupp, February 18, 1875; as edited in Berdrow, *Briefe*, p. 315.

125. Berdrow, *Briefe*, p. 84.

126. Krupp to Prokura, December 15, 1873: HAK, WA 4/269; also edited in Berdrow, *Briefe*, p. 297.

127. Krupp to Ernst Eichhoff, January 31, 1872: HAK, FAH 2 B 181; also edited in Berdrow, *Briefe*, p. 274.

128. Berdrow, *Briefe*, p. 333.

129. Meyer to Goose, April 6, 1877; as edited in Berdrow, *Briefe*, p. 350.

130. *Krupp 1812–1912*, p. 265.

131. Cited in "Die Krupps. Lebensabriss von Friedrich Krupp, Alfred Krupp und Friedrich Alfred Krupp," Essen, 1912, manuscript in HAK.

132. "Gemeinschaftliches Festlied," dedication of the Krupp monument, 1892: HAK, FAH 2 G 19.

133. Richard Ehrenberg, *Grosse Vermögen: Ihre Entstehung und ihre Bedeutung, Die Fugger-Rothschild-Krupp*, Jena: Gustav Fischer, 1902, p. 208.

CHAPTER 3: SCIENCE

1. F. A. Krupp to Armand von Ardenne, February 2, 1896: HAK, FAH 3 C 60, Bd. 2; also edited in Michael Epkenhans and Ralf Stremmel (eds.), *Friedrich Alfred Krupp. Ein Unternehmer im Kaiserreich*, Munich: C. H. Beck, 2010, p. 304.

2. Quoted by Lothar Gall, *Krupp: der Aufstieg eines Industrieimperiums*, Berlin: Siedler, 2000, p. 325.

3. Letter of January 8, 1885; quoted by Barbara Wolbring, *Krupp und die Öffentlichkeit im 19. Jahrhundert*, Munich: C. H. Beck, 2000, p. 200.

4. Gall, *Krupp*, p. 250.

5. Volker Wellhöner, *Grossbanken und Grossindustrie im Kaiserreich*, Göttingen: Vandenhoeck & Ruprecht, 1989, p. 147.

6. Quoted by Wolfgang König, *Wilhelm II und die Moderne: Der Kaiser und die technisch-industrielle Welt*, Paderborn: Schöningh, 2007, p. 236.

7. Krupp to editorial office [Redaktion] of *Berliner Börsenzeitung*, July 26, 1887: HAK, FAH 3 B 102.

8. Krupp comment on report of Hanns Jencke (21.8.1892), September 22, 1893: HAK, FAH 3 B 121.

9. Wilhelm Muehlon, *Ein Fremder im eignen Land: Erinnerungen und Tagebuchaufzeichnungen eines Krupp-Direktors 1908–1914*, Bremen: Domat, 1989, p. 61.

10. Ralf Stremmel, "Unternehmensziel Bildung. Der Kruppsche Bildungsverein als Sonderfall?" *Essener Beiträge: Beiträge zur Geschichte von Stadt und Stift Essen* 119, 2006, pp. 239–62, 249.

11. *Evening Telegraph*, April 2, 1902, quoted by Ralf Stremmel, "Von der 'Treue' zum 'Vertrauen'? Friedrich Alfred Krupp und seine Beschäftigten (1887 bis 1902)," *Zeitschrift für Unternehmensgeschichte* 51/1, 2006, p. 84.

12. Heinz Dieter Franke, "Friedrich Alfred Krupp und die Naturwissenschaften," in Epkenhans and Stremmel (eds.), *Friedrich Alfred Krupp*, p. 132.

13. Anna Caspary, "Das Leben von Frau Margarethe Krupp geb. Freiin von Ende" (manuscript), Teil 2b: HAK, FAH 3 M 77.

14. Franke, "Friedrich Alfred Krupp," pp. 141, 152–55; Rudolf Korn to Ernst Haeckel, June 5, 1902: HAK, FAH 3 D 159.

15. Ralf Stremmel, "Friedrich Alfred Krupp: Handeln und Selbstverständnis eines Unternehmers," in Epkenhans and Stremmel (eds.), *Friedrich Alfred Krupp*, pp. 34–36; Gall, *Krupp*, p. 328; Harald Regner, "Schumpeterian German firms before and after World War I: The innovative few and the non-innovative many," *Zeitschrift für Unternehmensgeschichte* 54/1, 2009, pp. 50–72.

16. Stremmel, "Friedrich Alfred Krupp," p. 41.

17. Wellhöner, *Grossbanken*, p. 159.

18. Wellhöner, *Grossbanken*, pp. 160–61.

19. Calculated from figures in HAK, WA 4.

20. Ralf Stremmel, "Globalisierung im 19. und 20. Jahrhundert. Ausgewählte Daten zum Export der Firma Krupp," in *Essener Beiträge: Beiträge zur Geschichte von Stadt und Stift Essen* 122, 2009, pp. 97–113.

21. Shellen Wu, "*Underground Empires*," Princeton University PhD diss., 2010.

22. Stremmel, "Friedrich Alfred Krupp," pp. 62–64.

23. Institut für Zeitgeschichte, Munich, ED 142/37, December 16, 1917, Muehlon letter to Friedrich Wilhelm Foerster, as copied in January 12, 1918, memorandum of Stellvertreter Generalstab der Armee.

24. Clive Trebilcock, *The Vickers Brothers: Armaments and enterprise, 1854–1914*, London: Europa, 1977, pp. 120–23.

25. Trebilcock, *Vickers*, pp. 125–27.

26. Gerald D. Feldman, *Iron and steel in the German inflation, 1916–1923*, Princeton, N.J.: Princeton University Press, 1977, p. 17.

27. König, *Wilhelm II*, p. 161; Michael Epkenhans, "Zwischen Patriotismus und Geschäftsinteresse: F. A. Krupp und die Anfänge des deutschen Schlachtflottenbaus 1897–1902, *Geschichte und Gesellschaft* 15, 1989, p. 199; see also Fahri Türk, *Die deutsche Rüstungsindustrie in ihren Türkeigeschäften zwischen 1871 und 1914*, Frankfurt: Peter Lang, 2007, p. 197.

28. Wolbring, *Krupp*, p. 210.

29. *Volks-Zeitung*, September 20, 1887: HAK, WA 41/2-100b; *Berliner Zeitung*, no. 438, September 20, 1887: HAK, WA 41/2-100b.

30. Wolbring, *Krupp*, p. 257.

31. Krupp to Hanns Jencke, October 14, 1897: HAK, FAH 3 B 126; also edited in Michael Epkenhans, "Grossindustrie und

Schlachtflottenbau 1897–1914," *Militärgeschichtliche Mitteilungen* 43, 1988, p. 95.

32. See Geoff Eley, *Reshaping the German right: Radical nationalism and political change after Bismarck*, New Haven: Yale University Press, 1980, p. 78.

33. *Germania*, November 14, 1899; quoted by Wolbring, *Krupp*, p. 273.

34. Eley, *Reshaping*, p. 144.

35. December 12, 1899, Reichstag session; quoted by Wolbring, *Krupp*, p. 284.

36. Telegram of Wilhelm II to directory board [Direktorium], July 11, 1900: HAK, FAH 3 B 35.

37. Wolbring, *Krupp*, p. 288.

38. Krupp memorandum for Wilhelm II, undated: HAK, FAH 3 B 36; Notes of Krupp for audience with Wilhelm II, undated: HAK, FAH 3 B 36; also edited in Epkenhans, "Grossindustrie," pp. 98 and 100.

39. Friedrich von Hollmann to Krupp, July 19, 1900: HAK, FAH 3 C 233; also edited in Epkenhans and Stremmel (eds.), *Friedrich Alfred Krupp*, p. 326.

40. Epkenhans, "Grossindustrie," pp. 74–75.

41. Angelika Schaser, "Margarethe Krupp: Entwurf eines Lebens im Zentrum der Krupp-Saga," in Epkenhans and Stremmel (eds.), *Friedrich Alfred Krupp*, pp. 191–92.

42. See Wolbring, *Krupp*, p. 310.

43. Article "Capri Sodoma," in *Propaganda*, October 15, 1902, quoted by Dieter Richter, "Friedrich Alfred Krupp auf Capri. Ein Skandal und seine Geschichte," in Epkenhans and Stremmel (eds.), *Friedrich Alfred Krupp*, p. 173. See also Carlo Knight, *Die Capri-Utopie von Krupp*, Capri, 2002.

44. *Vorwärts*, November 15, 1902: HAK, FAH 3 G 9; also Diana Maria Friz, *Margarethe Krupp: das Leben meiner*

Urgrossmutter, Munich: Deutscher Taschenbuch Verlag, 2008, pp. 354–55.

45. *Berliner Tageblatt*, November 30, 1902; quoted by Wolbring, *Krupp*, p. 319.

46. F. A. Krupp to Ernst Schweninger, September 19, 1902: Bundesarchiv Berlin, N 2281/90, quoted by Schaser, "Margarethe Krupp," p. 195; See also Isabel V. Hull, *The entourage of Kaiser Wilhelm II, 1888–1918*, Cambridge: Cambridge University Press, 1982, pp. 169–70.

47. Caspary, "Margarethe Krupp."

48. Quoted by Wolbring, *Krupp*, p. 322.

49. Margaret Lavinia Anderson, *Practicing democracy: Elections and political culture in Imperial Germany*, Princeton, N.J.: Princeton University Press, 2000, pp. 274–75.

CHAPTER 4: DIPLOMACY

1. Rudolf Herzog, *Die Stoltenkamps und ihre Frauen*, Berlin: Deutsche Buch-Gemeinschaft, 1917, p. 11.

2. Wilhelm Muehlon, *Ein Fremder im eigenen Land: Erinnerungen und Tagebuchaufzeichnungen eines Krupp-Direktors 1908–1914*, Düsseldorf: Donat, 1989.

3. Ernst Haux, "Bei Krupp 1890–1935. Bilder der Erinnerung aus 45 Jahren," manuscript, p. 66: HAK, FAH 4 E 16.

4. F. A. Krupp to Margarethe Krupp, December 31, 1900: HAK, FAH 3 D 173; also edited in Michael Epkenhans and Ralf Stremmel (eds.), *Friedrich Alfred Krupp. Ein Unternehmer im Kaiserreich*, Munich: C. H. Beck, 2010, p. 328.

5. Poem of 1906, sent to Gustav von Bohlen und Halbach by Margarethe Krupp, August 17, 1906: HAK, FAH 23/860.

6. Letter of Kaiser Wilhelm II to Bertha Krupp, December 12, 1902: HAK, FAH 4 E 782; also edited in Ralf Stremmel,

"Kaiser Willhelm II' und sein Idealbild vom Unternehmer: ein Brief aus dem Jahre 1902," in Wilfried Feldenkirchen, Susanne Hilger, and Kornelia Rennert (eds.), *Geschichte— Unternehmen—Archive*, Essen: Klartext, 2008, p. 70.

7. Klaus Tenfelde, "Krupp in Krieg und Krisen: Unternehmensgeschichte der Fried. Krupp AG 1914 bis 1924/25," in Lothar Gall (ed.), *Krupp im 20. Jahrhundert: Die Geschichte des Unternehmens vom Ersten Weltkrieg bis zur Gründung der Stiftung*, Berlin: Siedler, 2002, p. 149.

8. Lothar Gall, *Krupp: der Aufstieg eines Industrieimperiums*, Berlin: Siedler, 2000, pp. 323–24; Tenfelde, "Krupp in Krieg," p. 149.

9. Hansard, House of Commons, *Parliamentary debates*, vol. 8, p. 891, 26 July 1909.

10. See Ralf Stremmel, "Globalisierung im 19. und 20. Jahrhundert. Ausgewählte Daten zum Export der Firma Krupp," in *Essener Beiträge: Beiträge zur Geschichte von Stadt und Stift Essen* 122, 2009, pp. 97–113.

11. See Wolfgang König, *Wilhelm II und die Moderne: Der Kaiser und die technisch-industrielle Welt*, Paderborn: Schöningh, 2007, p. 161.

12. Muehlon, *Fremder*, p. 44.

13. Muehlon, *Fremder*, p. 60.

14. Alfred Hugenberg memorandum, "Krupp als gemischtwirtschaftlicher Betrieb?" April 3, 1914: HAK, WA 4/1957; also edited in Michael Epkenhans, "Grossindustrie und Schlachtflottenbau 1897–1914," *Militärgeschichtliche Mitteilungen* 43, 1988, pp. 109–14.

15. Quoted by Epkenhans, "Grossindustrie," p. 82.

16. HAK, WA 7f/1094; Tenfelde, "Krupp in Krieg," p. 47.

17. Tenfelde, "Krupp in Krieg," p. 37; Richard Foerster memorandum, "Die Sicherung des Werkes in Erz und Kohle," October 31, 1915: HAK, W 4/1426.

18. Gerald D. Feldman, *Iron and steel in the German inflation, 1916–1923*, Princeton, N.J.: Princeton University Press, 1977, pp. 68–69, citing meetings of April 6, 1917, and May 15, 1918, Rheinisch-Westfälisches Wirtschaftsarchiv Cologne, Historisches Archiv der Gutehoffnungshütte, 3000035/2.

19. See Lothar Burchardt, "Zwischen Kriegsgewinn und Kriegskosten: Krupp im Ersten Weltkrieg," *Zeitschrift für Unternehmensgeschichte* 32/2, 1987, pp. 71–122.

20. Burchardt, "Zwischen Kriegsgewinn und Kriegskosten," p. 82.

21. Holger Afflerbach (ed.), *Kaiser Wilhelm II. als Oberster Kriegsherr im Ersten Weltkrieg. Quellen aus der militärischen Umgebung des Kaisers 1914–1918*, Munich: Oldenbourg, 2005, p. 501.

22. Gustav Krupp von Bohlen und Halbach to Ernst Haux, April 7, 1917: HAK, FAH 4 C 73b.

23. Tenfelde, "Krupp in Krieg," p. 81.

24. Heinrich Potthof (ed.), *Friedrich von Berg als Chef des Geheimen Zivilkabinetts, Erinnerungen aus seinem Nachlass*, Düsseldorf: Droste, 1971, pp. 169–70; "Unser Kaiser ist doch ein lieber Kerl." *Kruppsche Mitteilungen*, no. 36, September 14, 1918, p. 219.

CHAPTER 5: TRADITION

1. Erik Reger, *Union der festen Hand*, Berlin: Klartext, 2007, pp. 305, 219, 220.

2. See Ernst Schröder, *Otto Wiedfeldt: Eine Biographie*, Essen: Beiträge zur Geschichte von Stadt und Stift Essen 80, 1964. Otto Wiedfeldt, "Die Vereinbarung im deutschen Baugewerbe vom Frühjahr 1908," *Deutsche Wirtschaftszeitung* 4/20, October 15, 1908, p. 924.

3. Gustav Krupp von Bohlen und Halbach to directory board [Direktorium], November 19, 1918: HAK, FAH 4 C 6.

4. Otto Wiedfeldt memorandum, concept, September 4, 1925: HAK, WA 4/1417.

5. Schröder memorandum, December 4, 1938: HAK, WA 40 B 1307.

6. Otto Wiedfeldt conversation with David Lloyd George, March 1, 1922: HAK, WA 4/1418.

7. Klaus Tenfelde, "Krupp in Krieg und Krisen: Unternehmensgeschichte der Fried. Krupp AG 1914 bis 1924/25," in Lothar Gall (ed.), *Krupp im 20. Jahrhundert: Die Geschichte des Unternehmens vom Ersten Weltkrieg bis zur Gründung der Stiftung*, Berlin: Siedler, 2002, pp. 150–51.

8. Walther Rathenau to Otto Wiedfeldt, October 30, 1919: HAK, WA 4/2004; see also Tenfelde, "Krupp in Krieg," p. 155.

9. Otto Wiedfeldt to Albert Vögler, November 3, 1919: HAK, WA 3/225.

10. Jeffrey R. Fear, *Organizing control: August Thyssen and the construction of German corporate management*, Cambridge, Mass.: Harvard University Press, 2005, p. 525.

11. Gerald D. Feldman, *The great disorder: politics, economics and society in the German inflation, 1914–1924*, New York: Oxford University Press, 1993, p. 280.

12. Gerald D. Feldman, *Iron and steel in the German inflation, 1916–1923*, Princeton, N.J.: Princeton University Press, 1977, pp. 367–68; citing Banking Section Fried. Krupp to Ministerialdirektor Schäffer, June 4, 1923, HAK, WA 4/2560.

13. Tenfelde, "Krupp in Krieg und Krisen," p. 134.

14. William C. McNeil, *American money and the Weimar Republic: Economics and politics on the eve of the Great Depression*, New York: Columbia University Press, 1986, p. 74; Fear, *Organizing control*, p. 492.

15. Wiedfeldt memorandum, September 4, 1925.

16. Toni Pierenkemper, "Von Krise zur Krise. Die Fried. Krupp AG von der Währungsstabilisierung bis zum Ende

der Weimarer Republik," in Lothar Gall (ed.), *Krupp im 20. Jahrhundert: Die Geschichte des Unternehmens vom Ersten Weltkrieg bis zur Gründung der Stiftung,* Berlin: Siedler, 2002, p. 186.

17. Wiedfeldt memorandum, September 4, 1925.

18. Wiedfeldt memorandum, September 4, 1925.

19. Wiedfeldt memorandum, September 4, 1925.

20. Fear, *Organizing control,* pp. 508–9.

21. Gustav Krupp von Bohlen und Halbach to Albert Vögler, September 20, 1925: HAK, FAH 4 C 45; Bernd Weisbrod, *Schwerindustrie in der Weimarer Republik: Interessenpolitik zwischen Stabilisierung und Krise,* Wuppertal: P. Hammer, 1978, p. 97; see also Alfred Reckendrees, *Das "Stahltrust"-Projekt: die Gründung der Vereinigte Stahlwerke A.G. und ihre Unternehmensentwicklung 1926–1933/34,* München: Beck, 2000, pp. 171–72.

22. Weisbrod, *Schwerindustrie,* pp. 440–41.

23. Weisbrod, *Schwerindustrie,* p. 179.

24. Hartmut Pogge von Strandmann, "Grossindustrie und Rapallopolitik: Deutsch-sowjetische Handelsbeziehungen in der Weimarer Republik," *Historische Zeitschrift* 222, 1976, p. 331.

25. Extract from a collection of the minutes of the supervisory board [Aufsichtsrat], 1947, here: minutes of the meeting of December 2, 1932: HAK, WA 40 B 1458.

CHAPTER 6: POWER AND DEGLOBALIZATION

1. See Urs Bitterli, *Golo Mann, Instanz und Aussenseiter,* Zurich: NZZ Verlag, 2004, pp. 524–25; also Tilmann Lahme, *Golo Mann: Biographie,* Frankfurt: S. Fischer, 2009, pp. 389–91 (quote from p. 390); and Diana Maria Friz, *Alfried Krupp und Berthold Beitz: Der Erbe und sein Statthalter,* Zurich: Orell Füssli, 1988, p. 36.

2. "Werden und Wirken eines Deutschen Wirtschaftsfuehrers, dargestellt nach Nuernberger Dokumenten," oD: HAK, FAH 24/13.

3. *Trials of War Criminals before the Nuremberg Military Tribunals*, vol. 9, *The Krupp Case, Case 10*, Washington, D.C., 1950, pp. 159–60.

4. Christoph Buchheim and Jonas Scherner, "The role of private property in the Nazi economy: The case of industry," *Journal of Economic History* 66/2, 2006, pp. 390–416; Christoph Buchheim and Jonas Scherner, 2009, "Corporate freedom of action in Nazi Germany: A reply to Peter Hayes," *Bulletin of the German Historical Institute* (Washington, D.C.), Fall 2009, pp. 43–50. Also see Jonas Scherner, *Die Logik der Industriepolitik im Dritten Reich*, Stuttgart: Steiner, 2008. See also Neil Gregor, "Nazism: A political religion? Rethinking the voluntarist turn," in Neil Gregor (ed.), *Nazism, war and genocide: Essays in honour of Jeremy Noakes*, Exeter: University of Exeter Press, 2005, pp. 1–21.

5. *Case 10*, p. 788.

6. Ernst Schröder memorandum, December 1, 1938: HAK, WA 40 B/1307, see below; see, on Norbert Frei, Ralf Ahrens, Jörg Osterloh, and Tim Schanetzky, *Flick: Der Konzern, die Familie, die Macht*, München: Karl Blessing, 2009, p. 427: "in rejecting the prosecution case, the whole argumentation of the verdict shows how the judges had fallen into a trap set by business."

7. Buchheim and Scherner, "Role of private property"; Buchheim and Scherner, "Corporate freedom." Also see Jonas Scherner, *Die Logik der Industriepolitik im Dritten Reich*, Stuttgart: Steiner, 2008.

8. Tim Mason, "The primacy of politics: Politics and economics in National Socialist Germany," in Jane Caplan (ed.), *Nazis, Fascism and the working class: Essays by Tim Mason*,

Cambridge: Cambridge University Press, 1995, p. 68, quoted by Buchheim and Scherner, "Private Property," p. 392.

9. Joseph Goebbels, "Unser Sozialismus," *Der Angriff* 5/84, April 22, 1931, pp. 1–2.

10. Berlin Bundesarchiv, R43I/1459, February 8, 1933, ministerial meeting; Harold James, *The German slump: Politics and economics 1924–1936*, Oxford: Oxford University Press, 1986, p. 381.

11. Jahresbericht und Bilanz für das Geschäftsjahr vom 1. Oktober 1934 bis 30. September 1935: HAK, WA 65/115.34/35.

12. Schröder memorandum, December 1, 1938, Anlage 24.

13. Aktenvermerk: Besprechung mit Chef des Admiralstabes Raeder, January 12, 1933: HAK, FAH 23/747.

14. Niederschrift über die Besprechung in Meppen am 24. März 1933, March 27, 1933: HAK, FAH 23/747; Werner Abelshauser, "Rüstungsschmiede der Nation? Der Kruppkonzern im Dritten Reich und in der Nachkriegszeit 1933 bis 1951," in Lothar Gall (ed.), *Krupp im 20. Jahrhundert: Die Geschichte des Unternehmens vom Ersten Weltkrieg bis zur Gründung der Stiftung*, Berlin: Siedler, 2002, p. 276; Adam Tooze, *The wages of destruction: The making and breaking of the Nazi economy*, London; New York: Allen Lane, 2006, p. 122.

15. Abelshauser, "Rüstungsschmiede der Nation?" p. 336.

16. Abelshauser, "Rüstungsschmiede der Nation?" p. 344.

17. Abelshauser, "Rüstungsschmiede der Nation?" p. 339.

18. Ralf Ahrens, "Die Finanzierung eines Konzerns der 'alten' Rüstungsindustrie: Krupp," in Johannes Bähr (ed.), *Die Dresdner Bank in der Wirtschaft des Dritten Reichs*, Munich: Oldenbourg, 2006, p. 341.

19. Peter Hayes, "Corporate freedom of action in Nazi Germany," *Bulletin of the German Historical Institute* (Washington, D.C.), Fall 2009, pp. 29–42.

20. HAK, WA 40 B/1347, Anlage 11; see also Ralf Stremmel, "Globalisierung im 19. und 20 Jahrhundert: Ausgewählte Daten zum Export der Firma Krupp," *Essener Beiträge: Beiträge zur Geschichte von Stadt und Stift Essen* 122, 2009.

21. Tooze, *Wage*, p. 340.

22. See Mark Spoerer, *Von Scheingewinnen zum Rüstungsboom: Die Eigenkapitalrentabilität der deutschen Industrieaktiengesellschaften 1925–1941*, Stuttgart: Franz Steiner, 1996.

23. Henry Ashby Turner, Jr., *German big business and the rise of Hitler*, New York: Oxford University Press, 1985, pp. 318–20. Abelshauser, "Rüstungsschmiede der Nation?" p. 290.

24. Gustav Krupp to Tilo von Wilmowsky, February 1, 1933: HAK, FAH 23/507.

25. Turner, *German big business*, p. 321.

26. Franz von Papen to Gustav Krupp, February 15, 1933; Gustav Krupp to Franz von Papen, February 16, 1933: HAK, FAH 23/793. These papers were discovered in the British Foreign Office only in the early 1990s, and were then returned to the Krupp archive. They were examined by Richard Overy; see his "'Primacy always belongs to Politics': Gustav Krupp in the Third Reich," in R. J. Overy, *War and economy in the Third Reich*, Oxford: Oxford University Press, 1994, pp. 119–43, although Overy omits any consideration of the extraordinary political initiatives of Ludwig Kastl.

27. Ludwig Kastl to Gustav Krupp, February 25, 1933: HAK, FAH 23/793.

28. Notiz Gustav Krupp zur Rede Hitlers vor dem RDI, February 22, 1933: HAK, FAH 23/793.

29. Ludwig Kastl to Gustav Krupp, March 8, 1933: HAK, FAH 23/793.

30. See Turner, *German big business*, p. 334.

31. Ernst Poensgen to Gustav Krupp, July 12, 1934: HAK, FAH 23/793.

32. Hans Otto Eglau, *Fritz Thyssen, Hitlers Gönner und Geisel*, Berlin: Siedler, 2003, p. 151.

33. Avraham Barkai, "Deutsche Unternehmer und Judenpolitik im 'Dritten Reich,'" *Geschichte und Gesellschaft* 15, 1989, p. 234.

34. Turner, *German big business*, pp. 336–37 (quote p. 337).

35. Gustav Krupp to Kurt Schmitt, April 26, 1934: HAK, FAH 23/793.

36. Edouard Houdremont to Col. Edson D. Raff, commander of Essen Zone, May 25, 1945: HAK, WA 7 f/1423. See also Andreas Zilt, "Edouard Houdremont (1896–1958)," *Rheinisch-Westfälische Wirtschaftsbiographien*, Band 17, Münster: Aschendorff, 1999, pp. 474–503, especially p. 492.

37. Letter to Dr. Adolf Fry (draft), September 29, 1934: HAK, WA 131/779.

38. *Kruppsche Mitteilungen*, February 1, 1935, p. 172: Abschiedsfeier für Professor Strauss.

39. Freiherr v. Verschuer to Reichsgruppe Industrie, Dr. Betz, July 5, 1935: HAK, FAH 4 E 221a.

40. Fr. Wiedemann (Adjutant des Führers) to Gustav Krupp, February 24, 1937: HAK, FAH 23/648.

41. Dr. Ballas, Aktenvermerk über eine Besprechung mit Ewald Löser, October 26, 1946: HAK, WA 40 B/914.

42. Ewald Löser, Finanzplan der Fried. Krupp AG und des Konzerns vom 4. August 1939: HAK, FAH 4 C 76; see also Abelshauser, "Rüstungsschmiede der Nation?" p. 358.

43. Ahrens, "Finanzierung," p. 337.

44. Schröder memorandum, December 1, 1938.

45. Schröder memorandum, December 1, 1938; trade figures from Albrecht Ritschl, "Die deutsche Zahlungsbilanz 1936–1941 und das Problem des Devisenmangels vor Kriegsbeginn," *Vierteljahrshefte für Zeitgeschichte* 39/1, 1991, pp. 103–23.

46. Quoted by Abelshauser, "Rüstungsschmiede der Nation?" p. 363.

47. Gustav Krupp to Ewald Löser (concept), August 1, 1942: HAK, FAH 4 C 44.

48. Fried. Krupp AG to Garbotz, Ministerium für Bewaffnung und Munition, April 24, 1940: HAK, WA 131/779.

49. See Rolf-Dieter Müller, "Die Mobilisierung der deutschen Wirtschaft für Hitlers Kriegsführung," in Berhard R. Kroener, Rolf-Dieter Müller, and Hans Umbreit (eds.), *Das Deutsche Reich und der Zweite Weltkrieg* 5/1, Stuttgart: DVA, 1988, pp. 463, 475, 532; Dietrich Eichholtz, *Geschichte der deutschen Kriegswirtschaft 1939–1945*, Munich: K. G. Saur, 1999 (originally 1984), pp. 119–20; Georg Thomas (ed. Wolfgang Birkenfeld), *Geschichte der deutschen Kriegs- und Rüstungswirtschaft 1918–1943/45)*, Boppard: Harald Boldt, 1966, p. 511. Tooze, *Wages*, pp. 349–51, is slightly confusing, as he dates the train conversation as April 8 but records that Todt was appointed as minister on March 17, 1940.

50. Gustav Krupp to Martin Bormann (concept), November 11, 1942: HAK, FAH 23/755.

51. Abelshauser, "Rüstungsschmiede der Nation?" pp. 324–25.

52. The German Industrial Complexes: The Krupp Complex, September 1945: HAK, WA 42/614. See also Abelshauser, "Rüstungsschmiede der Nation?" pp. 462–64.

53. Golo Mann to Hans-Dieter Müller, May 25, 1983, quoted by Lahme, *Golo Mann*, p. 391.

54. Zilt, "Houdremont," pp. 485–86; Bericht von der Reise an Rhein und Ruhr vom 15.–23. November 1944, Bundesarchiv Berlin, R 3, Nr. 1542, quoted by Klaus-Dietmar Henke, *Die amerikanische Besetzung Deutschlands*, Munich: Oldenbourg, 1996, p. 518.

55. Abelshauser, "Rüstungsschmiede der Nation?" p. 335.

56. Abelshauser, "Rüstungsschmiede der Nation?" p. 337.

57. "An die Führung der Ausschüsse und Ringe," in *Nachrichten des Reichsministers für Bewaffnung und Munition*, May 6, 1942: HAK, FAH 24/742.

58. See Ahrens, Osterloh, and Schanetzky, *Flick*, pp. 285–91.

59. Abelshauser, "Rüstungsschmiede der Nation?" p. 382.

60. Jörg Friedrich, *Der Brand: Deutschland im Bombenkrieg 1940–1945*, Berlin: Ullstein, 2004, p. 298.

61. Figures from Krupp archive, WA 40 B 1376.

62. Abelshauser, "Rüstungsschmiede der Nation?" p. 385.

63. Abelshauser, "Rüstungsschmiede der Nation?" p. 392.

64. See Ulrich Herbert, *Hitler's foreign workers: Enforced foreign labor in Germany under the Third Reich*, New York and Cambridge: Cambridge University Press, 1997.

65. Tooze, *Wages*, p. 537.

66. Abelshauser, "Rüstungsschmiede der Nation?" p. 405.

67. Robert Ley in a discussion with Ruhr coal managers, October 4, 1942, Hotel "Kaiserhof Essen": HAK, FAH 24/720, S. 85, 97, 101.

68. Erlass des Generalbevollmächtigten für den Arbeitseinsatz vom 26.8.1942, in Schreiben der Bezirksgruppe Steinkohlenbergbau Ruhr der Wirtschaftsgruppe Bergbau an die Direktionen, October 22, 1942: HAK, WA 41/6-85a.

69. *Case 10*, pp. 1316–17, September 9, 1942, Gussstahlfabrik, Einrichtung einer Fertigungsstätte für Teile von automatischen Waffen (Auschwitz); pp. 1319–20, September 7, 1943, Krupp letter to Oberstleutnant von Wedel; Wolfgang Benz and Barbara Distel (eds.), *Der Ort des Terrors*, Munich: Beck, 2007, pp. 460–61.

70. Friedrich, *Brand*, p. 353.

71. In the Nuremberg case against Krupp, it was assumed that all these women had died, but in fact at least four hundred survived the war and claimed compensation.

72. Henke, *Die amerikanische Besetzung*, p. 491.

73. *Trials of War Criminals before the Nuernberg Military Tribunals under Control Council Law No. 10, Case 10*, Vol. IX, Nuremberg 1950: International Military Tribunal, p. 131.

CHAPTER 7: REGLOBALIZATION

1. Will Tremper, *Das Tall Komplott*, Vienna: Molden, 1973, p. 297.

2. *Der Spiegel* 27, July 9, 1973, "Komplott gegen BB," p. 105.

3. See S. Jonathan Wiesen, *West German industry and the challenge of the Nazi past, 1945–1955*, Chapel Hill: University of North Carolina Press, 2001, pp. 205–97.

4. John J. Mc Cloy to Karl Brandt, February 13, 1951: HAK, WA 40 B/1300.

5. See Isabel Warner, *Steel and sovereignty: The deconcentration of the West German steel industry, 1949–54*, Mainz: P. von Zabern, 1996, pp. 116–17.

6. Bericht Maschke über "Die Geschichte der Entwicklung des Statement von Alfried Krupp von Bohlen und Halbach" vom 12.–17. April 1956: HAK, WA 130/147.

7. Ralf Ahrens, Jörg Osterloh, and Tim Schanetzky, *Flick: Der Konzern, die Familie, die Macht*, München: Karl Blessing, 2009, p. 703; *Der Spiegel* 38, September 17, 1958, "Flick—Der Eisenmann," pp. 22–33.

8. Hansard, House of Commons, *Parliamentary debates*, vol. 505, p. 197, October 15, 1952, and vol. 511, p. 872, February 16, 1953. See also Warner, *Steel and sovereignty*, p. 208.

9. See Warner, *Steel and sovereignty*, p. 75.

10. *Der Spiegel* 9, February 26, 1968, "Dem deutschen Volke," p. 68.

11. Werner Bührer, "Frankreich und das Ruhrgebiet— Mythos und Realität," in Andreas Wilkens (ed.), *Die*

deutsch-französischen Wirtschaftsbeziehungen 1945–1960: Kolloquium des Deutschen Historischen Instituts Paris 8.–10. Dezember 1994 = Les relations économiques franco-allemandes 1945–1960: colloque tenu à l'Institut historique allemand de Paris du 8 au 10 décembre 1994, Sigmaringen: J. Thorbecke, 1997, p. 231, quoting François-Poncet on April 29, 1950.

12. *Der Spiegel* 23, June 5, 1963, "Star im Osten," p. 37.

13. Lothar Gall, "Von der Entlassung Alfried Krupp von Bohlen und Halbachs bis zur Errichtung seiner Stiftung 1951 bis 1967/68," in Lothar Gall (ed.), *Krupp im 20. Jahrhundert: Die Geschichte des Unternehmens vom Ersten Weltkrieg bis zur Gründung der Stiftung*, Berlin: Siedler, 2002, pp. 482–83.

14. Berthold von Bohlen und Halbach, Aktenvermerk, September 29, 1951: HAK, FAH 24/444.

15. Sylvie Lefèvre, "Les sidérurgistes français propriétaires de charbonnages dans la Ruhr (1945–1954), in Wilkens (ed.), *Die deutsch-französischen Wirtschaftsbeziehungen 1945–1960*, pp. 246–47.

16. Ralf Ahrens, Jörg Osterloh, and Tim Schanetzky, *Flick*, pp. 506, 511.

17. Joachim Käppner, *Berthold Beitz: Die Biographie*, Berlin: Berlin Verlag, 2010, p. 109; Thomas Sandkühler, *"Endlösung" in Galizien: Der Judenmord in Ostpolen und die Rettungsinitiativen von Berthold Beitz 1941–1944*, Bonn: J.H.W. Dietz, 1996, p. 405; Bernd Schmalhausen, *Berthold Beitz im Dritten Reich: Mensch in unmenschlicher Zeit*, Essen: Pomp, 1991.

18. *Der Spiegel* 41, October 6, 1997, "Der Kampf um das Krupp-Erbe," p. 115.

19. *Der Spiegel* 47, November 20, 1995, "Einer hält die Hand drüber," p. 59.

20. *Kruppsche Mitteilungen* 2, March 1953, p. 60.

21. *Der Spiegel* 12, March 13, 1967, "Krupp-Krise— Schulden und Sühne," p. 23.

22. Carl Hundhausen, *Industrielle Publizität als Public Relations*, Essen: Girardet, 1957, pp. 13, 15; Edward L. Bernays, *Public relations*, Norman: University of Oklahoma Press, 1952.

23. Carl Hundhausen to Berthold Beitz, December 21, 1954: HAK, FAH 29/57; see also Wiesen, *West German industry*, pp. 107, 230; Louis Lochner, *Tycoons and tyrant: German industry from Hitler to Adenauer*, Chicago: H. Regnery Co., 1954.

24. Berthold Beitz interview with Golo Mann: HAK.

25. Wiesen, *West German industry*, pp. 141.

26. *Der Spiegel* 49, November 30, 1955, pp. 27f.

27. Staatssekretär im Bundeswirtschaftsministerium Ludwig Kattenstroth to Berthold Beitz, August 23, 1957: HAK, WA 130/144.

28. John J. McCloy to Alfried Krupp von Bohlen und Halbach, June 20, 1958: HAK, WA 66/99; see also Gall, "Von der Entlassung," p. 552.

29. Hansard, House of Commons, *Parliamentary debates*, vol. 617, p. 456, February 10, 1960, and vol. 765, p. 31, May 20, 1968.

30. William Diebold, *The Schuman Plan: A study in economic cooperation 1950–1959*, New York, 1959, p. 357; Warner, *Steel and sovereignty*, pp. 229–30.

31. Gall, "Von der Entlassung," p. 512.

32. Berthold Beitz speech, "Die Aufgaben von morgen," *Krupp Mitteilungen* 7, November 20, 1961 (Sonderausgabe 150 Jahre Fried. Krupp), p. 5.

33. Gall, "Von der Entlassung," p. 516.

34. Bührer, "Frankreich und das Ruhrgebiet," p. 234.

35. Auszug aus dem Manuskript der Ansprache zur Jubilarfeier der Firma Krupp am 17.1.1954 für die Presse: HAK, WA 63/80.

36. Beitz "Die Aufgaben von morgen," p. 5.

37. *Der Spiegel* 23, June 5, 1963, "Star im Osten," p. 37.

38. *Der Spiegel* 23, June 5, 1963, "Star im Osten," p. 37.

39. Hans-Peter Schwarz, *Adenauer: Der Staatsmann 1952–1967*, DVA: Stuttgart, 1991, p. 686.

40. *Der Spiegel* 23, June 5, 1963, "Star im Osten," p. 34.

41. Wortprotokoll des Empfangs des Generalbevollmächtigten der Firma Krupp, Berthold Beitz durch den Vorsitzenden des Ministerrats der UdSSR, Nikita Chruschtschow, May 15, 1963, translation by Tatjana Ilarionowa of document in Presidential Archive of Russian Federation, 3, Inventory 64, file 960, pp. 27–46: HAK, WA 60/500.

42. *Der Spiegel* 23, June 4, 1973, "Die Chinesen zahlen bar," pp. 25, 32.

43. Johannes Schröder "Der finanzielle Herzinfarkt. Liquidität bleibt oberstes Gebot des Wirtschaftens," *Handelsblatt*, July 27/28, 1962: HAK, WA 4/3641, p. 1.

44. Letter of Alfred Haniel, October 21, 1963, cited in Harold James, *Family capitalism: Haniels, Wendels and Falcks*, Cambridge, Mass.: Harvard University Press, p. 289.

45. Ausschnitt aus der Ansprache von AKBH bei der Jubilarehrung am 2. April 1966, *Krupp Mitteilungen* 3, May 1966, p. 67.

46. *Der Spiegel* 47, November 20, 1995, "Einer hält die Hand drüber," p. 65.

47. Grussadresse von Hermann Josef Abs anlässlich des 80. Geburtstags von Berthold Beitz, September 26, 1993, quoted by Gall, "Von der Entlassung," pp. 660–61.

48. Hermann Josef Abs to Berthold Beitz, September 25, 1968, quoted in Gall, "Von der Entlassung," pp. 575–56.

49. *Time*, August 11, 1967, "Germany: End of the Dynasty."

50. *Der Spiegel* 41, October 6, 1997, "Der Kampf um das Krupp-Erbe," p. 115. Diana Maria Friz, *Alfred Krupp und Berthold Beitz: Der Erbe und sein Statthalter*, Zurich: Orell Füssli, 1988, p. 120.

51. *Time*, "End of the Dynasty,"

52. Gustav Krupp to Hans Heinrich Lammers, May 16, 1944: HAK, FAH 24/689.

53. Keith Richards with James Fox, *Life*, New York: Little Brown, 2010, p. 231.

54. *Die Zeit* 41, October 1, 1998; Hanns-Bruno Kammertöns, "*Der Letzte Krupp*." *Arndt von Bohlen und Halbach. Das Ende einer Dynastie*, Hoffmann und Campe: Hamburg 1998.

55. Volker R. Berghahn, *America and the intellectual cold wars in Europe: Shepard Stone between philanthropy, academy, and diplomacy*, Princeton, N.J.: Princeton University Press, 2001, p. 198.

56. *Frankfurter Allgemeine Zeitung*, April 17, 1967, Wilhelm Throm, "Der Krupp-Konzern morgen."

57. Berthold Beitz interviews, *Der Spiegel* 47, November 20, 1995, p. 52; *Frankfurter Allgemeine Zeitung*, July 19, 1997.

58. See Yves Mény and Vincent Wright, *The politics of steel: Western Europe and the steel industry in the crisis years (1974–1984)*, Berlin: de Gruyter, 1987.

59. *Der Spiegel* 30, July, 22, 1974, "Andere würden sich die Finger lecken," p. 25.

60. *Capital*, July 1979, "Was die Perser mit Krupp vorhaben."

61. Josef Esser and Werner Räth, "Overcoming the steel crisis in the Federal Republic of Germany 1974–1983," in Mény and Wright (eds.), *Politics of steel*, p. 666.

62. Figures from published company reports.

63. *Der Spiegel* 32, August 9, 1982, p. 46, "Bis zum First."

64. *Der Spiegel* 5, January 31, 1983, p. 81, "Endloser Streit."

65. See Esser and Räth, "Overcoming," pp. 675–77; Josef Esser and Wolfgang Fach, "Crisis management 'made in Germany': The steel industry," in Peter J. Katzenstein (ed.), *Industry and politics in West Germany: Toward the Third Republic*, Ithaca: Cornell University Press, 1989, p. 234.

66. See John Zysman, *Governments, markets, and growth: Finance and the politics of industrial change*, Ithaca: Cornell University Press, 1983; Jürgen Beyer and Martin Hoppner, "The disintegration of organised capitalism: German corporate governance in the 1990s," *West European Politics* http://www.informaworld.com/smpp/title~db=all~content=t713395181~tab=issueslist~branches=26 - v2626/4, October 2003, pp. 179–98.

67. Andreas Platthaus, *Alfred Herrhausen: Eine deutsche Karriere*, Berlin: Rowohlt, 2006, pp. 245–47.

68. See Wolfgang Streeck and Kozo Yamamura (eds.), *The end of diversity? Prospects for German and Japanese capitalism*, Ithaca: Cornell University Press, 2003, especially the article by Robert Boyer, "The embedded innovation systems of Germany and Japan: Distinctive features and futures," pp. 147–82.

69. *Financial Times*, March 14, 1996, Michael Lindemann, "Turnaround at Hoesch Krupp," p. 31.

70. *Financial Times*, October 11, 1991, Charles Leadbeater and Andrew Fisher, "Attempt to reinforce German steel," Companies, p. 19.

71. Esser and Fach, "Crisis management."

72. See *Financial Times*, November 5, 1997, "Steel groups give in to lure of wedlock," Companies, p. 31.

73. *Financial Times*, March 19, 1997, Companies, p. 36; *Financial Times*, March 25, 1997, "Krupp meets its match," p. 19.

74. See *Economist*, March 27, 1997, "Auf Wiedersehen, shareholders."

75. *Financial Times*, October 21, 1998, Tony Barber, "Thyssen Krupp sales to grow for three years," Companies, p. 31.

76. *Der Spiegel* 39, September 27, 1999, "Fusion mit Thyssen/Krupp?" p. 115; *Die Welt*, July 2, 1999, "Das 'Endspiel der Giganten' hat begonnen," quoting Manfred Gentz.

77. *Wirtschaftswoche*, June 11, 2004, "Iran will sich von Thyssen-Krupp Aktienpaket trennen."

78. *Die Welt,* November 17, 1999, "Thyssen-Krupp zieht sich vom Stahl zurück."

79. *Economist,* January 25, 2007, "Ring of steel."

80. *Handelsblatt,* November 20, 2009, "Steinbrück wird Aufseher bei Thyssen-Krupp."

ILLUSTRATIONS

1.1 Friedrich Krupp (1787–1826)   10
1.2 The Krupp works, c. 1820   18
1.3 Therese Krupp (1790–1850)   22
2.1 Julius Grün, portrait of Alfred Krupp, 1880s   25
2.2 Registration of three steel tire logo, 1875   35
2.3 Print for the 1867 Paris World Exhibition   40
2.4 Krupp worker Wilhelm Engels, employed 1841–78   41
2.5 Export share of Krupp production, 1813–2010   45
2.6 The Krupp cannon at the 1851 London Great
     Exhibition   48
2.7 King Wilhelm I visits the Krupp works, 1861   55
2.8 "Shooting Festival of the Peoples," Meppen,
     August 1879   63
2.9 Workers' dwellings in Westend settlement, 1914   74
2.10 Villa Hügel, 1873   82
3.1 Friedrich Alfred Krupp and Margarethe von Ende,
     1882 (Teich Hanfstaengl studio)   90
3.2 Research Department, 1912   96
3.3 Friedrich-Alfred-Hütte in Rheinhausen, c. 1910   98
3.4 Otto Lang's statue of Li Hongzhang, Villa Hügel
     park, 1896   105
3.5 Military share of Krupp production, 1848–1919   115
3.6 Cortege of Friedrich Alfred Krupp with Kaiser
     Wilhelm II, 1902   120

4.1 Gustav Krupp von Bohlen und Halbach, 1906
(Kessler studio)   124

4.2 Hubert von Herkomer painting of Krupp
directorate, 1912   135

4.3 "Big Berta": the 42 cm Krupp cannon   137

4.4 Kaiser Wilhelm II with a worker in the Krupp
factory, September 1918   143

5.1 The Krupp family, 1923   146

5.2 Krupp inflation money, 1923   158

5.3 The Ruhr struggle: demonstration in April 1923   159

6.1 Nuremberg trial of Krupp directors, 1947   173

6.2 George Harcourt portrait of the Krupp
family, 1930   175

6.3 A submarine launching at the Germaniawerft
in Kiel, c. 1940   183

6.4 Ruhr steel industry profits, 1933–40   186

6.5 Geographic distribution of Krupp exports,
1933–42   200–201

6.6 Hitler congratulates Gustav Krupp von Bohlen
und Halbach on his seventieth birthday,
August 1940   203

6.7 The heavy railcar-mounted cannon "Dora,"
c. 1941   206

6.8 Forced labor at Krupp Essen works, c. 1943   217

7.1 Berthold Beitz and Alfried Krupp von Bohlen
und Halbach, 1967   227

7.2 Release of Alfried Krupp von Bohlen und
Halbach from Landsberg prison, February 1951   230

7.3 Inauguration of the Rourkela steelworks,
India, January 1960   250

7.4 Berthold Beitz meets Chou En Lai in Beijing,
May 1973 (Sven Simon photo)   254

7.5 Berthold Beitz versus the banker and the
     politicians: Hermann Josef Abs, Karl Schiller,
     and Franz Josef Strauss, 1967   258
7.6 Arndt von Bohlen und Halbach and Berthold
     Beitz at the transformation of the firm,
     December 31, 1967   263
7.7 A reconstructed version of the Krupp Stammhaus
     and the new ThyssenKrupp central office, 2010
     (Peter Wieler photo)   284

INDEX

A. Schaaffhausen, bank, 68
AB Bofors, 152
Abdul Hamid II (sultan of the Ottoman Empire), 83, 111
Abelshauser, Werner, 209
Abs, Hermann Josef, 228, 257–58, 268
Acciai Speciali Terni, 278–79
Adenauer, Konrad, 229, 232, 234, 238, 251–52
AEG, 154
Ahmadzadeh-Hervari, Mahmoud, 270
AKA. *See* Ausfuhr-Kredit-Gesellschaft mbH
Aktiengesellschaft für Unternehmungen der Eisen- und Stahlindustrie (Afes), 159, 213
Alfried Krupp von Bohlen und Halbach-Stiftung (-Foundation), 4, 6, 259–60, 262–68, 277–78, 283
Allied High Commission, Law 27, 231–35
Appian Group, 286
Ascherfeld, Adalbert, 48, 72, 85
Asthöwer, Fritz, 101
Augstein, Rudolf, 241

Auschwitz, 219
Ausfuhr-Kredit-Gesellschaft mbH (AKA), 255, 257

Bahr, Annelise, 260–61
Balfour, Arthur James, 130
Bang, Paul, 190
Bankhaus Delbrück, 101
banks, universal. *See* universal banks
Barchewitz, Ferdinand, 81
Bayerische Geschützwerke, 139
Bebel, August, 113–14, 121
Becker, Karl, 205–6
Beitz, Berthold, 5; Adenauer, first meeting with, 234–35; Alfried Krupp and, relationship of, 240–41; capital, securing adequate, 269; compensation for Jewish slave labor, agreement to, 244; Cromme, support of, 277; early and wartime activities of, 239–40; financial crisis of the 1960s, actions regarding, 256–60; the foundation, actions regarding, 259, 262–63, 265–68; globalization, activities promoting,

Beitz, Berthold (*continued*)
248, 251–55; honorary degree
for, 264; Krupp family, relations with, 267–68; literary
portrayal of, 226, 228; photo,
227, 254, 258; rebuilding
Krupp, 241, 243, 245, 247,
287; recruitment of management, 259–60, 275; sales
obligation, end of, 234; tension with management, 255,
274–75
Belgium, 106
Bennigsen-Foerder, Rudolf von,
275
Berg, Friedrich von, 144
Berliner Neueste Nachrichten,
112, 114
Bernays, Edward L., 242
Berthawerke, 214–15
Beyer, Burkhard, 23
Bierich, Marcus, 273
"Big Berta" 42 cm cannons,
136–37
Bismarck, Otto von, 1, 60, 70,
91, 109, 110
Blaustein, Jacob, 244
Bleichroeder, Gerson, 71
Bochumer Verein für Bergbau
und Gussstahlfabrikation:
as competitor of Krupp, 36,
43; joint-stock company,
change to, 67; Krupp foreman
employed by, 80; purchased
by Krupp, 246; Sayner Hütte
ironworks, political battle over,
60–61; steel casts, use of, 54;
worker layoffs, 1873-1879, 77

Bohlen und Halbach, Arndt von,
235, 261–63
Bohlen und Halbach, Berthold
von, 235, 237
Bohlen und Halbach, Gustav
von. *See* Krupp von Bohlen
und Halbach, Gustav
Bohlen und Halbach, Harald
von, 188, 235
Bohlen und Halbach, Irmgard
von, 235
Bohlen und Halbach, Waldtraut
von, 235
Bormann, Martin, 207, 214
Borsig, 77
Bosch, 267
Bosch, Robert, 191, 196
Boulton, Matthew, 18
Boyen, Hermann von, 53
Brandt, Willy, 253–54
Brazil: contracts with railways
in, 50; Krupp's international
ventures in, 249; military
products, as market for, 56,
107; steel-plant investment
in, 285
Brenner, Otto, 268
Britain. *See* Great Britain
Brown, John, 46
Brüning, Heinrich, 145, 170
Buchenwald, 221
Buchheim, Christoph, 176–77
Buddenbrooks (Mann), 9–10, 27
Bülow, Bernhard von, 119
Buschfeld, Wilhelm, 195
business model/strategy: of
Alfred Krupp, 42–44;
cartels/syndicates as postwar

strategy, 154–55; centralized form of management, retention of, 156; competition between states as marketing strategy, 59, 62–64; corporate culture, transition of, 289–94; corporate governance, financial crisis and the need for more effective, 256–59; deconcentration and codetermination rules, 235–37; Deutschland AG, 228, 236, 273–75, 288; family ownership, 5–6, 9–10, 78–80, 85, 149, 155, 165–66, 256; finance, the banks and, 65–72, 256–59; foundation control, 260, 262–67, 292–94; of Friedrich Alfred Krupp, 92–96; of Friedrich Krupp, 44–45; "fusionitis," 282; globalization (see globalization); heroic entrepreneurship, 6–7, 27, 87–88; holding company created in 1923, 159; image, recasting while holding onto the past, 241–47; joint-stock companies (see joint-stock companies); limited liability company, change to, 259; markets, technical improvements and the creation of new, 31; modernization of in the 1990s, 276–85; multi-division form (M-Form), 100; patriarchalism, 241; pricing, quality and, 30; profitability and, 4–5; secrecy regarding production techniques, 56–57; shareholders, impact of not having, 75; the state and, 51–65, 139–40, 161–62, 178–79, 198–202, 231, 233–35, 292; steel trust, resisting argument for, 160–66; of Therese Krupp, 23; traditional foundations of the twenty-first century German, 287; vertical integration, 38–39; workers and management, 72–78 (see also labor/workers)

capitalism: credit from banks, Alfred Krupp and, 65–72; personal, F. A. Krupp and, 121–22; public interest, 264, 294; Rhineland, 3–4, 65; vilified in Nazi Germany, 178. See also finance
Capri, 117–18
Carl Friedrich von Siemens Stiftung, 265
Carnegie, Andrew, 264–65
Carnegie Endowment, 264–65
Carroll, Earl J., 224, 231
cartels, 43–44
Castle, Barbara, 233–34
cast-steel block for the Chrystal Palace, 48–49, 53
Chandler, Alfred, 100
China, 51, 104, 253–54, 283
Chou En Lai, 253–54
Cobden, Richard, 47
coin-making equipment, production of, 18–20, 29, 31, 52

community, corporate existence as a way of rebuilding around an idea of, 293–94
competition, economic: Alfred Krupp's view of, 54; anti-competitive stance of imperial German government, 107–8; Tirpitz's efforts to promote, 116
Cromme, Gerhard, 275–78, 281, 289
Cyrankiewicz, Józef, 251

Daimler, 267
Deichmann, Wilhelm, 68
Delbrück, Clemens, 131
DEMAG, 166, 249
Deng Xiaoping, 253
Dernburg, Friedrich, 119
Der Untertan (The Loyal Subject) (Mann), 89, 91
Deschimag, 211, 239
Deutsche Bank, 102, 198, 214, 260, 275, 291
Deutsche Industriwerke Spandau AG, 181
Deutsche Morgan Grenfell, 280
Deutschland AG, 228, 236, 273–75, 288
Devon Ertsmaatschappij, 155
Diesel, Rudolf, 99
diesel engines, production of, 99
Dillon Read & Co., 160–61
Dinnendahl, Franz, 13
DINTA (German Institute for Technical Labor Training/ Deutsches Institut für technische Arbeitsschulung), 147

Dior, Christian, 243
Disconto Gesellschaft, 68–69, 102
Doenitz, Karl, 211
Dönhoff, August Count von, 110
"Dora" cannon, 205–6
Dortmunder Union, 69
Douglas, Hugo Sholto von, 109
Dresdner Bank, 101–2, 155, 161–62, 214

East Germany. See German Democratic Republic
Eccius, Otto, 133–35
Egypt, 49, 56
Ehrenberg, Richard, 87
Eichhoff, Bertha. See Krupp (née Eichhoff), Bertha
Eichhoff, Ernst, 70, 85
Eichhoff, Richard, 80
Eizenstat, Stuart, 244
Ende, Felix von, 127
Ende, Margarethe Freiin von. See Krupp (née von Ende), Margarethe
Engels, Wilhelm, 41
England: Alfred Krupp's trips to, 46; cannon, unsuccessful testing of, 56; as the challenge to continental European entrepreneurs, 44–45; 1851 London Great Exhibition, 47–48, 53; military products, as market for, 59; steel made through the Huntsman process in, 14–15. See also Great Britain
entrepreneurial activity: Alfred Krupp as definitive of, 26–27;

competition and, 54; as creative destruction, 9, 21; deglobalization and failure of, 106–8; innovative and *Bürgerlichkeit*, incompatible values of, 21
entrepreneurship, high-tech, 5
Erzberger, Matthias, 134
Estel, 272

F. A. Seilliére, 68
F. Asthöwer & Cie. Steel Works, 36
Feldman, Gerald D., 157
finance: banks and bankers, Alfred Krupp and, 66–72; banks and bankers, Friedrich Alfred Krupp and, 101–2; capital market, replacement of bank lending by, 291; crisis of the 1960s, 255–60; inflationary period, strategies during, 155–57; of investment during the expansion of the 1930s, 197–204; joint-stock companies (*see* joint-stock companies); relatives, credit from, 66; universal banks (*see* universal banks). *See also* business model/strategy
Flick, Friedrich, 207, 212, 233, 238
Foerster, Richard, 137
Ford Foundation, 264–66
Fould, Achille, 56
Foundation Initiative of German Business, 244
Fowles, E. L. Douglas, 222

France, 56, 231–32
François-Poncet, André, 232, 234, 248
Frankfurter Allgemeine Zeitung, 114, 119, 266
Freitag, Walter, 238
Fried. Krupp. *See* Krupp firm
Fried. Krupp Schlesische Industriebau GmbH, 213
Friedrich (crown prince of Prussia), 59
Friedrich Wilhelm IV (king of Prussia), 55
Fritz Thyssen Stiftung, 265, 280
Friz, Diana Maria, 261
Fry, Adolf, 193–94, 206

Gall, Lothar, 69, 91, 129, 156, 247
Gantesweiler, Carl, 72
General Electric, 167
German Democratic Republic (GDR), foundation activities in, 264
German Empire: anticompetitive actions by, 107–8; collapse of, 147; F. A. Krupp in the politics of, 108–16; "Kruppianer" as model for social relations in, 87; the Krupps and, 91; lobbying in the politics of, 60–61; military products, as a market for, 61–62; World War I (*see* World War I)
Germaniawerft: financial problems at, 103, 161, 163, 181–82, 184; the navy and pre-World War II production,

Germaniawerft (*continued*)
181–84; purchase and expansion of, 102–3; sale of, interest in, 210; strikes at, 142; submarine production at, 139
German Labor Front, 195
Germany: East (*See* German Democratic Republic); identification and parallel development with, 27–28; imperial (*see* German Empire); under National Socialism (*see* Nazi Germany); Weimar (*see* Weimar Republic). *See also* Prussia
Germany, Federal Republic of: business leaders in, characterization of, 6; "fusionitis" in, 282; new corporate governance, actions furthering the transition to, 288; steel industry, crises of, 268–69, 271–72; steel rationalization, failed efforts to achieve, 272–74
GHH. *See* Gutehoffnungshütte (Gute Hoffnung ironworks)
Girod, Hans, 215
globalization, 5, 32; acquisitions of foreign companies, 278–79; business model of Alfred Krupp and, 44–51; deglobalization under F. A. Krupp, 104–8; exports to advanced countries in the 1980s, 274; exports to developing countries in the 1970s, 270–71; geographic distribution of exports, 1933-1942, 200–201;

Iranian participation in Krupp, 269–71; post-World War I remains of, 155–56; pre-World War II cultivation of global markets, 184–85; products to compete with England, Friedrich Krupp and, 14–15, 44–45; recovery of the late 1870s and, 77; of the 1950s and 1960s, 248–55; transformation of the German business model in the 1990s/2000s and, 286–88
Goebbels, Joseph, 178
Goerdeler, Carl, 195–96
Goerens, Paul, 193, 195
Goetz, Carl, 196
Goldman, Nahum, 244
Goldman Sachs & Co., 161, 280, 291
Goldschmidt, Jakob, 193
Göring, Hermann Wilhelm, 185, 189, 198, 208, 211, 214
Göring office: foreign exchange earnings, vital status of, 201–2; profitability of Krupp, new method of calculation and, 202; Silesian expansion of Krupp, negotiations over, 211–12
Graf zu Eulenburg, Friedrich, 51
Great Britain: Alfried Krupp, opinion of, 208–9; armament sales by, 106–7; cooperation with Krupp, initiatives for, 106; deconcentration and Nazi influence, concerns regarding, 233–34; Krupp,

occupation and closing down of steelmaking at, 222; Krupp sale requirement, controversy over, 245; Krupp's dynamism, dangers perceived as associated with, 130; military products, as a market for, 63–64; steel interests, possible sale of stake in Krupp to, 164. *See also* England

Grundig, Max, 240

Grusonwerk, 100–101, 108

Gussstahlfabrik: British takeover of, 222; dismantling of in 1947, 223; employees at, 129, 140–41; expansion of, 97; labor during World War II, 215–16, 218; labor peace during turmoil of 1920, 150; labor unrest at, 142–43; losses at, 161, 163; military production at, 180–81; remnants of as centrally organized conglomerate, 247; separate production sites, aggregation of, 138, 212; site visits as marketing strategy, 55–56; statue of Alfred Krupp at, 86–87; wage rates, cuts of, 169; Wilhelm II's visits to, 108–9; women workers employed during World War I, 141; worker layoffs, 1873-1879, 77; worker layoffs, 1923-1924, 157–58; workers killed by French soldiers at, 158; World War I expansion of, 140–41; World War II bombing of, 210

Gutehoffnungshütte (Gute Hoffnung ironworks), 11–13, 28, 30, 33, 164–66, 188, 286

Haass, Heinrich, 47

Haeckel, Ernst, 95

Hallstein, Walter, 233

Hamm, Eduard, 188

Haniel, Alfred, 256

Haniel, Franz, 67

Haniel family, 164–65

Harkort, Friedrich, 49

Hartmann, Gustav, 126

Haux, Ernst, 127

Healey, Denis, 245

Heeres-Rüstungskredit-AG, 214

Helfferich, Karl, 126

Hennig, Klaus, 229

Herkomer, Sir Hubert von, 134

Herle, Jacob, 192

heroic entrepreneurship, 6–7, 27, 87–88

Herrhausen, Alfred, 253, 260, 273, 275

Herstatt, 66–68

Herzog, Rudolf, 123

Hess, Rudolf, 224

Heusinger von Waldegg, Emil, 182

Heydt, August von der, 33, 54, 65–66

Hiesinger, Heinrich, 283

Hindenburg, Paul von, 139

Hindenburg Program, 139–42

Hirschland, 162

Hirschland, Kurt, 193

Hitler, Adolf, 1; businessmen, meeting with, 189;

Hitler, Adolf (*continued*)
chancellor, appointment as,
188; Goerdeler, objection
to appointing, 196; Gustav
Krupp's avoidance of meeting
with, 187; Krupp ownership
structure, change in, 207;
military production, actions
regarding, 183, 205, 213–14;
munitions output, incensed
at low figures for, 205; photo,
203; remilitarization aspect
of work creation measures,
emphasis on, 179
Hoerder Verein, 77
Hoesch, 166, 186, 271–73, 277
Hollmann, Friedrich, 116
Hoogovens, 272
Hörder Verein, 67
Hossenfeldt, Vera, 261
Houdremont, Edouard, 193–94,
205, 209, 221, 239
Huber, Ernst Rudolf, 229
Hugenberg, Alfred, 133–35, 145,
148, 190
Humboldt, Alexander von, 57
Humperdinck, Engelbert, 82
Hundhausen, Carl, 242–43, 252,
287
Huntsman, Benjamin, 14

IG Farben, 244
Ihn, Max, 219
import-substitution strategy,
248–49
India, 249–51
Iran, 269–71, 277, 282

Isabella (Crown Princess of
Brazil), 56
Italy, 65
Itzenplitz, Heinrich Friedrich
von, 61
Ivan Programm, 212

Jackson, Robert, 2, 223
Jacobi, Haniel & Huyssen, 66
Jäger, Wilhelm, 32–33
Janssen, Friedrich, 231, 239–40
Japan, 51, 285–86
Jencke, Hanns, 77, 92–93, 100,
109, 131
Jewish Claims Conference, 244
Jews: anti-Semitic attacks, 111,
113; compensation for slave
labor by, 244; Nazi anti-
Semitism, 191–94; prisoners
as labor, 219–20; saved by
Beitz, 240; use of stereotypes
about, 57
joint-stock companies, 67, 87–
88; competition with, F. A.
Krupp's complaint regarding,
115; transformation of Krupp
into, 126–27, 277

Kádár, Janos, 252
Käppner, Joachim, 240
Kastl, Ludwig, 188–92
Kechel, Georg Carl Gottfried
von, 14–16
Kechel, Wilhelm Georg Ludwig
von, 14–16
Khrushchev, Nikita, 252–53
Klasen, Ludwig, 81

Klass, Gert von, 69
Klöckner & Co., 207
Klotzbach, Arthur, 170–71, 193, 195
Klüpfel, Ludwig, 127
Knapp, Georg Friedrich, 133
Kohl, Helmut, 273
Kohlhaussen, Martin, 291
Körner, Paul, 212
Korschan, Heinrich, 193
Krackow, Jürgen, 260
Kranzbühler, Otto, 176, 229, 231
Kriwet, Heinz, 279
Krosigk, Lutz Graf Schwerin von, 190
Krupe (Krupp), Arndt (Arnold), 11
Krupp, Alfred: anglicization of, 45–46; Annen works, acquisition of, 99; banks and bankers, views of and relations with, 65–72; Bismarck and, 60, 91; business model of, 42–44; England, trips to, 45–46; family and personal life of, business and, 78–86; formal studies and university education, skepticism regarding, 94; fraternization with competitors, lack of trust necessary for, 43; the German Empire and, 91; globalization, efforts regarding, 44–51; as heroic entrepreneur, 6–7; hypochondriac, nervous breakdowns and history as a, 79; Krupp as German icon, maker of, 1;

legacy of, 86–88; philosophy and personality of, 24, 26–28, 44, 69, 85, 294; portrait of, 25; production for war and peace, similar requirements for, 57–58; running of the business after his father's death, beginning of, 22–23; Stammhaus, making of legend regarding, 21; the state and, relations with, 51–65; the technical imperative and, 28–42; workers and management, view of and actions regarding, 72–78; at the world exhibition in 1851, 47–48
Krupp, Arnold, 11
Krupp, Arthur, 85, 211
Krupp, Friedrich: business and financial failures of, 16, 20–22; coin-making equipment, production of, 18–20; death of, 22; factory in Russia, dream of, 5; founding of firm to make "English steel," 13–16; initial business move of, 12–13; as namesake of the company, Alfred's insistence on, 7; novel, portrayal in, 123; practical skill in making steel acquired by, 17; silhouette of, 10; steel production in Russia, fascination with, 20, 49; supplies and location, problems with, 17
Krupp, Friedrich, Jr., 72, 78–79
Krupp, Friedrich Alfred: asthma of, 84, 92; birth of, 79, 84;

Krupp, Friedrich Alfred (*continued*)
business expansion under, 97–103; character of, 89, 91; death of, 119–20; deglobalization under, 104–8; father, relationship with his, 84–85; labor relations under, 93–94; management of the firm by, 92–94, 131; mergers and acquisitions by, 99–102; personal capitalism, disastrous end to, 121–22; personal scandal and marital conflict, 116–19; photo of, 90; politics, involvement with, 108–16; profits under, 103–4; science, embrace of, 94–96, 131; task of, 88; Wilhelm II and, 1, 91–92; will of, 126–27; woman not suited to lead Krupp, note regarding, 127–28
Krupp, Friedrich Jodocus, 11
Krupp, Helene, 13
Krupp, Hermann, 30–32, 72, 78
Krupp, Peter Friedrich Wilhelm, 12
Krupp, Petronella, 13, 20–21
Krupp, Therese, 22–23, 29, 52, 78
Krupp, Wilhelm, 13, 15
Krupp family tree, 295
Krupp firm: anticompetitive governmental actions and, 107–8; anti-socialist addresses to be signed by workers of, 120–21; business model/strategy of (*see* business model/strategy);

Chemical-Physical Experimental Institute, 96; company statute *(Generalregulativ)*, 76–77; compensation for slave and forced workers, 244; corporate logo of, 35; the depression of the 1930s, impact of, 168–71; early twentieth century expansion and technical advances, 128–30; employees, number of, 1812-2010, 303–4; employee shares, experiment with, 156; Essen, explosives dropped on during World War II, 213; export share of production, 45; financing concerns of the 1930s, 197–204; financing concerns of the 1960s, 255–60; foundation control, corporate restructuring to, 262–67; the French occupation in 1923, 158–59; German government and, foreign perception of relationship between, 130; Hoechst, hostile takeover of, 277–78; inflationary period, strategies during, 154–58; Iran, securing capital through participation of, 269–71; as joint-stock company, 126–27, 277; Krupp works circa 1820, illustration of, 18; literary portrayal of, 123, 125, 226, 228; major themes of, 4–7; management, early twentieth century changes in, 131–33; management, late

1980s changes in, 274–75; mergers and acquisitions by F. A. Krupp, 99–102; military production (*see* military production); modernization and mergers, 276–85; money printed by, 157–58; Nazi impact on personnel of, 192–97; Nuremberg trials and (*see* Nuremberg International Military Tribunal); ownership structure, alteration of, 207–8; paternalism of, 73; post-World War II deconcentration and scaling down of, 230–39; post-World War I tumult, tradition and adjustment in, 147–53; pre-World War I political conflict, 133–34; profits, 103–4, 131–32, 140, 177–78, 186, 199–202, 289; Prokura and management board of, 72, 76; prosperity in the 1920s, 166–68; remaking of, 239–47; revenues and profits/losses, 1811-2010, 297–302; sale of assets after World War II, 237–38; sales obligation, end of, 245; scientific research at, 96; shipyard, acquisition of, 101–3; size of, 2–3, 33–34, 39; survival of, reasons for, 287–88; Thyssen, attempted hostile takeover of, 280–81; Thyssen, discussion of merger with, 246; Thyssen, merger with, 281 (*see also* ThyssenKrupp); the Villa

Hügel for visitors, 81–83; workers' dwellings, photo of, 74; World War I and (*see* World War I); World War II and (*see* World War II). *See also* ThyssenKrupp

Krupp foundation. *See* Alfried Krupp von Bohlen und Halbach-Stiftung (-Foundation)

"Kruppianer," 87, 291

Krupp (née Ascherfeld), Helene Amalie, 11–13

Krupp (née Eichhoff), Bertha, 79–80, 84, 86

Krupp (née von Ende), Margarethe, 84, 90, 117–20, 127–29, 132

Kruppsche Mitteilungen, 130

Krupp von Bohlen und Halbach, Alfried: American business practices and production in big series, urging of, 202; amnesty and release of, 229–30; arrest of, 222; attempted biography of, 172; authority, acceptance of, 241; Beitz, appointment of and relations with, 239–41; Breslau, construction of new production location at, 213; chairman of the executive board, taking position of, 208; coal, efforts to acquire, 214; death of, 267; executive board, appointment to, 196–97; exports and cultivation of foreign clients, 248; fictional literature about

Krupp von Bohlen und Halbach,
Alfried (*continued*)
business life, contribution
to, 173–74; formal return
to head of scaled-down
enterprise, 239; foundation
control, determination to
convert to, 261–62, 265, 267;
management at the Bertha-
werke, adequacy of, 215;
Mehlem Agreement, signing
of, 235; new style of business
planning, necessity of, 256;
ownership structure, change
in, 207–8; patriarchalism of,
241; photo, 227, 230; political
links and Nazi party membership of, 208–9; profits,
dismissal of the significance
of, 289; statement renouncing
participation in steel production, signing of, 232–33; trial
and sentencing of, 176, 224;
withdrawal and personal
failures of, 260–61; workers
during World War II, actions
regarding, 216, 221
Krupp von Bohlen und Halbach,
Bertha, 2, 126–28, 132, 155,
168, 207, 261, 267
Krupp von Bohlen und Halbach,
Gustav: Alfried's first marriage, opposition to, 261; arrest and imprisonment by the
French, 158–59; British steel
interests, rejection of selling
large stake to, 164; business
conditions after World War I,

awareness of change in, 147;
democracy, worries about,
142–43; family moved from
Essen during turmoil of 1920,
150; family of, photo of, 146;
family of, portrait of, 175;
family wealth as a reserve,
postwar statement regarding,
149; financial support from
the state, seeking of, 161–62;
financing of investment in the
1930s, concerns regarding,
197–98; food crisis and labor
unrest at the close of World
War I, concerns regarding,
142; Fry, dismissal of, 193–94;
Führer, necessity of sup-
port of, 205; Germaniawerft
shipyard, consideration of
selling, 181–82 (*see also* Germaniawerft); indictment of at
Nuremberg, 1, 151, 223; legal
status of the firm, alteration
of, 207; literary depictions
of, 145–46, 172–73; management appointments in the
mid-1930s, 195–97; marriage
and entry into management,
132; photo, 124, 135, 203;
politics, activity in, 169–70,
179, 187–92; positive portrayal of in pacifist's memoirs,
126; pressures from the state,
difficulties posed by, 184; primogeniture, seeking of means
to avoid strict interpretation of, 261; Ruhr lockout,
concerns regarding, 168; the

steel trust, decision regarding, 44, 165–66; strikebreakers, forwarding of memo on supporting, 133; U.S. Steel, rejection of selling minority stake to, 156; wartime campaigns of British steel industrialists, resentment of, 167

labor/workers: Alfred Krupp's view of and actions regarding, 72–77; buying off after World War I, 149–50; codetermination rules and the reconstruction of the coal and steel industries, 236–37; Comme and, 276–77; compensation for World War II forced and slave workers, 244; control of, 42; domestic and foreign, comparative costs of, 220; "Essen Declaration" with ThyssenKrupp, 285; flexibility of, premium placed on, 288, 290; forced during World War II, 217–21; foreign during World War II, 215–16, 218–21; Friedrich Alfred Krupp's view of and actions regarding, 93–94; modernization of business strategies and, 279; Nazi labor activism and, 194–95; prisoners of war during World War II, 215–16, 218; recruitment of during World War I, 141; reduction of in 1923-1924, 157–58; reduction of in the 1970s,

271; Rheinhausen closing, protests provoked by, 276; Ruhr lockout, 168; slave during World War II, 214, 219; surplus workers after World War I, removal of, 148; unrest among during World War I, 142–43
Lammers, Hans Heinrich, 207, 261
Lange, Kurt, 198
"Law on the Organic Construction of the German Economy," 192
Lenin, Vladimir, 136, 252
Lennings, Manfred, 275
Ley, Robert, 208, 218–19
Liebknecht, Karl, 133–34
Li Hongzhang, 51, 104–5
Lloyd George, David, 153
Lochner, Louis, 242–43
Loewe, Ludwig, 111
Longsdon, Alfred, 36, 47, 62
Löser, Ewald, 182–84, 196–98, 205, 208, 210–11, 216, 224–25
Ludendorff, Erich, 139
Lukac, Alfred, 270
Luther, Hans, 161–62, 170

Maier, Charles, 264
Manchester, William, 172
Mann, Golo, 172, 209
Mann, Heinrich, 89, 91, 123, 125, 172
Mann, Thomas, 9–10, 27, 89, 108, 172
Mannesmann, 286

Martin, Emile, 37
Martin, Pierre-Emile, 37
Marx, Karl, 26
Maschinenbau Kiel (MaK), 247
Maschinenfabrik Augsburg, 99
Maschke, Hermann, 232
Mason, Tim, 178
McCloy, John, 229, 244, 265–66
Meissner, Otto, 188
Melchior, Carl, 191
Mendelssohn, 198
Menshausen, Carl, 111
Merkle, Adolf, 289
Metallurgische Forschungsgesell-
  schaft mbH (Mefo), 181
Meyer, Carl, 57, 62, 70–71, 86
Middelmann, Ulrich, 283
military production: artillery,
  beginning of orders for, 38;
  artillery, innovation and marketing of, 61–65; "Big Berta"
  42 cm cannons, 136–37;
  cannon-making equipment
  and workshops, expansion
  of, 58; cannon with a ring-
  constructed barrel, written
  history of, 62; competition
  between states for, 59, 62–64;
  "Dora" cannon, 205–6; expansion of capacity to produce,
  98–99; hidden rearmament
  after the Versailles Treaty,
  151–53; initial production of,
  32–33; Krupp cannon at the
  1851 London Great Exhibition, 47–48, 53; Krupp's
  business model and, 44; per-
  centage of Krupp production,

115, 180; pre-World War II
  rearmament, 180–87; pricing
  of, political conflict over, 111–
  16, 133–34; profits from, 103–
  4; return to in the 1970s, 271;
  ships and naval equipment
  (see Germaniawerft; ships and
  shipbuilding); during World
  War I (see World War I)
Moellendorf, Wichard von, 136,
  176
Mohammad Reza Pahlavi (shah
  of Iran), 269
Mommsen, Ernst Wolf, 260, 269
monopsony, 209
Muehlon, Wilhelm, 125–26,
  132, 134
Müller, Carl Friedrich von, 30,
  66–67
Müller, Erich, 174–75, 205–6,
  213
Müller, Fritz, 205, 222, 224
Müller, Johann Christian Friedrich von, 66

Navy League, 112–13
Nazi Germany: association
  of Krupp with, 221, 225;
  industrialists and the state,
  political relations of, 187–
  92; rearmament, business
  experience during, 180–87;
  the voluntarist perspective on
  business decisionmaking in,
  175–79; workforce of Krupp,
  impact on, 192–97. See also
  World War II
Nehru, Jawaharlal, 249

Nicolai, Friedrich, 16–17, 19, 52
Niemann, F. L., 67
NIROSTA, 129
Nuremberg International
    Military Tribunal, 1, 172–75;
    Alfried Krupp and Krupp
    directors, amnesty and release
    of, 229–30; Alfried Krupp
    and Krupp directors, trial
    of, 223–25; Gustav Krupp,
    trial of, 223; Krupp directors
    at, photo of, 173; room to
    maneuver, business decisions
    and, 175–79

O'Neill, Jim, 248
Oppenheim, 68
Orconera Iron Ore Co. Ltd., 39
OSRAM, 167
Ostpolitik, 228, 251, 253
Ottoman Empire, 108–9

Papen, Franz von, 187–88
Paris Geschütz cannon, 136
Patriotic Auxiliary Service Law,
    142
Pedro II, Dom (emperor of
    Brazil), 82
Peil, Friedrich, 51
Pfandhöfer, Eberhard, 12
Pferdmenges, Robert, 236
Phoenix, 107, 165
photographic department: adver-
    tising panoramas, creation of,
    39–40, 42; workforce, control
    of, 41–42
Piccard, Auguste, 243
Poland, 251

politics: Alfred Krupp and, 108;
    Beitz's globalization initiative
    and, 251–55; and business in
    Nazi Germany, 178–79; con-
    tinued relevance of, 292; F. A.
    Krupp and, 108–16; German
    coal and steel industry, post-
    World War II debate regard-
    ing, 231–36; Gustav Krupp
    and, 169–70, 179, 187–92;
    inflationary policies and, 157;
    Italian and personal scan-
    dal of F. A. Krupp, 118; the
    kaiser's anti-socialist speech,
    backlash from, 120–21;
    lobbying in German, 60–61;
    pre–World War I conflict,
    133–34; vulnerability of F. A.
    Krupp in, 121–22
Polysius, Gottfried, 270
Prien, Günther, 182
Protestant work ethic, 24, 26
Prussia: financial support from,
    seeking of, 52; Krupp artillery
    and military victories of, 58–
    60; military products, early
    efforts to interest in, 52–55;
    secrets of the state, Krupp's
    keeping of, 57; state railways,
    Krupp's interest in, 54

Raddatz, Carl, 226
Raeder, Erich, 181
railways, production for, 33–36,
    47, 50, 54, 151, 169
Rapallo Treaty, 252
Rathenau, Walter, 136, 154, 176
Rau, Johannes, 254, 280

RDI. *See* Reichsverband der
Deutschen Industrie
Reger, Erik (Hermann Dannen-
berger), 145–47
Reichsverband der Deutschen
Industrie (RDI), 170, 187–92
Renewal League (Erneuerungs-
bund), 147
Reusch, Paul, 168
revolutions of 1848, 53, 79
Rheinhausen, 97–98, 129, 221–
22, 237–39, 244–46, 276–77
Rheinmetall, 107–8, 116
Rhenish-Westphalian Coal
Syndicate, 100
Rhineland capitalism, 3–4, 65
Richter & Hagdorn, 47
Richthofen, Ferdinand von, 51
Rider of the White Horse, The
(Storm), 24
Ritscher, Samuel, 193
Robert Bosch Stiftung GmbH,
265
Robinson, Joseph S., 231
Röchling, Hermann, 208
Rockefeller Foundation, 265
Rohwedder, Detlev, 275
Roon, Albrecht von, 57, 59
Rötger, Max, 131–32
Ruhr Coal Mining Association,
133
Ruhr lockout, 168
Russia, 46–47, 49–50, 53, 59. *See
also* Union of Soviet Socialist
Republics (Soviet Union)

Sachwerte, 156
Salimi, Reza, 270

Sandkühler, Thomas, 240
Sauckel, Fritz, 210, 219
Saudi Arabia, 270
Saur, Karl Otto, 176, 211, 213,
215
Sayner Hütte ironworks, 60–61
Schacht, Hjalmar, 145, 170,
188–90
Schaeffler Group, 288–89
Schäfer, Dietrich, 113
Schäffer, Hans, 191
Scheider, Wilhelm, 275
Scherner, Jonas, 176–77
Schiller, Karl, 257–58
Schlessmann, Fritz, 222
Schmidt, Emil Ludwig, 94
Schmitt, Kurt, 192
Schneider-Creusot, 156, 286
Schöller, Alexander, 32
Schröder, Gerhard, 288
Schröder, Johannes, 199–201,
231, 255–56
Schulz, Carl, 78
Schulz, Ekkehard, 281, 283
Schuman Plan, 232, 236
Schumpeter, Joseph, 9
Schweinburg, Victor, 112–13
Schweninger, Ernst, 117, 119
science, Wilhelm II and, 92
secrecy, 56–57, 83
Seebohm, Hans-Christoph, 238
Seehandlung, the, 71
shareholder value, 289
Shaw, George Bernard, 6–7, 172
ships and shipbuilding: German
unification and plans for, 61;
naval gunnery, advances in,
64–65; ship shafts, production

of, 38; shipyards, acquisition of, 101–3, 211; submarines, production of, 103, 139, 182–83. *See also* Germaniawerft

Shooting Festival of the Peoples, 62–64

SIDECHAR, 238

Siemens, 100, 154, 288

Siemens, Carl Friedrich von, 191

Siemens, Friedrich, 37

Siemens, William, 36–37, 46

Siemens-Schuckert, 181

Skoda, 286

Smith, William Henry, 64

Social Democratic Party (SPD), 121, 232, 237

Sohl, Hans Günther, 246

Sölling, Friedrich, 33, 55, 67, 79

South Africa, 270

Soviet Union. *See* Union of Soviet Socialist Republics

SPD. *See* Social Democratic Party

Speer, Albert, 208–10, 212–13, 218

Spengler, Oswald, 145

Spethmann, Dieter, 273

Sprenger, Jean, 239

Springorum, Fritz, 188

Stammhaus: Alfred Krupp's residence in, 80; construction of, 19; legend, turned into, 21, 83; photographic department based in the, 39; reconstructed version of, 284–85

Stapelfeldt, Franz, 211

Stauss, Emil Georg von, 139

steel: Bessemer process, 36; carbon content of, 14; competition in German among producers of, 107–8; crucible process, scaling up of, 43, 48–49; hammers for working, 37–38; Huntsman process of making, 14–15; industry profits, 1933-1940, 186; living in the age of, Alfred Krupp on, 60; non-rusting, 129, 202; oxygen steelmaking, 246; puddling process, 35, 129; quality of pig iron for, 17, 19, 28; Siemens-Martin process, 36–37; sponge-iron process, 270

Steinbrück, Peer, 2, 292

Stettiner Vulkanwerft, 67, 103

Stewart, Michael, 245

Stinnes, 154, 156, 160, 256

Stinnes, Hugo, 145, 160

Stoltenberg, Gerhard, 255

Storm, Theodor, 24, 86

Strauss, Benno, 129, 193–94

Strauss, Franz Josef, 257–58

Strenger, Christian, 283

Stresemann, Gustav, 159

Stroschein, J. E., 112–13

Strousberg, Bethel, 71

Stumm, 114, 116, 121

Stumm-Halberg, Carl Ferdinand von, 109

Süddeutsche Reichskorrepondenz, 112

Switzerland, 56

tableware, production of, 31–32

Tallis, John, 47

Taylor, Telford, 224

technological innovation: by Alfred Krupp, 28–42; in cannon barrels, 49; gasification of coal for power generation, 274; in nonrusting steel, 129; in powder and explosives, 49; in rifle barrels, 33; in steelmaking (*see* steel); Widia, production of, 167

Tenfelde, Klaus, 128–29, 156

Th. Prosser & Son, 47

Thies, Moritz, 46

Thiess, Erich, 205

Thyssen, 107, 154, 156, 160–61, 246–47, 271, 273, 279–81

Thyssen, August, 100, 134, 145, 160

Thyssen, Fritz, 145, 160, 187, 190–91

Thyssen-Bornemisza, Heinrich, 160, 165

ThyssenKrupp: creation of, 281; headquarters, moving of, 165; international diversification of, 285; Krupp tradition, moves reasserting, 283–85; labor relations at, 285; reorganization of holdings and renewal of the executive board, 282–83; size of, 3; transition of corporate culture, as incarnation of, 292. *See also* Krupp

Tilly, Richard, 69

Tirpitz, Alfred, 112, 114, 116

Todt, Fritz, 205–6, 210

Todtleben, Franz Eduard von, 49

Tooze, Adam, 186, 216

Tremper, Will, 226, 228, 294

Turkey, 62–63, 185

Turner, Henry, 188

Uhlhorn, Diedrich, 18

Ulbricht, Walter, 252

Union der festen Hand (Reger), 145–47

Union of Soviet Socialist Republics (Soviet Union): exports in the 1930s to, 170; globalization under Beitz and, 251–53; hidden German rearmament and, 153; relations with, British and German interest in, 153; steelmaking equipment transferred to and resumption of production in Magdeburg, 222–23

United States: foundations in, 264–66; Iran, pressure on Krupp to reduce holding by, 282; as a market, development of, 47; railway products, as a market for, 77; steel mill constructed in, 285

universal banks: industrial development and the rise of, 66, 69; literary portrayal of, 226, 228

U.S. Steel Company, 155–56, 265

Valdunes, 286

Vargas, Getulio, 249

Vereinigte Stahlwerke, 163–66, 181, 199

Versailles Treaty, 151

Vickers, 106–7, 286

Vienna, 31–32
Villa Hügel, 2, 80–84, 86, 94, 116, 168, 222, 230, 243
Visconti, Luchino, 172
Vogel, Dieter, 280–81
Vogelsang, Günter, 259, 273
Vögler, Albert, 155, 165–66
Vogt, Oskar, 117
Voigts-Rhetz, Konstantin Bernhard von, 58, 62, 65
Volkswagen, 288
Vorwärts, 118–19
Vyshnegradsky, Ivan, 49

Wagener, Otto, 191
Waldthausen, Ernst, 67
Waldthausen, Julius, 67
Warburg, Max, 191
Weimar Republic: currency stabilization, business during the period of, 160–66; financial assistance from, 161–62; French occupation of the Ruhr Valley, 158–59; hidden rearmament in, 151–53; inflationary period in, 154–60; market economy in, 177; postwar revolution, 147–51; prosperity phase of, 166–68
weldless steel tires, 34–35
Wellhöner, Volker, 91
Wendel, 286
Westrick, Ludger, 234
Widia, 129, 202, 222
widows, role in development of the steel industry, 23
Wiedfeldt, Otto, 148–49, 153–56, 160, 162–64, 181, 251

Wilhelmi, Johann, 20
Wilhelm II (emperor of Germany): Bertha's duty to run Krupp, condolence letter stating, 128; Bismarck and, tension between, 109; caricatured in a novel, 89; F. A. Krupp and, 1, 91–92; Gussstahlfabrik, visits to, 108–9; Krupp prices, complaint regarding, 114; Krupp works, late World War I visit to, 143–44, 147; merger of Krupp and Grusonwerk, approval of, 101; as modernizer, 92; patent of 1906 restricting use of the Krupp name, 267; shipyard acquisition, encouragement and approval of, 102; size of Brazil battleship, protest regarding, 107; speech following F. A. Krupp's death, 120
Wilhelm I (king of Prussia, emperor of Germany), 1, 54–55, 59, 61, 86
Wilhelm (Prince of Baden), 55
Wilmowsky, Barbara von, 127, 267
Wilmowsky, Tilo von, 187–88, 196, 216, 229, 260, 267
Wolbring, Barbara, 114
Wolff, Otto, 165
Wollheim settlement, 244
women: in business during the early nineteenth century, 23; excluded from business during the early twentieth

women (*continued*)
century, 127–28; as workers
during World War I, 141
World War I: artillery pieces,
production of, 135–36; centralized planning for defense
procurement, development
of, 136; the Hindenburg
Program, 139–42; the kaiser's
visit to the Krupp factory,
143–44, 147; labor shortages,
responses to, 141; labor unrest during, 142–43; logistical
and organizational challenges
of business expansion during,
138–42; planning for lengthy,
absence of, 135–37; plan-
ning for the peace, limited,
137–38; shells and grenades,
production of, 136–37

World War II: acquisitions and
new construction during,
211–14; coal, supply of, 212,
214, 218; eastward shift of
production, 212–15; German
collapse and the immedi-
ate aftermath for Krupp,
221–23; labor, foreign, forced
and slave, 214–21; management, different and con-
flicting strategies of, 204–6,
208; Nuremberg trials (*see*
Nuremberg International
Military Tribunal); ownership
structure, alteration of, 207–8;
procurement priorities and
demands, constantly shifting,
209–13

Zaharoff, Basil, 6–7